THE RELEVANCE OF
ISLAMIC IDENTITY
IN CANADA

Culture, Politics, and Self

edited by
Nurjehan Aziz

MAWEN**Z**I
HOUSE

We acknowledge the support of the Canada Council for the Arts for our publishing program. We also acknowledge support from the Government of Ontario through the Ontario Arts Council.

Cover design by Peggy Stockdale

Library and Archives Canada Cataloguing in Publication

The relevance of Islamic identity in Canada / edited by Nurjehan Aziz.

Includes bibliographical references.
ISBN 978-1-927494-65-3 (paperback)

    1. Muslims—Canada—Ethnic identity.

    2. Islam and secularism—Canada.

I. Aziz, Nurjehan, editor

FC106.M9R44 2015   305.6'970971   C2015-905136-3

Printed and bound in Canada by Coach House Printing.

Mawenzi House Publishers Ltd.
39 Woburn Avenue (B)
Toronto, Ontario M5M 1K5
Canada
www.mawenzihouse.com

CONTENTS

Preface

There's a story about the great Urdu poet Mirza Ghalib (1797-1869). One evening during the time of the so-called Indian Mutiny, while on the road in Delhi he was stopped by British soldiers. "Are you a Muslim?" they asked. To which he replied, "Only half a Muslim. I drink wine but I don't eat pork." One might wish to draw a line between those precarious times and ours; or wonder if the answer would not draw a fatwa in parts of the world today. But that question, and its answer, neatly illustrate the concerns with which we conceived this volume. So much has been written recently about Islam and Muslims, that we felt that a fundamental question needed illumination: What does it mean to be a Muslim? Is it a public or a private identity, and as an identity does it make sense in a secular democracy such as Canada? What relation does it bear to historical, cultural, and ethnic identities? Is a total agnostic or an atheist a Muslim? Is a person who disavows being a Muslim still a Muslim?

The book, then, began as an exploration, and perhaps a naïve one. Not all our questions were answered, and we learned. The responses have been illuminating, thought-provoking, and also disturbing. To some, the question we posed does not even arise; Muslims is what they are. To others it's an irritant: when Ameen Merchant was posed the question, "Are you a Muslim?" over the phone, his immediate response, he tells us, was "No." But later he began to try to understand that response. To some, Muslimness is imposed from without, or it's one of several identities, or it's an identity that has only been recently awakened after 9/11 during the so-called war on terror; or it's something beautiful and personal. The responses to our questions have come from perspectives that are personal, historical, cultural, political, and philosophical. The question of reinterpreting or rereading the scriptures arose. While examining Tariq Ramadan's proposals for radical reform, Mohamed Alibhai asks, is it time for "thinking the unthinkable," for abandoning the idea of verbal revelation itself?

To our great surprise, however, one observation was almost universal: recently in Canada Muslims have found themselves the objects of vilification and discrimination. Being a Muslim then means being a victim. The niqab controversy in Canada appeared to be an almost hysterical culmination of this victimization and misunderstanding, when the Federal Court of Canada had to uphold a Muslim woman's rights, while physical attacks on Muslims accompanied verbal abuse and slander of their faith, bringing to some an eerie reminder of the vilification and finger-pointing of visible minorities elsewhere at other times in the name of security. But we live in a democracy, for every ignorant and bigoted demagogue there are many examples of true democrats. But if the attacks are not with machetes—we live in Canada, after all—they are still damaging. This is a historical juncture at which, whether we intended to or not (we didn't), these dispiriting observations from diverse perspectives will bear witness to what Haroon Siddiqui in these pages calls "Canada's newest dark chapter."

An Incompetent Muslim

SAFIA FAZLUL

There's no shortage of peculiar sights when walking down Yonge Street from the Eaton Centre to the Toronto Reference Library, but there's always one that never fails to make me smirk to myself. A five-minute walk from Wellesley Station is the Toronto Islamic Centre, right beside Seductions, one of North America's largest adult department stores with scantily clad mannequins coquetting at the window display.

Anyone with even a minimal understanding of Islamic views on modesty and sexuality would understand the irony behind this juxtaposition. I see humour in the irony, but also, more importantly, I see this small display as representative of the general live-and-let-live attitude of non-Muslim Canadians towards conservative Islamic culture, and of conservative Canadian Muslims towards liberal mainstream culture—at least when the delineation between the two is bold and clear.

The Toronto Islamic Centre occupies a small, obscure office on the second floor of a bubble-tea cafe, tucked away behind bars, eateries, clothing stores, and other manifestations of materialism and decadence. It is not a threat; it's just a benign representative of a culture that rightfully belongs on the cultural mosaic, an ideal of our society promoted by the Canadian government itself.

But imagine now the Toronto Islamic Centre as a ten-storey building with posters on its windows saying "Make Eid a National Holiday" or, more boldly, a neon sign proclaiming, "All Homosexuals Will Go To Hell"—what would happen to that laissez-faire attitude? Would years of bottled frustrations kept behind the façade of Canadian politeness burst into the public sphere?

And imagine the mannequins at the Seductions storefront wearing lingerie and hijabs to mock the garments of traditional Muslim women—would those Muslims who secretly detest liberal Canadian ideals finally take their opinions to the streets? Might there even be a violent outburst from the few fundamentalists?

The reason why any tension between traditional Muslims and liberal Canadians is lukewarm is because the two exist side by side with the unspoken rule of never spilling into each other. When the two streams try to make inroads into each other the tension becomes heated and the myth of the cultural mosaic as an inclusive policy unravels itself. Discrimination, although usually subtle and so politely delivered it is difficult to detect, rears its ugly head.

Take the hijab, niqab, and burqa for example. There is no uproar from Canadians about these garments being worn by Muslim Canadian women in their homes, at work or in school because they are a clear symbol of belonging to a subcategory of "Canadian." To deny the right to wear the symbolic garments would mean to attack the multicultural ideals that shape Canada. However, when these attires are worn in the public spaces where the dominant culture feels insecure or threatened, hostility rears its head: let's not forget the 2011 banning of the niqab in citizenship ceremonies (recently lifted) or the Parti Québécois's unsuccessful attempt to ban hijabs and other religious symbols in Quebec's public service in 2013.

When I learned of these government actions and other individual incidents such as the removal of a nine-year-old from a soccer game because she refused to remove her hijab, I was appalled and naively expected my fellow Canadians to also drop their jaws. That didn't happen. Indeed, most of the anonymous online comments on these stories were anti-hijab and anti-Muslim. Some were outright hateful and racist and made it clear that Muslims would never be considered Canadian unless they gave up their "backward" and "oppressive" religion.

On the flipside, an example of the hesitancy of some Canadian Muslims towards Canadian liberal values can be found in discussions of sex-education policies. The Muslims in Canada, especially those who are newly immigrated, encourage their youth to excel in school. The Muslim South Asian community I grew up in placed high importance on teaching its children everything—math, chemistry, English, music, biology—everything except sex education. That was for the "Canadian" children to learn. Sex education is not forbidden by the Quran so this is strictly a rejection of liberal values and not a claim to religious rights. I remember the parents in my community being very assertive on the subject: many complained angrily to the principal, many wrote notes to the teacher demanding their child be moved from the class, and many allowed their kids to attend the class but only to learn how Western culture was immoral.

I find that the concept of the cultural mosaic acts more like a map of categories to which you can insert yourself—a selection of labels. The problem I face then, as someone who isn't able to choose a category and lives on the fringes of being "somewhat liberal Canadian" and "somewhat conservative Muslim South Asian," is quiet rejection from both sides. My inability and unwillingness to pick a label for myself and live my life strictly under the rules of one category has brought me the experience of discrimination and exclusion, from both liberal or secular Canadians and traditional Muslim Canadians.

I became both a "Muslim" and a "Canadian" by surprise. I was Muslim first, way back as a carefree child in Oslo, Norway in the 1990s. Norway was nothing like Canada. The Norwegians overtly wanted you to become Christian and assimilate, and there was nothing you could do about it. In elementary school you were expected to partake in *all* class activities or get sent home. These activities included making Christmas cards, painting Easter eggs, walking with a candle for Saint Lucia ceremonies, walking in the "Søttene Mai" march (May 17 is Norway's Independence Day) to wave to the Norwegian king, and sing and act in all Christmas shows (I think I played baby Jesus once).

My parents were young and newly immigrated from Dhaka, Bangladesh. They worked, went to night school, and tried their best to get six hours of sleep. Religion was the last thing on their minds. As long as my older sister and I brought home straight As, wore nothing above the knee, and referred to ourselves as "Muslim" and to God as "Allah," they weren't concerned with innocent Norwegian brainwashing. They were aware, however, that being South Asian and Muslim was looked down upon in this new country. They repeatedly taught us to be proud of Bangladesh and Islam, to always see ourselves as equals and to defend our home country and our choice of religion.

The day I realized I would consciously identify as a Muslim was when I stubbornly defended Islam. We were making posters to hang around our classroom as Christmas decorations. The teacher wanted us to draw reindeer, Christmas trees, and of course Jesus. A Pakistani girl whose name I can't remember said something along the lines of "I'm not drawing Jesus because Jesus is a prophet and it's un-Islamic to depict prophets in art." She and I were the only Muslim kids in our class and already unpopular because we'd wear t-shirts instead of bathing suits to the swim class. She was ridiculed by the other kids; they made fun of her, Pakistanis, and Islam until she broke down into tears.

I yelled at the kids and didn't back down from my position that Islam was just as deserving of respect as Christianity. I said I was a Muslim and proud of it. Until that day, I had only called myself a Muslim because my parents told me to. That day onwards, I began to study the religion and found myself engulfed in true faith.

Now I'm usually the first in the room to say something defensive when anyone criticizes Islam. I'm like a guard dog: I know who to bark at but I'm not always aware of *why*. I don't agree with or believe everything that's written in the Quran. I'm admittedly an inconsistent Muslim. I don't know how to pray the prescribed way; I don't fast every single day during Ramadan; I dress however I want to and according to the weather; and I reject all Hadith teachings (I'm a Quranist). A few practising Canadian Muslims I've met have been forgiving of my inconsistency, but most have rejected me.

When my family and I moved to Canada, we lived in a modest apartment near the intersection of Victoria Park and Danforth Avenues, a popular area for Muslims, particularly new immigrants from Bangladesh, Somalia, and Ethiopia. Living in that area felt like a test of loyalty: are you going to remain a Muslim or are you going to go join those sinning "Canadians"? The continuing gossip in the neighbourhood was around this very question and every family was on watch to see whose kids would fail the test first.

As with most communities, the in-crowd was the most consistently Muslim group. The families that attended mosque together, whose kids enrolled in the same Arabic classes, and who made friends with similar people got to choose who was allowed in the inner circle. Exclusion was based on shallow details like how "Canadian" one looked or acted. For girls especially, attire made all the difference on how you were received. T-shirts and shorts made you less of a Muslim; having diverse friends made you less of a Muslim; having friends of the opposite gender made you less of a Muslim.

It was as though being a Muslim was something I had to wear on the outside at all times just to be validated. After moving away from the area, I was reluctant to insert myself in any Muslim community, South Asian or otherwise, because frankly I don't like others telling me how to practice my faith and I perceive religion to be a private struggle, not a group endeavour. However, I can't avoid the minority group I ultimately belong in and every now and then I'm met with snarky, discriminative comments. Recently, at a close friend's Iftar party, a stranger in a hijab asked me cockily why I had my nails manicured. "You can't pray with your nails manicured," she scoffed. I told her I don't remember reading that in the Quran and she and her friends spent the rest of the evening pretending I wasn't in the room.

I became a Canadian at the age of thirteen. The exact moment was when I stood in the citizenship court with my sister and mother. When I pledged allegiance to a queen I had no idea about, it struck me that there was a white, Christian woman somewhere out there who ruled over me, indeed I'd made a legal promise to become her subject, so I could no longer view myself as only a Muslim who answered to Allah. That moment another label was added to my forehead.

I remember that we bought a cake that day—complete with red and white icing—to celebrate being a part of this amazing country. We felt included that day because if anybody asked us now where we were from, we could answer "Canada" without hesitation. We forgot briefly that our skin remained brown and that meant a lifetime of "I know you're from Canada, but where are you *actually* from?"

The answer would remain "Bangladesh" and sooner or later the conversation would reveal that I'm a Muslim. Ever since 9/11, I find I've been questioned more about being a Muslim than ever before. Many of the non-Muslim Canadians who question me seem to feel entitled to my opinion about Islam and terrorism, as though I owe them an explanation for choosing a faith that is inherently "evil," "violent," and "un-Canadian." From my own experience and what I hear from other Muslims, I find that this is the subtle but glaring form of discrimination that Muslims face in Canada. We've all been painted with the same brush and are held individually accountable to explain the actions of over 23% of the world's population (there are about 1.6 billion Muslims in the world).

I can't count the number of times I've had to explain terrorism—the big, complex topic of terrorism in which I have no degree or diploma—to bosses, coworkers, classmates, neighbours, and even friends I thought I'd chosen carefully. I've found that they don't actually have much interest in understanding the issue, but rather are testing me to see if I belong—if I am Canadian enough to be included.

If I don't hate Muslim terrorists enough to want our troops to bomb their countries up, then I'm accused of supporting terrorists.

If I can't give a satisfactory explanation of why I'm a woman who chooses to be Muslim, then I'm a misogynist with an oppressive family. If I don't admit that the Quran encourages violence against all non-Muslims, then I'm a liar and not to be trusted. Essentially, I'm not seen as a Canadian unless I agree to the misconceptions most non-Muslim Canadians have about Islam.

I've felt the most discriminated against as a Muslim in the work-place. One odd job I had back in university made me feel forced to talk bad about Muslims just to feel that I was part of the team. When I first entered that company, I got along well with everybody. I don't wear the hijab and I dress in the contemporary secular fashion so that nobody knew I was a Muslim until it randomly came up in con-versation one day. Things changed quickly after that revelation.

Suddenly I wasn't invited as frequently to after-work get-togethers and I was made fun of in a negative connotation. Most of the jokes were related to being "backward," which is so often a word used to describe Islam by Islamophobes. I haven't held on to those insulting memories but one exchange still sticks with me. I asked the manager for a day off for Eid al-Adha and I was met with a surprising joke:

"What is 'Eidie'?" he said mockingly. "You're not going to blow things up, are you?"

I was offended and appalled but knew the consequences of defend-ing myself. I knew that if I didn't laugh and let it go, I'd be seen as a stereotypical serious Muslim who can't take a joke. If I tried to edu-cate my boss about Eid al-Adha, he'd just make another demeaning joke about sacrificing animals and being backward. I had to accept his insult just to prove that I was also deserving of the same respect as the non-Muslim workers.

There is strong but subtle discrimination against Muslims. I don't regret that I don't belong to any specific category in this false cultural mosaic; not belonging wholly to one side has given me the privilege to see from both sides. I feel proud of the harmony Canadians as a whole manage, especially when walking by the Seductions store and the Toronto Islamic Centre, but it's worrying to me what actually lies beneath the politeness and civility. Would the people inside Seductions look at me twice if I walked in with a hijab? Would the people in the Islamic Centre accept the way I choose to practice my religion? Either way, I just continue down the street.

Identity Fragments

AMEEN MERCHANT

Late last year I received a request for a donation from a charity. A donation request from Amnesty International or Greenpeace, yes, but a donation form in Urdu script and an Indian Gandhi stamp? How unusual. It brought a smile to my face. It had come all the way, across land and ocean, from a mystic's shrine in Ajmer, Rajasthan to Vancouver, BC. I'd never been to that shrine. How did they get my address? How did they know my name?

Bulk Data Buying, I said to myself, and set the envelope aside. I did not send a donation. That envelope is still at the side on my desk, somewhere under a pile of printouts and scanned documents.

In March this year, one day the phone rang. Although the ringer had been turned off, the display panel flashed: "Unavailable name and number." Sometimes calls from India announce themselves this way. I picked up the phone and said "Hello?"

Without any introduction, a male voice asked: "Are you Muslim?"

"No." I hung up.

That answer stayed with me for a few weeks. Why did I say "No"? Was it because I did not want to talk to a total stranger? Was it because I was in the middle of working out a chapter in my new novel and did not want to talk? Could it be denial? Did I feel put on the spot, to choose my faith or to disclose the lack thereof? The ease with which the "no" rolled off my tongue was both surprising and reassuring.

The surprising part was the succinct and definitive nature of the reply. The reassuring part was the honesty within it.

There has been no such call since.

The first night of the crescent

I went to an Anglican high school in Madras (Chennai), the oldest school in Asia, founded in 1715, where I read passages from the Holy Bible to the students' morning assembly. At age seven, I took on the responsibilities of performing puja with my Hindu neighbour at a little temple we both had set up in the backyard of his house. He performed the morning rituals and I offered the evening aarti. On the eve of Christmas, I accompanied our housemaid, a Tamil Christian, to Fatima Church for midnight mass. To this day, I can sing the hymn "The Lord's My Shepherd" from memory. I remember other hymns too. For fourteen years, before I left India for graduate work in Canada, I fasted during the entire month of Ramadan, the holiest month in the Muslim calendar. I was the only one in our family to do so. In the sweltering heat and humidity of a south Indian summer, with the temperatures pushing into the forties, I attended school and took the bus to work, my mouth parched, my stomach knotting into spasms, and my eyes always on the clock, silently urging the hands to move faster to the sunset hour. I don't believe I took on this task to demonstrate my religious commitment and fervour. Nor did I do it in the hopes of being granted a favourable place in the afterlife. I undertook the fasting ritual of Ramadan for just one reason: It made my mother really happy.

These are my first memories of religion and its role in my life. By age five I spoke Tamil, Hindi, and English fluently. At the same age, without any conscious understanding of the sacred and the divine in a conventional or formal way, I was a Christian, a Hindu, and a Muslim all at once. In other words, a devotee above division, fluid and boundless, culturally grounded, but also unfettered and free.

The separations and differences in the path to God did not exist in thought, word, or action.

It was and is how it has always been.

I was all of eighteen months when my father took our family—my mother and my two brothers—with him from Bombay (Mumbai now) to Madras (Chennai now). A Hindi-Gujarati-speaking family from an Indian sect of Islam, uprooted from its place of history and familiarity, and replanted in a whole new geography with a Dravidian language, an unfamiliar culture and cuisine, and an entirely different way of seeing, living, and being in the world.

The only cultural link for my mother, removed from her familial and social network and far away from the Bombay of her life and time, was the community hall of the Ismailis in Madras. And every month, on the eve of the first moon, she would dress me up in the "special occasions" clothes and take me on the bus with her to the hall, always referred to as the "jamatkhana" (community hall, quite literally) for an evening of cultural and spiritual reconnection. This was perhaps the only time when I was keenly aware of my Muslim heritage, our difference in Chennai made apparent for just one evening in thirty days, all based on the waxing and the waning of the moon.

Otherness and its contents

Notions of cultural and communal "otherness" are first and always imposed from without. It is a difference articulated for you without consent or explanation, an imposition that both silences and defines the place and space of your being, even if that being is not how one sees oneself. While seldom meaningful or nuanced, these markers of self and belonging, of difference and separation, draw their power from the dominant collective that proscribes the role and status of the other, for the other and always without the consent or participation of the other. Culled first from essences of the visible, this enduring taxonomy of reductive stereotypes and half-truths establishes itself entirely by semiotic deductions of appearance, behaviour, and engagement. The arc of this narrative is short, for its mission is to contain difference, silence difference, and to entrench difference. As such, it privileges homogeneity over heterogeneity, singularity over multiplicity, and interpretive imprisonment over the potential of unmediated possibilities. In a nutshell, it is a narrative that is wholly invested in a full and complete failure of the imagination.

For all my assumptions of cultural fluidity and freedom, there were moments in my childhood and early adulthood when my otherness as an outsider, a person from "Bombay" in "Madras," a "Muslim," became too visible in the eyes and words that framed my personhood, my legitimacy as an Indian citizen questioned without cause or provocation.

The one sure time when my "Muslim" background was singled out by my schoolmates (and later by my work colleagues) was during cricket test matches. Cricket, a national Indian obsession, and a magnificent one at that, brought all corners of the country to a standstill. From roadside transistors that blared by-the-minute commentary from tea-stalls to showrooms and offices where workers gathered during breaks around black-and-white television screens, everything was Cricket all the time. The sport also served as an easy conduit for all sorts of simmering and diffused resentments. In short, cricket test matches brought out the jingoism that was always lurking, waiting for an opportunity to raise its ugly head, right at the drop of an Indian wicket. This fevered intolerance, long on the brew, reached its peak when India's arch-rival Pakistan made it to the finals, and then it spilled over without care or restraint. Every ethno-religious pejorative was dusted off and hurled, sometimes casually and most times with malice and vehemence. The Mughals (particularly Aurangzeb), Partition, circumcision, cow slaughter, ritual, and attire—it was open season and nothing was spared. Accusations of disloyalty to India followed as naturally as night follows day. Those five-day test matches were my first glimpse of something resembling a personal hell.

To be suddenly aware of otherness is always startling no matter how many times it may have happened in the past, it is always the first time when it happens again.

In Canada, September 11, 2001 was the turning point. One day, in the year 2002, on my arrival at Vancouver airport, I was stopped, searched, interrogated at the airport while still holding a valid Canadian passport and all boarding passes. From 2002 to 2004, and always on the Vancouver-New York-Vancouver route, I was selected for extra screening. It happened like clockwork no matter how professionally, courteously, and respectfully I presented myself to the officer at the clearance point. I could draft the profile parameters myself: Single man, brown complexion, a Muslim first name, under the age fifty, presumably of Middle-Eastern/Near-Eastern origin. My Canadian passport identified my city of birth as Bombay, India, but that didn't seem to make any difference. In a span of two years, this kind of incident had occurred nine times. To me, this was my otherness made visible always after my return flight from New York's JFK airport to Vancouver. I dreaded that moment. I remember the tenth time it happened. I had been cleared by Customs and Immigration, and while I was waiting at the carousel to pick up my luggage, I was approached by an officer and asked to step aside. Having kept my calm the previous times, I found my voice this once—it finally seemed too obvious to be just a random occurrence—to lodge a complaint alleging racial profiling. I asked to see the airport personnel supervisor. When he walked into the screening area, I requested him to give me his contact card so that the next time I was pulled aside based on my name, my skin pigmentation, and my travel itinerary, I would be able to call him to come and be a witness to the frequency with which my number fell into place in the eyes of the trained profilers in the arrivals area. I was overwhelmed with a sense of humiliation. "For once," I said to him, "it would be nice to feel good about returning home without being made to feel like a criminal."

To this day, I double-check to make sure I have that card in my wallet every time I get ready for an international flight.

Since the attacks on the World Trade Centre in 2001, it seemed as if the diversity and multifaceted aspects of Islam that I had seen and celebrated had been demolished along with those towers. That one act of terror and violence had concretized all the hoary, negative stereotypes of the faith and its followers in the eyes of the world. The dialectic of the "West" and the "Other" was here to stay, and Muslims in the US, Canada, and Europe were implicitly and explicitly designated "the enemy within." To get a sense of how the word "Muslim" was received post-9/11, I embarked on a small experiment. While the results of the exercise were neither conclusive nor definitive, they did reveal the process by which essences congeal and consolidate a monolithic view of a people and a faith, aided and abetted incessantly by a media culture dedicated to locate the "other" amidst us.

Facebook markers

Early spring 2015, I posed a question to my hundred and fifty friends on Facebook: "What do you hear, see, feel when you hear the word 'Muslim'?" This was by no means a reliable sample to qualify as a study, but my motivation for this impromptu survey was to find out how the word played in favour or in opposition to the constant barrage of media stories relating to the Iraq war, the rise of ISIL (Da'esh), and issues of multiculturalism and assimilation of Muslims in Canada. This was also perhaps the first time that many of my Canadian friends realized that I was a "Muslim," and I was interested in how this new fact might change or influence their responses to my question.

Ambivalent about my own status as a "Muslim," for I was far removed from all traditional interpretations of what makes a believer or follower, I hoped to find a response that clarified my own faith for me in the way of an outsider looking in. I was hoping for a response that took the word out of the religion and recast it in a spiritual and cultural frame.

The answers to my question, especially from my North American and European friends, were illuminating and informative. They ranged from "I think Mathematics" to "I see a lost friend of a misinterpreted religion" to "Seldom do I see women." A response from

Iceland said: "I've been accused of being an Islamist because of my support for Muslims as fellow human beings." Another confessed: "It happens when I hear the name of any religion—hackles up. And with Islam I particularly associate 'Taqqiya.'" An acquaintance from Bombay, no doubt shaken by the terrorist attack in her city, was unsparing: "Fanatics is what comes to mind immediately. But I do have dear Muslim friends for whom their religion is a very personal issue that they will never allow to be manipulated."

Finally, a friend from Paris said something that seemed to fit my own cultural celebration of Islam: "The food that lines the streets of my neighbourhood in Paris in the evenings during Ramadan. (The pastries especially, due to my sweet tooth, but also the chick pea soup, really delicious.) I see headscarves, Sufis, poetry, music, whirling. (And then the word Sunni, and trying to remember the differences— total failure there.) Green and blue tiles."

The diversity of these honest and unbiased responses was reassuring. It told me that not everybody is swayed by the relentless and essentialist portrayals of Islam and Muslims by the media. These short, fleeting thoughts held the promise of alteration, correction, and revision.

This experiment also held one unexpected revelation: there was no response from my Muslim friends on Facebook.

Subject to change

Acknowledging, accepting, and living my life openly and honestly as a gay man did not just change my sense of self in the world; it changed my relationship with the world around me. Every religion, no matter how compassionate, merciful, and benevolent, always draws the line of exclusion when it addresses or condemns sexuality. But when the awareness of marginality has been constant in one's life, as it had been with mine, one's negotiations with it in the here and now—dislocation, displacement, immigration, race, ethnicity, and sexuality—change, and adaptation within these subject positions also becomes a necessary constant. The fact that my own community, itself marginalized within the context of traditional Islam, a progressive and visionary community that embraced science and spirituality with equal zeal, would still disallow me the honesty to be my true self was not a surprise. If I had learned anything about religion in all the years, it was this: irony and religion are mutually exclusive. To practice dishonesty just to belong can only scar and corrode the soul, and that was a price I was never going to pay. The choice was made for me, and I've chosen to be a fundamental humanist by including everything else that has informed and made my personal history. As a man, a son, a brother, a spouse, a cultural Muslim, an immigrant, an Indian Canadian, a writer, and a proud citizen, I celebrate these subjectivities with a sense of belonging to each one of them equally. To privilege one over the other would be to corrupt the spirit and to sully the self, to tip the balance into discrimination from within.

In the past fifteen years since 9/11, I've had many responses and reactions to the portrayal of Muslims and Islam in mainstream Canadian and world media. I distinctly remember a front and centre story published in the *Vancouver Sun* during the runup to the Iraq war. It featured Dr Sunera Thobani and Osama bin Laden side by side—one, a woman voicing her opposition to war, and the other the mastermind behind the most shocking and heinous terrorist attack of the twenty-first century. That they both were Muslims seemed to escape the scrutiny of the journalist. Nationalism conflated opposite trajectories and divergent narratives into one essence: otherness. The backlash against Muslims was up and running. In a moment of pure schadenfreude, a temporal satisfaction in the misery of Muslims who would deny me my own core and identity, I reasoned that perhaps the sense of their visible otherness was necessary. That, should they allow themselves the introspection, it could only lead to perspective, comprehension and change. But spite is always the wrong emotion. To see marginality as static and rooted is to misunderstand it. To understand marginality as an exchange, an inevitable dialectic—the self changed and also affecting a similar change in its sphere of engagement—is vital. It is also inherently anti-essentialist.

As a child growing up in India, I did not have many toys. My parents bought me books—handwriting books, colouring books, and illustrated books like the *Amar Chitra Katha* and *Chandamama*. This might also account for my complete disinterest in cricket. However, there was one toy that I cherished and have now come to see as a metaphor for all the marginalities that have made me who I am—self and whole. It was a rustic kaleidoscope. A long tube-like contraption with the viewer at one end and at the other end a double glass compartment that held broken strips of coloured bangles, all of them equal in length. You held the tube in your hand and fixed your eye to the viewing end as you raised it to a source of light. Ever so slowly, you turned the tube in your hand and a geometric pattern came alive at the other end, vibrant and astonishing. One more turn, and the strips of bangles rearranged themselves into an entirely new form. No one pattern was like the other. Once it was all blue and red, and next it was green and yellow with small flecks of purple. The possibility of infinity in a limited number of coloured bangle strips was a revelation. No one strip was like the strip next to it, but they were all equal and they worked in unison, in a concert that made each element important and necessary to make it whole. And multicoloured change was the gift.

Subjectivity is also one such gift. My sense of my Muslim identity may not be another's definition of what a Muslim ought to be and it also may not be in line with scripture and sacred text. Then again, my subjectivity is also not anybody else's. It is multifarious, absorbent, and always subject to change. And it is my own.

My answer was the correct one: No.

I am a Muslim. But I am also not just a Muslim.

Mosques and the Making of Muslim Identity

NARENDRA PACHKHÉDÉ

The Mosque *in Venice*

This year at the 56th edition of Venice Biennale, the most political edition of the prestigious art event in years, there was an interesting art project titled *The Mosque*. A disused fourteenth-century church, Santa Maria della Misericordia, which had ceased its religious operations in 1969, was made into *The Mosque*.

Swiss-born, Iceland-based artist Christoph Büchel was commissioned by the Icelandic Arts Centre to represent Iceland in Venice. Working in collaboration with the Muslim Communities of Venice and Iceland, he premised the concept for *The Mosque* in both the historical context of Islamic culture's profound influence on the City of Venice, and the sociopolitical implications of contemporary global migrations. Enriched for centuries by trade with the East and shaped by Islamic art, architecture, and language, Venice was home to a Muslim prayer room (though not a mosque) as early as 1621, in a space inside the thirteenth-century palazzo today known as the Fondaco dei Turchi. Nevertheless and in spite of its inextricable links to the Muslim world, the City of Venice has to this day never permitted the establishment of a mosque in its historic centre.

The Mosque, curated by Nina Magnúsdóttir, was to function for a full seven months of the Biennale, as a place of activity and worship for the Venice Muslim Community while at the same time offering educational and cultural programs to the general public.

Interestingly, the Cannaregio site of *The Mosque* is adjacent to a section of the historic city known as the Jewish Ghetto, where long-standing political restrictions on Jewish rights and residences were instituted into law in 1516—and subsequently applied also to Muslim merchants worshipping in Venice in the seventeenth century.

In the period leading to the Biennale, two crucial events played into the narrative. First, the attack on the Paris office of the French satirical weekly *Charlie Hebdo* in January 2015 that heightened anti-Muslim sentiments in Europe. Second, later that summer Venice underwent a mayoral campaign. While the more liberal candidate, Felice Casson, supported the project, the right-wing candidate Luigi Brugnaro did not, describing the installation as a "mistaken initiative, which was done without taking into account people's feelings in Venice." Brugnaro got elected as the mayor for a five-year term.

Under attack, *The Mosque* was shut down two weeks after it opened. The Icelandic Art Centre is suing the city of Venice and the matter is in the courts.

The installation and subsequent forced closure, in a paradoxical way, gave a reply to Okwui Enwezor, the curator of the 2015 Venice Biennale, who posed this question to frame the Biennale International Art Exhibition entitled *All the World's Futures*: "How can the current disquiet of our time be properly grasped, made comprehensible, examined, and articulated?"

The mosque in Mississauga, Ontario

There is an eerie similarity in the narratives surrounding *The Mosque*, the art installation, and the Meadowvale Mosque in the city of Mississauga, Ontario. More than a decade in the making, the Meadowvale Mosque evoked the same anxieties and contestations as Christoph Büchel's *The Mosque*.

Unlike Venice, Mississauga has many mosques dotting its

landscape and serving various interests of the diverse Muslim community. Broadly speaking, though the Muslims see themselves as part of a worldwide human diaspora, their simultaneous affinity with the *ummah*, or global Muslim community, can make their relationship to "multiculturalism" seen to be a tenuous one. This is a double-edged sword, which they put to use as a strategy for resisting their racialization and marginalization. In the Greater Toronto area, attempts to build mosques with a distinct Islamic architectural design have engendered deep-seated neighbourhood resistance, since they appear to challenge the political and spatial order of city planning in place.

On October 22, 2014 there was an attack on Parliament Hill in Ottawa in which Canadian soldier Nathan Cirillo was shot dead. This immediately spurred anti-Islamic rhetoric in the nation. The following summer, the city of Mississauga was in the midst of a municipal election for a replacement to the aged mayor Hazel McCallion, who had ruled the city for decades and was against the mosque project. The proposed Meadowvale Islamic Centre's 20,000 square-foot Sunni mosque with a soaring 88-foot minaret was a key issue in the election campaign for the influential Muslim community of the city. The issue spilled over into the September vote of approval for the mosque. Kevin Johnston, who ran a campaign to stop the mosque, was publicly reprimanded for hate-mongering. The anti-mosque rhetoric claimed that the neighbourhood would experience loss of Canadian values, loss of property values, rape, untold violence, and traffic chaos! Despite such opposition, the city of Mississauga, by a vote of 11 to 1, approved a two-storey mosque for the Meadowvale Islamic Centre.

The Muslim community historically has evolved around a mosque for a range of reasons, from praying to mobilizing the community. The construction and use of mosques has been part of a process of making new demands upon public space. In her seminal work, *Making Muslim Space in North America and Europe*, historian Barbara Daly Metcalf argues that it is ritual and sanctioned practices that are a priority, and it is these practices that create "Muslim space," which does not require juridically claimed territory or formally consecrated or architecturally specific spaces. For Canadian anthropologist Regula Burckhardt Qureshi, this multiplicity marks the history of the Islamic "built space" for the people's use. "Islamic praxis transcends local space primarily by aural, not visual communication."

The mosque as Muslim presence

In general estimation, the mosque becomes a facility that unites people in worship rather than a building per se. The act of worship and the construction of a place of worship invoke many forms of contestations largely premised on a fluid concept of secularization and the role of religion in public life. Mosques have clearly become places for the representation of Muslim presence.

The building of mosques as "Islamic projects" embodies the Muslim subjectivity, which is shaped relationally through mutual self-exposure in the public sphere. In this way, exposure to others becomes a constitutive act in contributing to an ongoing version of subjectivity. The narratives of these contestations establish and become important as a means of defining their political subjectivity and help them to make sense of their identity in transformation. Simultaneously the mosque provides the material condition for sociopolitical life to come into effect and therefore to enable a challenge to the traditional modes of representation in Canada, as pointed out by Canadian Urbanists Kanishka Goonewardena and Stefan Kipfer.

Muslim subjectivities have been shaped through the collective practice of consciousness-raising and performativity. Scholarship in urban geography and the thrust of multicultural planning enable us to understand how social relations and institutionalized forms of power interact to produce changes within the built environment. Further, they help us to understand the agency of the religious groups who through their deliberative engagement with the planning process influence the very configuration of materiality of the built environment.

Resistance to a project designed to serve its city's minority and immigrant populations brings to light issues of segregation and inequality that continue to drive contemporary conflict the world over. It also highlights the role of urban space as a mediating factor in the construction of citizenship and identity, which "takes on renewed urgency as cities of difference are overlain by the effects of neoliberal urban policies and the privatization of space, as well as economic dislocations and the potential rise of nationalisms, possibly producing new geographies of inequality, separation, control and fear in Canadian cities (Walks 2009, 351)."

Mosque and city

In the late twentieth century, with the growth of political Islam, there is a greater urgency and a growing concern with understanding the mosque both in its overarching historical setting and its contemporary role and positioning in cityscapes—the mosque in the life of the city and its residents, as a sociopolitical, cultural, and public space.

It now looks pretty certain that at the very inception of Islam—i.e. in the Prophet's own scheme of creating a site for addressing and forging a new community—and then across the succeeding centuries, the mosque well exceeded the function of a place where the faithful merely congregated for worship. At the heart of its expanded function lies the *khutba*, the address delivered to a congregation by the imam (the one leading the prayer) from the pulpit (the *minbar* of the mosque), this being an integral part of the prayer ritual. The *khutba* was not meant just to inculcate Islamic dogma or precepts in the believers, but also to orient the community towards the important public issues of the day.

"Given the open-ended character of the Islamic congregation, the Islamic pulpit is well regarded as being laden with social agency for insinuating a sense of the public into people at large, i.e. across divisions of class, status, ethnicity, occupation and language," says historian Iftikhar Khan.

Far from being a stand-alone, functionally delimited space for worship, for the larger part of its history the mosque was part of a complex of interlinked institutions that in time became more elaborate through the contributions of succeeding generations of Islamic rulers and social elites. This complex included the key Islamic institutions of *waqf* (community endowments) and the *madrasa,* which attracted to itself a diverse body of students from different parts of the Islamic world. It drew in another large cluster of institutions, which included hospitals for teaching medicine, observatories for the study of astronomy, and schools for mathematics, philosophy, and science.

During the postwar influx of immigrants, the opportunities for Muslim communities to establish religious institutions in accordance with Islamic requirements became the defining characteristic of the settlement process. Migration networks, organizational structures, and authoritative frames on which this infrastructure was built were taken as an important structuring feature of Muslim religious activity in the West. "The establishment of a religious infrastructure and the integration of migrants were considered two sides of the same process and thus inextricably linked to one another," according to anthropologist Thijl Sunier.

He continues, "By the 1990s two key concerns arose in response to this settlement trend. One, how to reconcile Islam with the Western conceptions of liberal secular democracy anchored in its 'Judeo-Christian' roots; and two, how to accommodate and govern the increasingly diverse society." As we saw in the Meadowvale Mosque case in Mississauga, the presence of Islam was primarily seen as an identity issue. In governance-speak, how to accommodate a new religious presence wherein the entailed process is political and various parties engage in negotiations about the establishment of religious accommodation. Interestingly, while the governments of the day play the role of a referee and are assumed to be impartial, except for instances of radicalization the development of Muslims and their subjectivities remains largely untouched. "The development of an Islamic religious infrastructure is part of the larger and more fundamental process of the rooting of Islam under changing circumstances in which perceptions about the future of society play a crucial role. This is informed by a combination of Islamic normativity and ideas about their position in society, which predicates the envisioning a future Islamic landscape in the country of settlement (Sunier 1996)."

Canadian mosque-scape

The Canadian mosque-*scape* offers a rich terrain for investigating Muslim subjectivities, sociological pathologies, and architectural dogmas, together with mundane and routine identity politics. In addition to its iconography, it offers a sense of temporal depth to the long history of Muslim settlement in Canada.

There are about 140 mosques in Canada. Largely, there have been two distinct types of mosques, repurposed and purpose-built. Storefront mosques, such as the Hamza Mosque on Queen Street in Toronto, have often been a starting point for the community before they transition into purpose-built mosques such as Vaughan's Baitul Islam Mosque (1992) and the more recent Ismaili Centre in Toronto (2014).

In the 1950s the Muslim community of London, Ontario began efforts to establish a mosque and succeeded in building one in 1964. In the same period the Islamic Centre of Quebec in Montreal took initiatives towards building its first mosque. By 1973 British Columbia had its first Jami Mosque in Richmond, designed by architect Alexander Resanovic. And currently, in 2015, Iqaluit's Muslim community has begun work to build its first mosque in Nunavut.

The story of Al-Rashid, Canada's first built mosque, constructed in 1938 in Edmonton, Alberta, is largely unexplored beyond the historical narrative. The local Muslim settlement consisted primarily of Lebanese and Syrians, who employed the services of a Ukrainian master-builder, Mike Drewoth. The mosque appeared more like a church, demonstrating the limits of Drewoth's expertise and exposure. As the community grew, the need for a larger space became imminent.

In 1982, the community decided to shift the premises and begin a new mosque, now called the Canadian Islamic Centre. The community at the same time wanted to preserve the historic building for posterity, and the city relented by offering a site at Fort Edmonton Park, where the structure, by means of a delicate maneuver, was shifted and also named a heritage property. It opened to the public in 1992. Meanwhile the new Canadian Islamic Centre (Al-Rashid Mosque) took a different architectural form, with a dome and minaret.

Late nineteenth-century Victorian-era Toronto had had its share of Moorish-style architecture. A classic example is the former Athenaeum Club on Church Street, which has retained its facade in a new condominium complex. Similarly, the interiors of Massey Hall and the Keg Mansion (formerly Massey Mansion) are two other examples using Moorish style. Postcolonial realities challenged this Western Orientalist fashion of using Islamic religious architecture as decoration. "As the new Muslim world became foregrounded, different architectural styles came into prominence, characterized by three phases—the Orientalist colonial, nationalist, and neo-Islamist—each of which shared the same historicist discourse on Islamic architecture," according to architect and historian Nasser Rabbat.

The Revolution in Iran and the first Gulf War and the publication of Edward Said's seminal book *Orientalism* marked a turning point in the perception and study of Islam in the West, offering a vocabulary to the politics of identity on one hand and, on the other, defining the relationship between form and cultural identity. In Canada and the West, the representation of Muslim identity takes the visual form of a dome and minaret. We see this archetypal and stereotypical motif in posters at anti-Muslim rallies. As Nebahat Avcioglu says, "Such a regime of referential singularity not only sustains the category of identity as a logical boundary between 'us' and 'them' but also reconfigures the colonial trope, *image-as-identity*, into one of postcolonial, *identity-as-image* (2007, p 92)."

The mosque as a dynamic space

Mosque One: Oral Histories of Toronto's First Mosque, a project of the

Tessellate Institute, a Toronto-based think tank, offers a compelling narrative of Toronto's early history of Muslim settlement and efforts to organize the community and build a mosque. The website of Jami Mosque, Toronto, says that in 1911, Rajjab Assim, an Albanian Muslim, with help from other Muslims in the city, established the Muslim Society of Toronto. In 1968, to pursue its religious affairs, an old Presbyterian church on Dundas Street was converted into the first mosque. Two years later, the congregation outgrew the small mosque and the community split along ethnic and theological lines. The 1970s had in fact seen a new wave of Muslim immigrants from South Asia, many of whom were members of the Tablighi Jamaat, a conservative Muslim Missionary movement. With the dispersion of the congregation, the memory of its first days faded away.

Both the Toronto Mosque (at Dundas) and the Al-Rashid Mosque had some distinguished visitors who attempted to forge a solidarity between members of the Canadian Muslim community and the Nation of Islam. Two key representatives who visited Canadian mosques were El-Hajj Malik el-Shabazz (Malcolm X) and Muhammad Ali.

Interestingly, a small Toronto mosque, el-Tawhid Juma Circle, demonstrates the shifting Muslim subjectivities. El-Tawhid Juma Circle, started in 2009, is a place of unison for straight, lesbian, gay, bisexual, and transgender worshippers. Born-Muslim or new convert, with any orientation or gender, one can lead the prayers and offer a sermon. Juma Circle demonstrates the urgency of internal dialogue within the Muslim community.

There is a growing tension within the mosque complex in Canada, which calls for reforms with respect to the role of women. In the early twentieth century, women were active members of Muslim congregations. They were appointed to the boards, raised money, and negotiated with the municipal authorities. In the religious affairs of the mosques, the idea of separation was minimal or nonexistent. Zarqa Nawaz's *Me and the Mosque* (2005), poignantly captures the tensions in a mosque and the evolving diminished role of women in its community. This dynamic was also captured in the 2013 report from the Hartford Institute, titled *The American Mosque Report*, which painted a dismal picture of the lack of inclusion of women in mosques in North America.

Younger members of the Muslim community have started blogs (see 30Masjids.ca) and think tanks such as the Tessellate Institute in Toronto, which document their Islamic heritage in Canada. And mainstream television hosted a multiseason run of *Little Mosque on the Prairie*, a satirical look at a small-town Muslim community, created by Zarqa Nawaz. There is thus a pronounced effort in bringing Muslim religious life into the public realm beyond the idea of the mosque. This year (2015), for the first time a Canadian prime minister hosted an *Iftaar* (an evening meal to end the Ramadan fast) dinner at his residence in Ottawa.

Reexamining Relations Between Men and Women:

Partnership as a New Paradigm for Reading Islamic Religious Texts

MONIA MAZIGH

He is beginner of the heavens and the earth. How could He have a child when He has had no companion.

Qur'an 6:101, "Al-An'am"

Economic and cultural globalization, the rapid growth of new markets, the decreasing role of agriculture in the lives of the Arab Muslim peoples, the introduction of satellite television and the spread of mobile telephones, the growing popularity of education among the youth, and increasing urbanization have all contributed to the fact that the Arab Muslim family no longer resembles that which prevailed in Arabia in the seventh century at the time of the Revelation to the Prophet Muhammad or that of the colonial and postcolonial periods.

Today we are witnessing the emergence of societies that are undeniably disconnected from the traditional religious view, which is centred on women's dependence upon men as guardians of the family. Only in the light of the new economic and social realities, accompanied by a critical rereading of Islam's founding texts, can the new role of women and men as guarantors of family unity be reexamined and reinterpreted.

This essay will attempt to show that in order for Islamic discourse to be relevant to the Muslim societies of today it must embrace the economic, social, and cultural realities generated by globalization in order to synthesize a new jurisprudence. Such a revolution—for it would indeed be that—cannot be imposed from without by Western feminism, which is insensitive to the cultural specificities of these countries, nor by foreign military intervention justified for example by calls for the "liberation" of Afghan women from the *burqa*, but instead must be implemented by a critical reexamination undertaken from within. Far from moralizing, it would be deeply innovative and creative.

The role of the man as provider and manager of the household finances, known as *qiwamah*, can no longer be sustained in a world where Muslim women increasingly work in factories and in the public service, to name only two areas. It would be far more pertinent to speak of partnership, *musharaka*.

I will argue that the concept of partnership should henceforth prevail in marriage as the principle that regulates relations between men and women. In Islam the notion of *musharaka* applies to economic matters and commercial contracts. Likewise the principle of risk-sharing, which is categorically opposed to the taking of interest, *riba*, where one of the parties possesses the capital and thus enjoys a dominant position while the other must pay the interest and thus becomes subordinate. I will show that marriage constitutes a contract similar to commercial contracts; it follows that in our day Islamic marriage contracts should be drawn up based on the model of partnership, *musharaka*, instead of *qiwamah*.

The notions of the dominant man and the subordinate woman, as derived from the most traditionalist and widespread interpretation of Sura IV, Verse 34, were over the centuries propounded by male religious power in close alliance with male political power. *Qiwamah* became the ultimate justification of men's superiority over women. It thus contributed to the prevalence of a juridical and legal literature not only biased against women, but also to its acceptance of practices and social traditions prejudicial to them. For example, Ibn al-Jawazi, a twelfth-century Muslim scholar, writes: "The wife must know that she is as a bondswoman to her husband."[1] Today, several rereadings of this verse reject the traditionalist definition of guardianship and open the door to new ways of understanding, placing emphasis on the shared responsibilities of men and women.[2] As the Moroccan scholar Asmaa Lamrabet argues, "a new reading of the relevant verse shows that its subject is not masculine privilege but rather one of responsibility and limitation incumbent upon men in the material administration of conjugal space as determined by the socioeconomic context of the day."[3]

My contention here goes beyond a simple reinterpretation of *qiwamah*. I maintain that the literal, traditional understanding of the principle of guardianship that it expresses is no longer either viable or acceptable. I believe that it has led to the development of self-contradictory societies that find no difficulty in using technology to spread a religious message while simultaneously denying women the right to work to broaden their horizons or to provide for their family's economic needs. The religious message itself is as contradictory as it is incoherent. On the one hand, the population is encouraged to embrace a neoliberal economic system (market economy, mass consumption) while at the same time it is being exhorted to lead a simple, modest life of religiosity. The transposition of *musharaka* into the family unit would reestablish equilibrium between women and men and eliminate such contradictions. Henceforth, tasks would be shared, based not only on the sole criterion of gender, but also upon ability, educational level, the nature of the task itself, and the financial situation of the partners.

Applying the principle of partnership would make it possible to sustain coherent relations between women and men, which would in turn contribute to making up internally coherent societies, in harmony with the economic, social, and technological realities of the modern world.

—〜—

In those verses of the Qur'an in which God speaks of Himself, it has been noted that He frequently uses the term "companion" or "associate" to negate any possible association with another being, and to insist upon His Uniqueness and Perfection. God, the reader understands, has need of neither "companions" nor "associates" to create and to govern the world. The verse, "To Him is due the primal origin of the heavens and the earth; how can He have a son when He hath no consort? He created all things and He hath full knowledge of all things,"[4] and Verse 163 of the same Sura, "No partner hath He," are examples of how the two words are used to describe relations that can be attributed to humans but of which God, in His Perfection, has no need. These words can be found in many places in the Qur'an.[5] When speaking of Himself, God never uses the term "spouse" or "wife" instead. This is not the place for linguistic arguments; my aim is more modest: I argue that the word "companion" as descriptive of relations between women and men is an ideal one, towards which any relationship of a human couple should aspire, even though God has no companion.

According to the Oxford English Dictionary, the word "companion" indicates "one who associates with or accompanies another; a mate, a fellow; an associate in some specific or legal relation, a colleague, partner." The online Free Dictionary defines "companion" as "A person who accompanies or associates with another; a comrade; a domestic partner."[6] From these definitions, three key notions can be derived: accompanying, sharing, and associating. All are flexible, contemporary notions that can be readily used to describe a couple's relationship today in the West. The Qur'an, which is fourteen centuries old, uses the same term.

Relations in the prophetic era between women and men were notable for their rigidity and conformism, both characteristic of the traditions of the day and corresponding to specific socioeconomic circumstances. Today, these traditions are in crisis; the socioeconomic organization of the Arab Muslim countries has come to resemble a hybrid, a combination of the traditional and the modern. Ever increasing numbers of Muslim women work at home and outside the home, bringing home money to provide for the needs of their families, while also assuming the burden of child-rearing, housekeeping, and protecting family traditions. More and more Muslim families aspire to a certain form of modernity, including the financial independence of the wife and her equality with her husband. Nonetheless, the traditional image of the wife still predominates in traditional religious discourse, even among "liberals," and above all in popular culture and the popular imagination.

Even though in our day the Muslim wife tends to share the financial burdens of the family unit, the Muslim husband remains the one who takes decisions regarding the family. Relations between men and women in the Arab Muslim countries remain deeply ingrained with the traditionalist concept of *qiwamah*. The man is described and perceived explicitly or implicitly as the provider and the woman as his subaltern, as protector of the man's material (money) and immaterial (children) wealth, placing her in a state of perpetual domination.

The motivation underlying my challenge to the traditionalist perspective is the first marriage contract between the Prophet Muhammad and his wife Khadija. In most of the traditional Islamic texts, their marriage is cited as a relationship of serenity, in which the woman, Khadija, represents the perfect spouse, who supported her husband in his newfound prophetic mission, bore him model children, and never either betrayed him or lacked respect for him. Without calling these aspects of the relationship into question, it should be noted that Muslim jurisprudents and historians have paid less than full attention to one of the most striking aspects of their marriage. Firstly, it must be recalled that Khadija became acquainted with the Prophet as a business partner before becoming his life partner. Her confidence in him was founded upon her experience of his personal qualities and opened the door to their commercial partnership. Only later did their commercial relationship evolve into a matrimonial partnership. The notion of *qiwamah* did not arise; Khadija did not become the wife who would stop working to look after the family home. On the contrary, Khadija's wealth enabled the Prophet to spread his message without having to perform the kind of traditional work done by other Prophets in the past.[7] Khadija also provided moral support. Her business continued to provide the financial underpinnings of their marriage and of the Prophet's mission for the length of their life together.

Some may object that at the time of the Prophet's marriage to Khadija Islam had not yet been firmly established; it would have been inappropriate to upset the prevailing order, particularly since the verse dealing with *qiwamah* had not yet been revealed. Nevertheless, their marriage—seen against contemporary custom—could be considered as nonconformist, not to say far ahead of its time on multiple levels. It contained the seeds of the transformation in man-woman relations that would take place far in the future. The marriage was that of a young man, the Prophet, and a widow, Khadija, substantially older than him; a marriage between a poor man of the highest honesty and integrity and a wealthy woman without a business agent; a monogamous marriage when the practice of the day would have allowed, or even incited, Muhammad to take several wives, which he was only to do later, after the death of Khadija.

Prophet Muhammad's first marriage contains precious secrets and lessons in life for all Muslims, men and women alike. Considering that theirs was a monogamous marriage with children, covering a substantial portion of the Prophet's adult life, it should be seen by Muslims as the norm for marriage in general. Contrarily, the marriages contracted later in his life should be seen as exceptions, irrespective of the strength and character of his later wives.

There exists in Islamic jurisprudence a rigid distinction between commercial and marriage contracts. It is this rigidity that must now be called into question. In fact, these contracts, all of which are mentioned in the Qur'an as contracts, engagements, pacts, or witnessing, differ in the manner in which they are drawn up, applied, and dissolved. But they nonetheless constitute contracts governed by the divine criteria of Justice and Equality. The first example of this type of contract is the one established between God and humanity according to the Qur'an. He has created it, and as the counterparty, humanity owes him recognition and belief: "And mention when your Lord took from the Children of Adam—from their generative organs—their offspring and called to them to witness of themselves: 'Am I not your Lord?' they said 'Yea! We bore witness'." [7:172] Later the idea of a contract between the Creator and His creatures is taken up again: "Those who live up to their compact with God and break not their solemn promise" [13:20]. The idea of Justice is implicit in this unprecedented contract, for God reminds human beings of their pact with Him and expects it to be honoured.

The second kind of contract concerns the marriage between a man and a woman: " . . . and they have taken from you an earnest solemn promise." [4:21]

The third kind of contract is that which governs human economic activity—the commercial contract: "O those who have believed! Live up to your agreements." [5:1]

Of primary interest are marriage and commercial contracts, for it is the permeability—hidden by jurists throughout the centuries—between these two types of contracts that may well serve as a new paradigm for the amelioration of man-woman relations.

Commercial contracts form the basis of the Islamic economic system, which is governed by the Qur'anic verses in which God forbids usury and interest:

> ➤ "God eliminates usury and makes charity greater." [2:276]

> ➤ "O those who have believed! Be God-fearing of God and forsake what remains of usury if you have been ones who believe." [2:278]

> ➤ "O those who have believed! Consume not usury, that which is doubled and redoubled; and be God-fearing of God so that perhaps you would prosper." [3:130]

The prohibition of usury and, by extension, of interest forms the fundamental concept underlying an economic system that is just and equal. These two practices lead inevitably to a skewed and unequal economic relationship in which the one who possesses capital or land exploits the one who does not. Islam prohibited the use of interest and created a system founded on partnership. This does not mean that Islam is against private property or investment; Islam favours an economic system in which those who possess capital and those who offer their services as managers or employees enter into partnership on an equal footing. Islamic jurisprudence speaks of the *mudharaba*[8] and the *musharaka*[9] models.

In a *musharaka*, several individuals enter collectively into a partnership that ensures them a portion of the profits corresponding to their initial investment. In a *mudharaba*, one party contributes the funds while the other acts as manager. Profits are then shared according to an arrangement agreed upon at the beginning. In a *mudharaba*, in the event that the enterprise fails, the investor loses his capital while the manager loses the fruit of his labour. It is at this juncture that the notion of shared risk becomes operative. It is also here that the concept of equality assumes its full importance, in contrast to the principle of financial equity where each investor must receive the same amount of money irrespective of the risk incurred.

The notions of equity, justice, and risk-sharing that occur in business and economic relations are nowhere to be found in the traditional system of man-woman relationships in Islam. The "scholars," in fact, whether voluntarily or involuntarily, have set them aside. In terms of man-woman relations, Islamic jurisprudence, both conservative and reformist, has settled upon Qur'an 4:34 as the foundation:

> Men are supporters of wives because God has given some of them an advantage over others and because they spent of their wealth. So the ones in accord with morality are the ones who are morally obligated and the ones who guard the unseen of what God has kept safe. And those whose resistance you fear, then admonish them and abandon them in their sleeping places and go away from them. Then if they obey you look not for any way against them. Truly God has been lofty, great.

Here the central idea is that man possesses an advantage over woman. This advantage, which some traditionalists have interpreted as purely physical (by analogy to nature: the cock with his red cockscomb as against the combless chicken, or the power of the ox to pull the plow as against the submission of the cow who bears calves) and which some reformers have interpreted primarily in economic and rarely in moral terms, is the most controversial provision of the Sura, and it is one which even today governs relations between men and women in Islam.

But this verse was revealed in response to conditions particular to a time and place. The mission of the Qur'an was and is to change beliefs. As such, the Qur'an's message is one of belief in and obedience to God and justice and equality on Earth. These are the principal objectives of the divine message. In this light, the notions of equality, partnership, and risk-sharing should govern man-woman relations exactly as they govern economic relations in Islam. Islam is a message of universal harmony. Relations between men and women cannot be based on distinction between dominant and dominated parties on the one hand, while on the other hand Muslims boast of an equitable economic system.

If the principles of equality, partnership, and risk-sharing were applied to man-woman relations, not only would Islamic society be more harmonious and less contradictory but it would also be more coherent; in such a society economic relations would not be the exception but a continuation of relations between men and women.

Some may criticize this thesis, asserting that God in the Qur'an has instituted the *qiwamah* of man over woman, and that no human interpretation can cause it to vanish. In my view, the appropriate response would be to insist that *qiwamah* should be based on merit. In other words, abilities should be the determining factor, not gender. If the wife is superior in education and is able to read to the children, she should be awarded the *qiwamah*; and if the man is skilled with his hands, capable of repairing a leaking faucet or fixing the floor, he too should be awarded the *qiwamah*.

The Qur'anic texts have set forth the broad guidelines that govern relations between spouses, but it is up to men and women to apply them to the realities of life. In this regard, I will use the argument of the Islamic thinker Muhammad Shahrour to which Amira el-Azhary Sonbol also refers in her article on polygamy.[10] Shahrour draws a connection between the number of wives a man can marry and the question of slavery in Islam. According to him, the intention was to gradually diminish both these practices. God wished to show Muslims that the path to be followed was not that of slavery. Without explicitly forbidding the institution, the Qur'anic texts were revealed to encourage Muslims to redeem and to free their slaves. In drawing a parallel with slavery, Shahrour was able to conclude that the Qur'an, without forbidding polygamy, discourages Muslims from taking more than one wife. Based on this analogy, I argue that the principle of gradation can be applied to man-woman relations and to the notion of *qiwamah* in a continuous progression toward *mushraka*. Though *qiwamah* may have been practical in the context of the Revelation and the socioeconomic reality of the time, it has today become a source of misunderstanding among families. Its erroneous interpretation and its absolute application have institutionalized injustice towards women and their subordination to men. It is time to reexamine the concept and to replace it with the notion of partnership, which is far more universal and better adapted to today's realities.

Equality, partnership, and risk-sharing in man-woman relations

The notions of equality, partnership, and risk-sharing are in full conformity with man-woman relations and are furthermore not contradictory to the fundamental principles of Islam.

The equality of which I speak is not that of Western feminism, which some might see as being imposed or imported from abroad into Muslim societies. The idea of equality that I put forward is one of contribution and opportunity. Under the traditional paradigm, when a man and a woman decide to marry, the contract upon which their relation is based is one under which the man offers the woman a dowry (a financial contribution) by virtue of which the woman becomes his wife. She owes him obedience while he must provide for the needs of the family. This is the patriarchal model that has existed for centuries, and which existed in Arabia at the time of the Prophet Muhammad without ever being called into question in the Qur'an. Nevertheless, the Qur'an did not impose this model upon religious scholars. In fact, their interpretations led to its adoption as the one and only possibility. Today, however, man-woman relations in the Arab-Muslim countries are a meld of patriarchal tradition and Western modernity, in which women suffer from both the weight of tradition and the financial demands of modern life.

Using the model I propose, inspired by Islamic commercial contracts and founded upon equality, partnership, and risk-sharing, man-woman relations would be more supple, more harmonious, and more closely aligned with the socioeconomic realities of the Arab Muslim countries.

Under this model, a husband and a wife would no longer simply be two individuals who have agreed to enter into a marital relationship, they would above all be partners, fully congruent with the definition of "companion" or "associate" as given by God in the Qur'an. Such a definition would be more accurate and more thorough in describing a man's and a woman's role in a marriage contract. The term "partner" not only connotes a joint project, it also points to equality. In contrast to the notion of a spouse, which from the inception of the relationship denotes imbalance between the two parties, the idea of partnership creates the very harmony that the Qur'an evokes.[11]

To this new relationship each partner brings a different contribution. One partner may contribute financially and the other, manual labour. Likewise, one partner may provide education or know-how, while the other provides material goods and furnishings. It is the combination of these diverse contributions that will determine whether such a relationship can survive and overcome life's obstacles. Such a couple would no longer be a mere platform for divergent interests, but instead would be a place of shared effort. In such a partnership, nothing requires that the man be the unique purveyor of funds and only the woman looks after the children or the household. The woman may well work, while the man may be better qualified to look after the children because of his patience and his love for them. There are women who discover after a first birth that they do not have patience with children, or that they do not know how to deal with them. In a traditional patriarchal relationship, such women have no choice but to suffer in silence. But in a marriage founded upon partnership, such situations can be avoided.

The concept of risk-sharing is crucial in Islamic commercial contracts. It is fully coherent with the logic of partnership: there is neither a dominant (lender or financier) nor a dominated (debtor) party. The two partners share the risk inherent in the relationship without the lender exploiting his financial advantage by receiving a given amount at a certain time—interest or usury—above and beyond his initial investment. Nor is the debtor exploited, for in contributing his education or his experience he may also receive the fruit of his efforts proportional to his initial investment, whether tangible or intangible. In both cases, he need not repay the lender or his partner any more than what that individual has invested or loaned. Both partners are motivated to ensure the success of the relationship, and to see that the fruit of their effort surpasses both their initial investment and their expectations.

In like manner, when a man and a woman enter into a marriage contract, the woman must be seen as a partner. In such a relationship, both partners are equal in terms of remuneration, with each partner receiving a yield proportional to his or her original investment. For example, if a woman is better educated than a man[12] (in the UAE in 2005, literacy rates for girls exceeded those for boys, with 97% of the girls attending school compared to 95% of the boys) and her work outside the home is better paid, a more just partnership would have the husband remain at home to look after the children. The wife would not be penalized for not remaining at home as she would under the traditional model; she would be the party that finances the partnership. In some societies, this model is becoming more and more prevalent. Furthermore, except for the patriarchal traditions powerfully anchored in Arab Muslim mentalities, nothing in the Qur'an can be seen as prohibiting this kind of relationship.

But should the two partners decide that their relationship would be stronger still if both husband and wife joined the labour market, the two partners would have to share in the upkeep of their children and the household chores according to their initial investment, i.e. according to their respective qualifications. He (or she) who earns more would spend more, and he (or she) who is better educated would be more involved with the children's education. In Arab Muslim countries, such a situation is virtually nonexistent. There, if the husband is the better educated and also the partner with the highest earnings, the wife will end up doing everything. At most, he would be called upon to provide for the family's needs and assure the children's education; she would end up performing household chores, helping the children with their homework, cooking, and administering the household, and also working outside the home. Such a partnership would be considered, under the model I propose, usurious. The wife would, in effect, be paying interest to the husband in the form of domestic labour, educating the children, and financial contributions above and beyond her initial contribution and her education. If the children fail in their studies or fall into delinquency, the wife would be blamed. The principle of risk-sharing is absent.

Under the principle of partnership, such a situation could not occur. If the man is better educated than the woman, it is his responsibility to look after the children's homework and education. His too is the responsibility to contribute substantially to the household expenses. The woman need not contribute more to the relationship than her original investment, while the man does not exploit the fact that he is a man by doing nothing or spending his time in cafés. If the couple's children fail in life, the man will be blamed because he did not fulfill his responsibilities, and vice versa. Risks are shared according to the initial investment of the contracting parties.

Of course, real-life situations are more complicated and multifaceted than those I have outlined above. Man-woman relationships are complex. However, I remain convinced that the idea of a domestic partnership would enable Muslims to rear a generation of children for whom there would no longer be a contradiction between what they see and learn at home and what goes on outside the home. What they would see is a continuation of the partnership principle. Today, we are trapped in a contradiction. On the one hand, we now see families in which the mother is called upon to play a greater role in educating the children and contributing to family expenses, while on the other, men continue to occupy decision-making positions in the public and private sectors. The partnership idea has been explored by certain Islamic legal scholars, but always within a context of traditional marriage.[13] But if marriage came to be perceived and experienced as a partnership, in which the woman is a companion and not a dominated wife, and in which men and women act as economic and spiritual associates, it would be relatively easy to extend the paradigm to both the public and the commercial spheres.

Qiwamah and the Canadian context

In this section, I would like to explore whether the application of the new paradigm of partnership between married men and women can be relevant in a Canadian context.

I will base my reflections on the results of two main studies: "Canadian Muslim Women: A decade of change—2001 to 2011"[14] and "Understanding Trends in American Divorce and Marriage."[15] The second study was conducted mainly in the United States and on a smaller scale in Canada, the author asserting that results can easily be extrapolated to Canada.[16]

In Canada, the Muslim population is young, urbanized, and multiethnic.[17] There is also an increasing number of young Muslims born and raised in Canada.[18] In 2011, the Canadian Muslim female population reached 513,380,[19] making up 3.1% of the female population of Canada. According to the National Household Survey mentioned in the first study, Muslim family structures reflect the social and economic transformations that the community went through in the last few decades. Even though traditional marriage still provides the most widespread family structure in Canadian Muslim families, there is a large number of single-parent families (12.63%) and a few persons are in common-law partnerships (2.27%).[20]

From both studies, we understand that Canadian Muslim women are increasingly more educated and active in the labour market.[21] In her four-year empirical study of Muslim marriage and divorce in North American communities, Julie McFarlane identifies three broad causes of marital conflicts: gender role and authority, Islamic family traditions, and domestic violence and abuse. We understand from MacFarlane's study that despite the fact that there is an increasing number of educated Muslim young couples, a misunderstanding about their "Islamic" responsibilities persists during the marriage. Some women are under the impression that they should be "good wives" by staying at home, raising the kids, and taking care of the household. On the other side, some men believe they have financial responsibility similar to what their fathers had. Thus each side has different expectations of the other. Tensions and conflicts will emerge in the marriage when these expectations turn out to be impractical.

Even though many of them were born and raised in Canada, the traditional concept of *qiwamah* seems to be prevalent among Muslims living in Canada. Their "Islamic identity," when it exists, is shadowed by the old concepts imported from their home countries or learned from their parents.

In her survey, MacFarlane finds that "some women who asked their husbands to consider different sharing of responsibilities in the home—for example, sharing household tasks where they both worked outside the home—or expressed aspirations such as returning to school, were accused of being a bad Muslim wife."

Introducing the concept of partnership to the Canadian Muslim youths will help them establish a coherent view of their identity as both Canadians and Muslims. Marriage shouldn't be an exceptional relationship in the lives of young Muslim couples. Instead, a sense of continuity should prevail between marriage and other aspects of lives such as financial, economic, and social.

—៳៳—

In conclusion, I would like to emphasize that the new paradigm I am proposing for man-woman relations does not mean that the life of a couple would only be considered from a purely materialist and mercantile viewpoint. I am not advocating the commercialization of these relationships. In all traditions, marriage remains above all a moral and spiritual commitment between two persons. For centuries Arab Muslim societies have perpetuated the patriarchal model as the only possible one for marital relationships. However, besides this traditional contract there exists an entire Islamic jurisprudence of commercial contracts that is much more flexible, broader, and better adapted to the requirements of modern life and that would also extract the woman from the dominated position she currently finds herself in despite the many attempts to extricate her.

I am well aware of the obstacles and resistance that my thesis can be expected to encounter. I am likewise aware that not only will it not win unanimous support, but also it will face opposition from traditionalist minds and from entrenched religious authorities. For all that, I remain convinced that only through creativity and innovation can Arab Muslim societies move forward and evolve towards the divinely inspired ideal.

—៳៳—

This article was originally written in French. I would like to thank Fred A Reed for translating it to English. I really benefited from the thoughtful comments of my friends Mohamed Ben Jemaa and Dr Salah Bessalamah. Their reflections and questions on the original manuscript helped me improving this article. All remaining errors are mine.

Anti-Muslim Bigotry Goes Official
—Canada's Newest Dark Chapter

HAROON SIDDIQUI

INTRODUCTION

Turning back the clock a thousand years, 9/11 reignited the argument of the Crusades: Islam and Christianity cannot coexist. The new twist is that Islam is incompatible with the secular West. I will argue otherwise, and submit that it's the West that is becoming incompatible with its own secular, democratic values. Whipped into an exaggerated fear of terrorism, it has been steadily eroding the very democratic values that it claims the terrorists hate us for. It has let bigots and demagogues as well as governments make us so paranoid about fellow citizens who happen to be Muslims that we are repeating the mistakes of the past in dealing with minorities. Worse, Stephen Harper's misuse of the powers of the state to isolate, even bully Canadian Muslims arguably posed a greater threat to Canadian democracy than the misguided actions of a handful of homegrown radicalized Muslims, whom our security forces have under closer scrutiny than they do other more numerous potential violent misfits.

ISLAM AND SECULARISM

Is Islam compatible with secularism and democracy? Of course it is, as much as Christianity or Judaism or any other faith is. The contrary view—that there is an inherent clash between Islam and secular democracy, and the two cannot co-exist—is most vigorously advanced by a small minority of archconservative Muslims, on the one hand, and by the growing hordes of Islamophobes in the West, on the other. Without that ostensibly unbridgeable divide, both groups would lose much of their raison d'être.

This is not to say that there is no tension between Islam and secular democracy—there is plenty, obviously. But it emanates mostly from geopolitical conflicts between the West and the Muslim world—long unresolved conflicts such as those around Palestine;[1] the military invasions and occupations of Muslim lands; the control of resources, especially oil; and the Western realpolitik of cavorting with oppressive autocratic Muslim allies, despite constant proclamations of fidelity to democracy and universal human rights. Our allies have included the Shah of Iran, General Zia ul-Haq of Pakistan, Air Marshal Hosni Mubarak and General Abdul Fattah el-Sisi of Egypt, Saddam Hussein of Iraq for many years, and the royal houses of Saudi Arabia, Jordan, and other Arab kingdoms to whom we sell tens of billions of dollars of armaments, whose torture chambers we use for extraordinary renditions and whose ruthless crushing of democratic uprisings, such as the Arab Spring, we wink at.

In the domestic context of nation states, the tension between the secular and the religious is no different in the case of Islam than other faiths. The right to religious freedom sometimes clashes with other fundamental rights, such as gender equity. Catholic women remain in the pews and cannot make it to the pulpit; Hindu women are not on the same elevated rung as male Brahmin priests; Jewish women suffer the indignity of being skipped over by the rabbi as he counts to the ten men required to begin the communal service; and Muslim women are relegated to the back of the congregation or in dingy basements or hot mezzanine enclaves. All are told that they have the option of quitting such faiths or finding more liberal congregations within their faiths, if any. Such are the uneasy democratic compromises when fundamental rights clash, and the courts generally refuse to be drawn into creating a hierarchy of rights between competing constitutional values.

I suggest that the more appropriate question of the age is this: Can secular democracies adhere to their most fundamental principle of not burdening all Muslims with collective guilt? Can they separate out the overwhelming majority of law-abiding Muslims from the minority of terrorists in far-off lands—Iraq, Afghanistan, Nigeria, Yemen, etc—and from home-grown terrorists, many of them Christian converts to Islam angry at Western wars on Muslim nations? Conflating the Muslims "there" and the Muslims "here," and the handful of violent Muslims here with the entire Muslim citizenry of the West is a major cause of the confusion and anger in Western minds about Islam and Muslims.

The debate about the clash of civilizations between Muslims and non-Muslims is, in fact, a smokescreen often used by Islamophobes and those whose religious or geo-political interests are served by demonizing Islam—far-right parties across Europe, several evangelical Christian groups in the United States, and those who unfortunately equate supporting Israel with opposing Arabs and Muslims, as well as Islam. Such individuals and groups have been well funded in the United States, according to the Washington-based Center for American Progress. Its 2011 report *Fear, Inc.: Exposing the Islamophobia Network in America*[2] catalogued how seven foundations dispersed $42.6 million between 2001 and 2009 to anti-Muslim groups. The report listed five "misinformation experts"—Frank Gaffney at the Center for Security Policy; David Yerushalmi at the Society of Americans for National Existence; Daniel Pipes at the Middle East Forum; Robert Spencer of Jihad Watch and Stop Islamization of America; and Steven Emerson of the Investigative Project on Terrorism. The report also named five groups that helped spread the Islamophobia movement across the US, including Brigette Gabriel's ACT! for America; Pamela Geller's Stop Islamization of America; and David Horowitz' Freedom Center. Together, they all helped poison public discourse and public opinion by successfully setting the agenda for populist politicians and media.[3] In February 2015, the Center for American Progress issued a follow-up report, *Fear, Inc. 2.0,* further detailing "the Islamophobia network's efforts to manufacture hate in America."[4]

No incongruity in being secular and Muslim

Whether Islam is compatible with secularism is not the same as whether Muslims are. As with the followers of any faith, not all Muslims are observant. To presume otherwise is to fall into yet another cliché about Muslims. While Muslims have a strong identity as Muslims, only a third are estimated to attend the Friday prayers worldwide. The participation rate among Muslims living in the West may be lower still. Even those Friday congregants may not all be presumed to be preoccupied with living their lives fully in accordance with Islamic theological dictates, which range from orthodox to liberal streams of *fiqh,* theological jurisprudence, of which there are as many as five, with hundreds of differences between them.

On, then, with the issue at hand: can Islam and secularism coexist?

Unlike strains of Hinduism and Buddhism that advocate renunciation of the worldly for the spiritual, Islam emphasizes *deeni-wa-dunyawi,* the spiritual and the worldly. Muslims cannot abandon one for the other. They must pray five times a day but no sooner have they done so than they must step out into the world and engage with it. For them, there's no sitting atop a mountain or under a tree to attain nirvana. Their faith dictates active participation in the societies in which they live, including secular ones.

Materialism, derided by some faiths, is not antithetical to Islam, which recognizes the right of private property and the accumulation of wealth—so long as it is ethically acquired by *halal,* legal, means and a prescribed portion of it distributed to the less fortunate through *zakat,* charitable giving.

The tension between the moral and the immoral, as defined by faith, is common to all believers, not Muslims alone. This is not to ignore the reality that observant Muslims must resist the ubiquitous temptations of *haram*, prohibited activities, such as gambling, obscenity, pornography, alcohol and drug consumption, abortion, the taking and giving of interest, etc. Some "radical Islamic groups claim that a Muslim cannot be bound by a constitution that allows interest (*riba*), alcohol (*khamr*) and other behaviour which contradicts Islamic teachings," notes European scholar Tariq Ramadan, who adds, rightly, that no observant Muslim is forced to participate in any such activity.[5]

What of the laws and norms that may force a Muslim to act against his or her religious entitlement? One can think of only one, polygamy. But the Qur'an says, "Marry of the women who seem good to you, two or three or four; and if you fear you cannot do justice (to so many) then only one . . . that will be more suitable, to prevent you from doing injustice."[6] The Qur'an also warns the believers, "You have it not in your power to do justice between the wives, even though you may wish it."[7] Far from conferring a license, this makes polygamy virtually impossible. But that's not how the verses were interpreted for hundreds of years. However, monogamous marriage is now the norm for the overwhelming majority of Muslims who accept the strong Qur'anic qualifiers. Yet polygamy remains religiously permissible and culturally acceptable in some parts of the Muslim world. But our concern here is only with those few Muslim men in secular states who may wish to have more than one wife, contrary to legal norm. Happily, there is a catch here as well: under Islamic law, Muslims are required to obey the law of the land where they live, so long as the law does not conflict with the basic tenets of the faith—belief in God and His messenger Muhammad; five daily prayers; *zakat*; dawn-to-dusk fasting in the lunar month of Ramadan for the physically fit; and performing the Hajj pilgrimage to Mecca and Medina, if health and finances permit. Polygamy is decidedly not one of those five essential obligations. That leaves only two options for men desirous of more than one wife—either migrate to another jurisdiction that permits it or face prosecution, just as the men of the Fundamentalist Church of Jesus Christ of Latter-Day Saints in British Columbia have, after years of prosecutorial neglect.

Other clashes, much in the news of late, between Muslims and secular society—adjustment in the work schedule for the Friday noon congregational prayers as well as for the two annual religious holidays of Eid al-Fitr and Eid al-Adha, or the wearing of hijab at work or, in some cases, separate swimming pool hours for men and women, etc.—are no different than the negotiated accommodations for other faiths, such as for the Sikh turban or the Jewish kippa or the annual Hanukkah or Diwali, not to mention the nettlesome issues of life-saving blood transfusions for followers of Jehovah's Witness or exemptions from war-time conscription for Quakers.

According to the Qur'an, Muslims can live in any place, any country so long as they are not being persecuted there: "Was not Allah's earth spacious [enough] that you could have migrated therin?"[8] There is thus no incongruity in being Muslim and being a Canadian or American or European or a resident of any democratic, secular state anywhere. In fact, Muslims are freer to practice Islam in democracies than in some Muslim states, which impose sectarian restrictions on either Sunnis or Shiites and, especially, the smaller branches or off-shoots of Islam, such as the Alevis, Alawites, Ahmadis, Bahais, and others. Many Muslim states also deny their citizens basic freedoms, including the right to free speech and assembly, and control the contents of Friday sermons and prosecute imams who do not toe the official religious and political line.

Muslims at home in Canada

I have long argued that, contrary to the literalist readings of the Qur'an by the ultra-orthodox and, lately, militant zealots, Canada is an ideal place where the spirit of Islam and Islamic values, especially the injunction of *sulh-e-kull*, complete peace, can be practiced better than elsewhere in the world. Canadian ideals are, at their core, Islamic ideals. The Charter of Rights and Freedoms, in guaranteeing freedom of religion, echoes the Qur'an, which urges no coercion in religion: "Whoever will, let him believe, and whoever will, let him disbelieve."[9] In outlawing racism, the Charter follows a Qur'anic precept: "We have created you male and female and have made you [into] nations and tribes that you may know one another."[10] The Charter also reflects the message of the Prophet Muhammad's famous last Hajj sermon delivered in 632 AD about the equality of human beings: "an Arab has no superiority over a non-Arab nor a non-Arab has any superiority over an Arab; also a white has no superiority over a black, nor a black has any superiority over a white—except by piety and good deeds."[11] Such injunctions are routinely violated by ostensibly Islamic states, which tolerate, indeed in some cases foster racism and bigotry towards their black or non-Arab residents.

The sense of justice that prevails in Canada is essentially Islamic. The Islamic injunction to care for the needy, sick, and weak is embodied in our universal medicare. The precepts of *zakat* are reflected in Canada's social services, which help the underprivileged through taxation. Canada also lives up to the first revealed words of the Qur'an: "Read! In the name of thy Lord . . . He Who taught (the use of) the Pen."[12] There is more freedom to read and write in Canada than in most Muslim nations.

Canada's harmonious balance between individualism and collectivity reflects an Islamic principle. The British North America Act, the Indian Act, the Official Languages Act, the various sections of the Charter, especially Sec. 27[13] and Sec. 15(b),[14] and the Multiculturalism Act are all nods to collective rights, in the same way that Islam enjoins the believer to defer to the common good, to balance between individual and collective rights, and between tribal instincts and universal responsibilities. Islam abhors ethnocentric particularism, as does Canada. Canada avoids extremes, just as the Prophet did. Muslims are as multicultural, multilingual, multiracial and multiethnic as Canadians.

This is not to pretend that Canada has been immune from post-9/11 anti-Muslim bigotry.

ISLAMOPHOBIA IN CANADA

Western prejudices against Islam and Muslims are historic. Contemporary anti-Islamic tirades—VS Naipaul's *Among the Believers*, Salman Rushdie's *The Satanic Verses*, and the Danish and the *Charlie Hebdo* cartoons of the Prophet Muhammad are newer versions of the ridiculing of the Prophet by Dante Alighieri, Francis Bacon, and those who caricatured him as the beast of the Apocalypse. Still, since 9/11, gratuitous insults to the Prophet Muhammad have increased exponentially across the West, as have the fear and demonization of Islam.

If in the United States, nearly half of the 50 states took panicky legislative steps to stop the *sharia*, Muslim law, that could not possibly have been introduced, Ontario had its own *sharia* hysteria in 2004-05. At issue was the province's 1991 Arbitration Act, which permitted Christians and Jews to use religious arbitration in business disputes and such family matters as divorce and the distribution of marital assets, under the aegis of the churches and *Beit din*, the rabbinical court. However, no sooner had a small group of Muslims sought permission to do the same than panic broke out. It didn't seem to matter that all faith-based arbitration could easily have been made compatible with Canadian law by making such settlements appealable in the courts, as recommended by New Democrat Marion Boyd, former Ontario cabinet minister and certified feminist, in a report commissioned by Premier Dalton McGuinty.[15] But the public furor was such that he had no realistic choice but to either allow such arbitration for all faith groups or none at all, and he opted for the latter.

If the Swiss voted in a 2009 referendum against the building of minarets, mosques across Europe have been desecrated with pig blood; dozens of American municipalities have held up the construction of Islamic centres; American protestors have marched in front of mosques shouting obscenities; and in Canada dozens of mosques have been vandalized and several niqabi and even hijabi women have been harassed in public places.

If a disturbing number of Americans and Europeans have persuaded themselves about the imminent takeover of their nations by Muslims, who constitute about 1 per cent of the American population and 3.8 per cent in the European Union, the story in Canada has not been all that different. A 2013 poll showed that nearly a third of Canadians believed that Muslims had too much power, even though Muslims constitute about 3 per cent of the Canadian population. The anti-Muslim sentiment has been the most pronounced in Quebec, where 43 per cent thought that Muslims had too much power, according to the Forum Research poll.[16] That sentiment echoed the old anti-Semitic trope about Jews controlling the world and, sure enough, the poll also showed that 32 per cent of Quebeckers thought that Jews had too much influence. While 57 per cent of Quebeckers did not like Muslims, 56 per cent did not like Hasidic Jews, according to a Crop poll released about the same time.[17] Anti-Muslim and anti-Jewish views were predominant among separatists, according to Forum President Lorne Bozinoff.

An Angus Reid poll showed even higher dislike of Muslims among Quebeckers, nearly 70 per cent. Anti-Muslim feelings, however, were not confined to the separatists, Reid said, reporting that in the rest of Canada, more than half of respondents viewed Muslims negatively. The old, the less educated and the less wealthy held the most negative views about Muslims and Islam, as did the supporters of the Conservative Party, in contrast to the supporters of other political parties.[18]

An earlier poll, done in 2011 by the Montreal-based Association for Canadian Studies, of 1,500 Canadians, showed that 56 per cent of respondents saw the conflict between the West and the Muslim world as "irreconcilable," with only 33 per cent holding out any hope of it ever being resolved. Jack Jedwab, executive director of the association, said that while a decade ago, there were concerns about tensions between "whites and all visible minorities," the poll showed that "what's emerging is a focus on Muslims vs non-Muslims. The outlet for people's prejudice has been displaced by the focus on Muslims."[19]

These were alarming findings for a constitutionally multicultural nation that prides itself on celebrating pluralism.

Quebec pathology

Quebec's Islamophobia had been simmering since the 2007-08 crises on "reasonable accommodation" of religious minorities, Muslims in particular. Provincial soccer and tae kwon do federations had banned hijabi girls under the thinly disguised excuse of safety. Media were sensationalizing stories of ostensibly outrageous requests for accommodating religious sensitivities. The provincial government of Liberal Premier Jean Charest established a commission, co-chaired by eminent academics Gérard Bouchard (a separatist) and Charles Taylor (a federalist). It held months of public hearings and concluded that there was no crisis—"trivial incidents" had been blown out of proportion, mostly by the media; Muslims and other religious minorities were not making unreasonable demands; and opposition to the hijab, from both rightwingers and leftist feminists, was often "irrational."[20]

The commission's report defused the crisis, temporarily. Muslim-bashing returned in 2012 with the election of the separatist Parti Quebecois, which introduced a Charter of Quebec Values, proposing to ban all religious attire and symbols, such as the kippa, hijab, and the Sikh turban from the public sector. The real target were Muslims—the Pauline Marois government being confident that the Montreal Jewish General Hospital and institutions of other faiths would take up its offer of opting out of the charter for five years. That would have freed them from the dictates of the charter and cleared the way for the government to ban the hijab from the public sector and fire thousands of hijab-wearing women from daycare centres, schools, and the health sector. PQ strategist and cabinet minister Jean-François Lisée admitted that much: "We are not dummies. Nobody will be at the doors of Jewish hospitals taking kippas off of doctors' heads. That's not the case."[21] But the Jewish General took a principled stand and refused the opt-out option and announced that it would take the government to court. Opposition to the bill kept gathering momentum and the Marois government was defeated in the 2014 election—and with it the charter.

Anti-Muslim sentiments, however, did not disappear. In February 2015, a judge in Montreal refused to hear a routine case unless the defendant, Rania El-Alloul, removed her hijab, which she refused to, saying that it was an integral part of her faith.[22] The Quebec council of judges refused to intervene, citing judicial independence. We can be reasonably certain that it would have had something to say had the judge erred on the side of anti-Semitism or racism.

A month later, Concordia University library staff was culling "controversial" and "inappropriate" books and documents in an office run by the Muslim Students' Association. The irony of a post-secondary institution censoring reading material in the twenty-first century seems to have been completely lost on all concerned. "This is totally crazy," said Salam Elmenyawi, president of the Muslim Council of Montreal. "Are we going to go back to the Dark Ages and start burning books now?"[23]

Philippe Couillard, the Liberal leader who succeeded Marois as premier, had made an ill-advised election promise to implement a lighter version of the PQ's Charter of Quebec Values. He did so in two separate bills in June 2015, to bar the niqab for all public sector employees and also for anyone receiving a public service, including health care; and to curb honour killings and forced marriages[24] (found among some Sikhs, Hindus, and Arab Christians but wrongly assumed to be exclusively Muslim practices). The measures were described as overkill by Nathalie Des Rosiers, dean of law at University of Ottawa and a former general counsel for the Canadian Civil Liberties Association. Murder is murder and laws also exist to take preventive measures for forced marriages, she said; the bills were introduced only to "target one group," Muslims.[25]

More than bigotry at work

There is an argument that the Quebeckers' hostility towards Muslims does not all spring from bigotry but rather from a skewed sense of secularism in Quebec, as in France. Secularism was to be the antidote to the absolute truths of religion, and the secular state was to remain neutral between faiths. But it has drifted into a fundamentalism of its own, becoming intolerant of religions—Islam, in particular. This is especially true in France and Quebec, partly because of their histories. In France, any public assertion of faith butts against the legacy of the Revolution, manifested in *laïcité,* which does not recognize religious, racial, ethnic, and other identities (at least in theory, while in practice, as the Taylor-Bouchard Commission wryly noted, the French state funds religious schools, churches, and chaplaincy services, observes Catholic holidays, and ordains that the state funeral for the president be a mass at Notre-Dame Cathedral—yet the state does little to curb the widespread discrimination that denies Muslims the equality promised by *laïcité*). In Quebec, the Quiet Revolution won the Catholic population freedom from the political and social clutches of the Catholic Church. Now with increasing immigration of Muslims to Quebec and the visible presence of their religious symbols, such as the hijab and the niqab, old-time Quebeckers, especially women, react viscerally. That may be an explanation for irrationality but not an excuse for state-sanctioned bigotry.

As dismaying as it was to see a provincial government of two different political persuasions, the Parti Quebecois and the Liberal Party, target Muslims, Stephen Harper was doing so on an unprecedented scale nationally.

HARPER AND MUSLIMS

Mr Harper is a bigot. Mr Harper does not like Muslims.
              —Dennis Edney, lawyer for Omar Khadr

In times of terrorism, the balance between security and civil rights tilts to the former. The public expects its leaders to stand up to terrorists with resolve. Harper, however, took a leaf out of George W Bush's book in stoking fear of Muslim terrorism. But unlike Bush and Barack Obama, both of whom tried to delink terrorism from Islam and Muslims, the prime minister mined, indeed fanned, anti-Muslim prejudices. Going well beyond being tough on terrorists, he not only made anti-Muslim talk respectable but also initiated a range of policies and legislation that constituted cultural warfare on Muslims.

Not until you enumerate all his actions, as I do below, do you realize how extensive and systematic he was in maligning Muslims and mollycoddling Islamophobes.

Waging jihad on terror

In 2011 the prime minister declared that the biggest threat to Canada was "Islamicism," invoking the vocabulary of those who say they are not against Islam—no, not at all—but rather against "Islamism," "political Islam," "radical Islam," "militant Islam," or "extremist Islam," terms that lack precision and can mean whatever one wants them to mean. Such a formulation is tailor-made for those who believe that terrorism involving Muslims is "Islamic," while the terrorism of, say, Anders Breivik is not "Christian," even though there are parallels between him and Muslim terrorists. Just as they use religious terminology to justify their barbarism, so did he in killing 77 fellow-Norwegians, most of them teenagers, in 2011. They invoke Islam, he invoked Christianity, which he thought was being undermined by Muslims in Europe and by governments that were enablers of multicultural concessions to Muslims. Muslim terrorists see themselves as warriors against American and NATO invasions and occupations of Muslim lands, while he saw himself as a soldier in the war against the imagined takeover of Europe by Muslims. Their terror is no more "Islamic" than his was "Christian," yet the Harperites made it a point to identify Muslim terrorists with Islam.[26]

When Harper decided in 2014 to commit Canada to the American war on the Islamic State caliphate (IS or ISIS), he, his ministers, and his MPs took up a mantra of war against "jihadists," "jihadism," "violent jihadism," "jihadi terrorism," "the international jihadist movement," "jihadist monsters," etc. And the government promoted its anti-terrorism legislation by posting images of religious-looking

Muslims—in one case, using a misleading photo.[27] On August 2, 2015 when the prime minister called an election for October 19, he invoked ISIS, thrice, as well as the threat to Canada of a "violent global jihadist movement."[28]

Harper used "public fear to advance his political agenda at the expense of Canadian Muslims," wrote Faisal Bhabha on the blog, The Harper Decade. In his essay entitled "Does Harper care about Canadian Muslims?,"[29] the Osgoode Hall Law School professor and former vice-chair of the Human Rights Tribunal of Ontario, noted that on "the day of the April 2013 Boston Marathon attack, the Harper government announced plans to rush debate of new legislation intended to revive the anti-terrorism detention and investigative powers that expired in 2007 . . . Within days of the January 2015 *Charlie Hebdo* attack in Paris, French President Francois Hollande spoke publicly to reassure French Muslims of their civil rights, acknowledging that Muslims were 'the first victims of fanaticism, fundamentalism and intolerance.' Stephen Harper, meanwhile, was quick to capitalize on the French tragedy. As with the Boston attack, he drew an implausible link to events in Canada. He went on to irresponsibly associate local mosques with the 'international jihadist movement.' The Prime Minister's resort (sic) to smearing peaceful places of congregation and worship[30] was, for many, cruel and unforgivable."

Holding a kangaroo court

The Harperites' penchant for tarring Muslims with the terrorist brush was starkly on display at hearings of the Senate committee on national security, held in the fall of 2014 and spring of 2015. The committee did not invite groups representative of Canada's more than one million Muslims. Instead it preferred anti-Muslim activists such as Ayaan Hirsi Ali, a Somali-born critic of Islam who lives in the United States and is a favourite of Islamophobes. It also invited a handful of Canadian Muslims who have made a career of attacking other Muslims. Such witnesses claimed that Muslim militants were crawling under every Canadian minaret. Using parliamentary immunity, they hurled unsubstantiated, indeed false, accusations against Canadian Muslims. The majority Conservative senators harried the witnesses who refused to go along with the prescribed party line—as illustrated in an exchange with Shahina Siddiqui.

The hijab-wearing Siddiqui (no relation) is head of the Winnipeg-based Islamic Social Services Association. She has been honored for her social justice activism and inter-faith work with the YMCA-YWCA Winnipeg Peace Medal and the Grass Roots Women of Manitoba Award, among others. She has worked with federal, provincial and local security and police forces and also helped produce an antiradicalization booklet. There was a marked contrast in the way the Conservative senators treated her and the hero's welcome they gave an anti-Muslim Montreal blogger, Marc Lebuis of Point de Bascule (Tipping Point), who said that mosques and Muslim organizations in Canada were "controlled and financed, proven, by countries known to harbour the most radical fringes of Muslim, the Wahhabism fringes."

When Siddiqui pushed back—"Please do not treat Muslim Canadians as if they are the enemy because we are not . . . Don't give in to fear and propaganda, otherwise we will tear each other apart"— she was upbraided by Conservative Senator Lynn Beyak, who told her, thrice, to stop being "thin-skinned" in reacting to increased hostility towards Muslims. She berated Siddiqui that Canadians are "tired of hearing excuses. If 21 Christians were beheaded by Jews, they would be called 'radical extremist Jews.' And if pilots were burned in cages by a Christian, they would be called 'radical violent Christians' . . . What would *you* answer to people who are legitimately concerned?" (emphasis mine).[31] In Beyak's bigoted view of the world, this Muslim from Manitoba had to answer for the atrocities committed by the Islamic State in Syria and Iraq.

Siddiqui told me later that the committee hearing felt like the "Tea Party in action. It was a very charged atmosphere—more like an inquisition." The Ottawa-based National Council of Canadian

Muslims described the committee proceedings as "a witch hunt."[32]

Following the hearings, I tracked down three individuals whom Lebuis had singled out.[33]

He had said that Jamal Badawi, former professor at the Sobey School of Business, St Mary's University in Halifax, and also a prolific author on Islam, "started" or "is behind" several Muslim organizations that are part of "the network of the Muslim Brotherhood infrastructure in North America," and that Badawi urges Muslims "to become judges and officials" in order to "take advantage of their position of influence to stop applying current national legal provisions that are incompatible with sharia law." Lebuis was echoing such American Islamophobes as Frank Gaffney, who have said that the Muslim Brotherhood had infiltrated the American government.[34]

Badawi told me he has never urged Muslims to infiltrate the government in order to advance sharia. "I challenge those who make this false allegation to produce evidence, such as a recording in my voice or quotes from my writings to back up their allegation. I consistently urge Muslims in Canada, USA, Europe and elsewhere to positively integrate in their societies, to fulfill their duties as citizens and to be beneficial to all."

Lebuis called Toronto lawyer Faisal Kutty "the spokesperson of two Al Qaeda funding organizations," who "consistently defends and promotes people who are known and banned in certain countries."

Kutty teaches law at Osgoode and also at Valparaiso University, Indiana. He has written extensively on radicalization, including what Muslims must do to stop it. He said he has worked with the Royal Canadian Mounted Police and the Canadian Security Intelligence Service, and been consulted by the US House Homeland Security Subcommittee on Intelligence. He told me, "I've never served as a spokesperson for any terrorist organization. A lawyer representing a client is a far cry from a spokesperson . . . By their spurious logic, all criminal lawyers must be closet criminals as well . . . I have unequivocally condemned violence of all kinds. I have always urged Canadians, including Muslims, to fulfill their patriotic obligation to defend our country but also to be vigilant in holding our government and its agencies accountable."

Lebuis accused Hamilton lawyer Hussein Hamdani of having lobbied Ottawa to stop using "Islamic" in relation to terrorism by Muslims, and having done so with "a delegation of Islamist leaders linked to the Muslim Brotherhood infrastructure operating in Canada." Since 2005, Hamdani had been a member of the federal government's Cross-Cultural Roundtable on National Security, which fosters dialogue between the government and leaders of various cultural communities on national security matters. In 2012 he spoke to Vic Toews, then minister of public safety, at the minister's invitation. "Mr Toews came to the Hamilton mosque, with four officials from his ministry, and nine or ten of us met him there," Hamdani told me. "I did say that the language used by Prime Minister Harper and others in Ottawa was counterproductive. I compared it with that of President Obama, who always asserts that Muslims are part of the American family and part of the solution to terrorism. Yet nowhere has Harper made clear that Canadian Muslims are part of the Canadian family, that they are partners in this battle against terrorism."

The RCMP and CSIS did stop associating terrorism by Muslims with Islam or mosques, and instead started being precise about terrorist groups and individuals. Still, Hamdani said, "the suggestion that I somehow strong-armed the government of Canada into changing is amusing. Clearly, the Conservatives have not changed," even if the security agencies had. "It is shameful that Islamophobes who used to be on the fringes are being brought into the centre by this government. Such people defame others without providing any evidence—'the world is flat and Islamists are taking over Canada.' And the people maligned do not have the wherewithal to defend themselves. That's what's really disconcerting."

Within weeks of Lebuis's accusation, the Harper government removed Hamdani from the federal advisory committee.[35] The decision was seen as a partisan payback for Hamdani having held a fund-raiser for Liberal leader Justin Trudeau. Still, the manner of

Hamdani's dismissal was vicious, with the government accusing him, without offering any proof, of having "links to radical ideology."

Dr Myrna Lashley, chair of the Cross-Cultural Roundtable, was "very, very shocked" about the government's allegation. "This is not the Hussein that I know," Lashley, a psychiatrist at Montreal's Jewish General Hospital, told the *Hamilton Spectator*. "He has never demonstrated any of this stuff that they're talking about. I can tell you that he has been one of the biggest supporters of Canada on the roundtable. He has done a lot to reach out to Muslim youth to sing the praises of Canada, to talk about unity. He's certainly adamantly against ISIS and al-Qaeda."[36]

On June 5, Hamdani told a gathering of Muslims in Mississauga that the Harperites "want Canadians to be afraid of Muslims because then they can say, 'we are the only party that will protect against the hordes, locusts and animals that are coming and who are already in the land.'" The public meeting where Hamdani spoke was an initiative of Dawanet, a community group. Organizer Mohammed Hashim told *Toronto Star* reporter Noor Javed that Muslims were feeling the effects of the rhetoric and policies of the Conservative government but were too scared to speak out. "There is a paralysis. People are just afraid to say anything. 'Is CSIS (Canadian Security Intelligence Service) going to watch me?' 'Are people going to think I am a jihadi?' 'Are people going to fire me?' The whole point of the event is to send a message back to the community: Let's stand up to the government for exploiting us, and stoking fear. Let's stand up against the rhetoric of Islamophobia."[37]

That rhetoric was in full flow in the Senate committee's report, released July 8.[38]

Being McCarthyesque

The committee's Conservative majority painted a picture of rising "Islamist fundamentalist menace," aided and abetted by Canadian imams spreading "extreme ideas," who ought to be "trained and certified." That prompted *The Globe and Mail* to ask, editorially: "Would clerics have to wear a crescent symbol on their lapels?"[39]

The committee offered no proof of the alleged complicity of the imams, citing merely the hearsay from some of its favourite witnesses: "The committee heard testimony from members of the Muslim community and others that *some* foreign-trained imams have been spreading extremist religious ideology and messages that are not in keeping with Canadian values. These extreme ideas are *said to be* contributing to radicalization and raise serious concerns if they continue to go unchecked" (emphasis mine).

Canada must fight not only terrorism but also extremism, the committee said, and offered ideas for thought control. There should be criminal bans on "the glorification of terrorists, terrorist acts and terrorist symbols connected to terrorism and radicalization." Yet, paradoxically, the committee recommended that those who criticize Muslim extremism be granted unfettered freedom of speech and be protected from "vexatious litigation," presumably by Muslims.

Ottawa should also stop foreign money from promoting extremist views, since "wealthy Saudis, Qataris and Kuwaitis are using charities as conduits to finance Canadian mosques and community centres" in order to "promote their own fundamentalist brand of Islam, Wahhabism, here in Canada." The committee offered no evidence of such financial flows doing religious brainwashing. Nor did it address Siddiqui's suggestion that if foreign funding was indeed a problem, Ottawa could easily ban it—for all faith groups.

The committee report "reads like a colonial document dictating a primarily one-way relationship with minority communities and suggesting the state has final say on determining who can participate in our communities," said Ihsaan Gardee of the National Council of Canadian Muslims. The report "stigmatizes and marginalizes" Canadian Muslims. Particularly misplaced was the attack on the imams, he said, not only because of the suggestion that only Muslim religious leaders need to be vetted but also because Canadian imams have long been in the forefront of addressing the "false narratives" used by radicals.[40]

The three Liberal senators on the committee refused to sign the report. Senator Grant Mitchell, committee co-chair, said that its recommendation flew in the face of evidence that Canada faces a terrorist threat from right-wing racist ideologies as well, and "not just from one group," Muslims. Also, "the committee's Conservative majority think it's time to get the state in the business of deciding who is allowed to preach and teach which religion, and implicitly what they get to say while preaching and teaching. But just for Muslims."

The Senate committee's work was reminiscent of the 1950s Red Scare tactics of Joseph McCarthy, the American senator who used his committee hearings to ruin the lives of many Americans by falsely accusing them of being Communist sympathizers.

A contemporary comparison is with the infamous 2011 US Congressional hearings, by the security committee of the US House of Representatives, on "home-grown radicalization" of American Muslims. The committee chair, Republican Peter King, claimed, without offering any proof, that "80-85 per cent" of America's 1,900 mosques were "controlled by Islamic fundamentalists. This is an enemy living amongst us."[41] The Canadian Senate committee's work was far more reprehensible, considering that Congress acts independently of the White House, whereas parliamentary committees take orders from the prime minister, especially one commanding a majority, like Harper, who was also known to dictate nearly every aspect of the government's parliamentary activities. It doesn't take much speculation to say that the Senate committee's work was orchestrated by the Prime Minister's Office.

Passing draconian laws

The Senate committee's recommendations came only weeks after the enactment of two sweeping laws that were widely criticized but sent a particular chill among Muslim Canadians.

The Anti-Terrorism Act empowered 21 federal agencies to share or exchange personal information without accountability or transparency; lowered the threshold for and lengthened the duration of preventative detention without charge; and created a new offence of "promoting terrorism in general," among other sweeping changes.[42] It was described as "the most dangerous legislation we've had in recent Canadian history" by Tom Henheffer, executive director of Canadian Journalists for Free Expression, which mounted a constitutional challenge, along with the Canadian Civil Liberties Association. "It will lead to a massive, massive chill on free speech and huge violations of privacy rights."[43]

In May 2015, the government proclaimed the Orwellian-sounding Strengthening Canadian Citizenship Act,[44] which, in fact, weakened citizenship protections for dual citizens who can now be stripped of citizenship if convicted of terrorism, treason or spying offences—at the discretion of the Minister of Citizenship and Immigration, without due process.[45] An estimated 950,000 Canadians hold dual or multiple citizenships. An undetermined number are either eligible for other nationalities or on whom the countries of their birth continue to claim rights of prosecution, such as Iran and Egypt.

Citizenship and Immigration Minister Chris Alexander said the law was needed to protect Canadians from "jihadi terrorism" within our borders.[46] He did not clarify whether naturalized Canadians deemed dangerous would be deported back to countries from which many had fled due to persecution. Or, whether yet others would be sent back to countries where there is the death penalty, despite long-standing Canadian policy of not transferring even convicted criminals there. Or, what the government would do with stateless persons, such as Palestinians, who had found refuge in Canada.[47]

Audrey Macklin, law professor at the University of Toronto, wrote: "From antiquity to the late 20th century, denationalization was a tool used by states to rid themselves of political dissidents, convicted criminals and ethnic, religious or racial minorities. The latest target of denationalization is the convicted terrorist, or the suspected terrorist, or the potential terrorist, or maybe the associate of a terrorist. He is virtually always Muslim and male."[48]

The medieval practice of taking away citizenship was a favourite of the British, who shipped off convicts to America and then Australia in the 18th century, and from colonial India to Burma in the 19th.

The Harper government's intentions became clearer during the October 2015 federal election campaign when, using the law for the first time, it moved to strip the citizenship of four people convicted and sentenced for their role in the 2006 "Toronto 18" terror plot to blow up sites in protest against Canada's military mission in Afghanistan. One was Saad Gaya, born in Montreal to Pakistani immigrants who came to Canada more than 30 years ago and had given up their Pakistani citizenship.

The policy raised troubling issues of double punishment, two-tier citizenship and deportation of even the Canadian-born based on their parents' original citizenship. But for Harper, it was just another extension of his campaign to target Muslims for political gain.

Maligning Muslims

In 2014, the Harper government passed its ominously-named Zero Tolerance for Barbaric Cultural Practices Act,[49] outlawing what was already outlawed—polygamy, family violence, "honour-killing" and forcing children under sixteen to leave Canada for marriages abroad—crimes that in the public mind are associated with Muslims.

Khadijah Kanji, programming coordinator for Toronto's Noor Cultural Centre, noted that seventeen women in Canada have been victims of honour-based killings compared with hundreds of aboriginal women who have gone missing or been killed by their intimate partners—about whom Harper steadfastly refused national calls for an inquiry.

The real purpose of the act did not become clear until a year later, when in the middle of the election the Conservatives announced with fanfare that they would set up a special RCMP hotline for Canadians to snitch on neighbours and others whom they suspected of engaging, or intending to engage, in a barbaric cultural practice.

"There's a low-frequency thrumming in the background of this election campaign—the political equivalent of the tension track used in movies to provoke anxiety and foreboding ... Instead of economic issues and the timeless election slogan of jobs, jobs, jobs, the drum-beat today seems to be Muslims, Muslims, Muslims," observed Neil Macdonald of CBC News.[50]

Vilifying Omar Khadr

Throughout their years in office, the Harperites ran a campaign against Omar Khadr, the only child soldier held at Guantanamo Bay. Not only did the government not make any attempt to have him released, it also opposed his transfer to Canada, ignoring calls by the United Nations Committee against Torture and numerous human rights groups.[51] Even after Khadr was released and transferred to Canada, the government did everything it could to keep him in fed-eral maximum security prison; deny media access to him; and oppose his bail until the day he was ordered released by the Alberta Court of Appeal on May 7, 2015 after nearly thirteen years of incarceration.

Ottawa lost in the courts at every turn, including at the Supreme Court thrice. Judges at different levels rejected every one of the Harper government's specious arguments: that Khadr was a danger to public safety, when, in fact, he had been a model prisoner; that freeing him would irreparably harm relations with the United States, even though the American State and Justice departments had made it abundantly clear that that was not the case; and that granting him bail would give Canada a bad name for reducing sentences levied abroad.

The government's game was political all along—Khadr was to be the poster child of Ottawa's tough stand against terrorism. Keeping him in federal custody allowed the government to deny him media exposure and control its narrative. The more the case dragged on in courts, the more publicity the government got for its anti-terrorism stance and its line that Khadr had committed "heinous crimes" and that Ottawa's "thoughts and prayers" were always with the family of the American soldier killed in Afghanistan, not this Canadian.

The courts saw through the Harper government's "lies" about

Khadr, said his longtime lawyer Dennis Edney of Edmonton, on the day the young man was released. "Our judicial system is something to be incredibly proud of."

"The Harper government says he committed a heinous crime. What it doesn't say is that we were the only Western country that didn't request one of their detainees to return home. We left a child, a Canadian child in Guantanamo Bay to suffer torture. Not only did we leave a child to suffer torture, we Canada participated in this torture."

Edney had a message for the Harperites: "Let me say to these guys: Why don't they get a camera and sit with me and challenge me and show me just how stupid I am. Show me and prove to the Canadian public that whatever I have said about Omar Khadr is not true. I would like to ask them, 'Why don't they talk about the truth? Why don't they talk about their own representatives from the department of foreign affairs who went to Guantanamo over the years and provided written reports, and every one of those reports talked about Omar Khadr being a wonderful guy.'"

Edney said it was ironic that Canada was spending millions abroad campaigning against child soldiers and "rehabilitating child soldiers in Sierra Leone," yet "gave no mercy to a young boy of 15 dropped into an abandoned house by his father" in Afghanistan.

"My view is very clear: Mr Harper is a bigot. Mr Harper doesn't like Muslims."[52]

Edney was to repeat his accusation a week later, in Ottawa after the Supreme Court ruled against the government for the third time: "I've come to the conclusion, an honest conclusion felt by many, many Canadians throughout Canada, that Mr Harper is a bigot, and Mr Harper doesn't like Muslims, and there's evidence to show that."[53]

I cannot recall a contemporary Canadian prime minister being so accused so publicly by a respectable public figure.

Boycotting Muslim groups

Even those Western governments that may be ambivalent towards their Muslim citizenry pay lip service to them and their organizations.

Not Harper's government. It boycotted the main Muslim groups, Sunnis and Shiites alike, except for two small tightly knit groups, the Ismailis and Ahmadis, the latter considered by many Muslims as heretics or non-Muslims.

The government wouldn't even deal with the nonpolitical and noncontroversial Association of Progressive Muslims of Canada, which confines itself to holding Canada Day celebrations and two annual dinners, one on Parliament Hill and the other at Queen's Park, to mark the two annual festivals of Eid al-Fitr and Eid al-Adha, where it honours selected Canadians, most of them non-Muslims. (Its only dubious selection was to have honoured me as well, in 2005.) The group invites MPs and MPPs of all parties but the Harper Conservatives never responded, according to Mobeen Khaja, president. After years of silence, the Conservatives organized their own Eid dinner, in 2011, away from Parliament Hill, an event to which guests were bussed in from Montreal, reportedly from ridings that Multiculturalism Minister Jason Kenney thought could be in play in the 2015 election. Harper attended and claimed, falsely, "Eid on the Hill is an idea that was a long time coming."[54] That prompted Khaja to tell me: "They are playing games. The government brought together people and groups I had never heard of"—the Association of Islamic Charitable Projects and the India-Canada Organization, whose representatives Bessame Derbas and Daljit Singh of Montreal, respectively, were acknowledged by Harper.

It turned out that Daljit Singh was, in fact, Baljit Singh, an imposter. The *Montreal Gazette* and the *Suburban* weekly later reported that Baljit Singh Wadyal came to Canada as a refugee in 1995 after spending four years in an American jail for trafficking a kilogram of heroin,[55] a period during which, he claimed in his refugee application, he was being persecuted in India where he was, in fact, reportedly under investigation for murder.[56] In 2006, he was reportedly charged by Montreal police for uttering a threat following an accusation of domestic violence; in 2009, the Minister of Public Safety had his refugee file re-opened; and in 2010, the Immigration and Refugee

Board ruled that his refugee status be annulled. Yet he was close to Kenney and other Conservatives, who were either unaware of what other government departments knew or saw no wrong in involving him in the Eid dinner in Ottawa and having Harper thank him from the podium.

It was not the first instance of the Harper government getting tripped up by questionable characters from among its anointed ethnic power brokers.

Another example of Harper pointedly avoiding outreach to Muslims and mainstream Muslim organizations was his long resistance to doing what American presidents and British prime ministers have routinely done at the White House and 10 Downing Street, namely, host an Iftar party, the breaking of the fast during the month of Ramadan, for a broadly representative group of American and British Muslim groups, respectively. When Harper finally did, in 2015, he and Kenney avoided inviting to 24 Sussex Drive anyone from mainstream Muslim groups, preferring instead to have three dozen mostly unknown guests. "This event certainly came as a surprise to many, given the government's record that has alienated, marginalised many Canadian Muslim communities," Gardee of the National Council of Canadian Muslims, told *iPolitics*.[57]

Not only did the Harperites ignore Muslim organizations, they attacked Liberal leader Trudeau for his outreach to Muslims. When he visited the Al-Sunnah Al-Nabawiah mosque in Montreal in 2011, a place that was later said in a leaked American intelligence document to have been linked with Al-Qaeda in the 1990s, the Tories kept hammering him for "consorting with religious extremists," even though Trudeau said he did not know at the time of the visit what the FBI would later reveal, nor did he ever go back to that mosque after that American report.[58]

The boycott of the Muslim community did not happen overnight. Stockwell Day, Harper's predecessor as leader of the Conservative Party—or the Canadian Alliance, as it was then called—tried to reach out to Muslims, using his God talk and social conservative credentials.

Even after Harper formed the government, Minister Kenney visited the Islamic school at the Canada headquarters of the Islamic Society of North America (ISNA) in Mississauga, a Toronto suburb, on November 29, 2008, and struck all the right notes:[59]

"We really do appreciate this opportunity to get to know each other better and to begin a closer dialogue between the Government of Canada, the Conservative Party of Canada, and the Muslim community in general, ISNA in particular . . .

"This school . . . is a shining example of what is best about Canada . . .

"Some people say you can't be absolutely true to your religion and absolutely loyal to Canada. And I say that's nonsense. Those of you here who were involved in this demonstrated that you can be, in fact, you are better Canadians by being good Muslims . . .

"Too often in Canada we speak about Muslims as though they are all of one monolithic culture, when, in fact, we know that Islam is a universal faith that is practiced and respected in every country in the world, and that it has within it an amazing cultural diversity that is indeed reflected in the Muslim community in Canada . . .

"There are negative stereotypes which exist in Western societies about Islam, about Muslims. We know that sometimes this creates a more difficult life for people of the Muslim faith. But my message to you is that this is nothing new in our history."

This conciliatory approach, however, was soon abandoned, and even the link to this speech was eventually removed from Kenney's official and personal websites.[60]

Wooing the victims of Muslim bigotry

The Conservatives particularly courted immigrants who came to Canada fleeing persecution from Muslim-majority nations—the Ahmadis and Christians from Pakistan, Coptic Christians from Egypt, and Bahais from Iran. These groups have good reasons to resent the Muslim societies they fled because of persecution. But the Harper government exploited and fanned their "old country" fault lines, instead of following the long-standing Canadian tradition of tamping down ancestral conflicts and bringing old warring factions together.

On November 19, 2013, Immigration Minister Alexander and two Conservative MPs, Bob Dechert from Mississauga-Erindale, the riding with a strong Coptic Christian presence, and David Anderson, parliamentary secretary to then minister of foreign affairs, John Baird, met a delegation of Coptic Canadians on Parliament Hill.[61] This was a time of turmoil in Egypt—General Sisi had overthrown Mohamed Morsi, Egypt's first elected president. Security forces were killing Muslim Brotherhood protestors by the hundreds, a crackdown condemned by human rights groups worldwide. But the Coptic delegation was singing Sisi's tune. Maher Rizqallah of the Coptic Canadian Association said the Brotherhood's "objective is to dominate, to impose its law on all nations and to extend its power across the entire planet . . . It is widely recognized now around the globe that the Muslim Brotherhood is the root source of Islamic terrorism."

Alexander responded that as someone who had "worked very hard in my previous capacity as parliamentary secretary for National Defence to get the Afghan Taliban and the Haqqani group (a Pakistan-based Afghan tribal ally of the Taliban) listed as terrorist groups, I strongly support listing all those groups that raise funds, practice, espouse terrorism, including the Muslim Brotherhood." (This was contrary to the stance of our American and European allies, who considered the Brotherhood a peaceful group, with which they maintained relations and welcomed its active participation in the democratic process after the fall of Hosni Mubarak).

Another member of the Coptic delegation, Sheref Sabawy, said that the Brotherhood's successful participation in the post-Arab Spring era was "just an attempt to deceive the international eye . . . In the name of protecting Canadians, it is imperative that the Government of Canada add Muslim Brotherhood to the list of known terrorist organizations. Can you promise us that?"

Anderson said that while he couldn't do so, he could promise to convey the message to his minister, adding an assuring note: "We've heard Minister Alexander's commitment tonight."

The Harper government did not name the Brotherhood a terrorist organization but it did support the Sisi government, with Harper welcoming the general's coup as a "return to stability."[62]

While any ethnic or religious group has a right to make its views known to government and it is the duty of government to listen, what was telling about the largely unreported meeting was how eager the Conservative MPs, including a cabinet minister, were to placate the Coptic delegation and not challenge any of its assertions.

Protecting religious freedom selectively

As part of wooing the Coptic, Ahmadi, and Bahai communities, the Harper government promised during the 2011 election to establish an Office of Religious Freedom to monitor the plight of religious minorities worldwide. Harper unveiled the policy at a campaign rally at a Mississauga Coptic Church. Later he announced the position of a new Ambassador of Religious Freedom at the Ahmadiyya mosque in Vaughan, a suburb of Toronto. And when the government organized a citizens' consultative meeting regarding the initiative, it invited four Christians, one Jew and one Bahai, no Muslims, even though much of the policy was aimed at Muslim-majority states. "No opportunity was given to mainstream Muslim groups," Wahida Valiante of the Canadian Islamic Congress told me. "Overall, the Muslim community is totally excluded by this government." Only at a second meeting was one imam invited—"at the last minute, as an after-thought." That was Abdul-Hai Patel of the Canadian Council of Imams. He told me that he came away with the impression that "they only want to champion the cause of minorities in Muslim nations."

The leader of one such minority, the Ahmadis, His Holiness Hadhrat Mirza Masroor Ahmed, was consulted by Foreign Minister Baird in London in January 2012 about the Office of Religious Freedom.[63] In December 2014, Harper revisited the Ahmadi mosque in Vaughan and thanked that community for speaking out against the killing of two Canadian soldiers—Patrice Vincent in Saint-Jean-sur-Richelieu, Quebec and Corporal Nathan Cirillo at the National War Memorial in Ottawa—by two Christian converts to Islam.[64] What the prime minister did not say was that all the mainstream Muslim groups and imams and leaders had also condemned the killings, including the Muslim Council of Greater Hamilton, which laid a wreath in honour of Cpl. Cirillo at the armoury in his native Hamilton, and Muslims in Ottawa who laid a wreath at the National War Memorial.[65]

Christians from Pakistan were also the centre of much attention by the Harper government. A junior cabinet minister in Pakistan, Shahbaz Bhatti, was murdered in 2011 for taking up the cause of a poor Christian woman falsely condemned to death for allegedly defaming Islam. Six weeks earlier, a much more well-known and important politician, Salman Taseer, governor of Punjab, the most populous province, was also gunned down for speaking out on behalf of the same woman. Bhatti's assailants were unknown. Taseer's murderer was a member of the elite security unit assigned to guard him; more shockingly, his assassin was hailed a hero, with nearly 500 clerics signing a statement calling him "a true soldier of Islam." The Harper government's reaction was to send Minister Kenney to Pakistan for the funeral of Bhatti, a Christian, but not for the funeral of Taseer, a Muslim.[66]

The Harper government also misused the Office of Religious Freedom on the international stage. It went to bat mostly for Christian and other minorities in Muslim nations, but rarely for the beleaguered Muslim minorities elsewhere, such as the Uighurs in China or the heavily persecuted Rohingas in Myanmar, or Shiite Muslims in Saudi Arabia and Pakistan.

Discriminating against Muslim refugees

The Harper government did not help the Sunni Muslim majority of Syria, the chief victims of Bashar al-Assad's murderous crack-down since 2011. Ottawa agreed to take only 1,300 Syrian refugees

and dragged its feet even on that miniscule target. Under widespread public criticism and sustained United Nations pressure, the
government announced in January 2015 that it would take 10,000
refugees—but prefer "persecuted minorities," Christians, Yazidis
and others. This upending of long-standing non-discriminatory
Canadian refugee policy drew the wrath of the Canadian Council
of Refugees, Canadian Council of Churches and Jewish Refugee
Action Network, among others. The *Toronto Star* editorialized that
"Syrians from every religious and ethnic camp are suffering. This
war is an equal opportunity killer."[67] Amnesty International Canada
said that Ottawa should be "protecting those in the greatest need, on
a non-discriminatory basis," rather than favouring non-Muslims.
A.I. Secretary-General Alex Neve told me: "Clearly there's nothing
wrong at all with offering protection to refugees from persecuted
ethnic and religious minorities. Such groups continue to experience
serious human rights violations. It is also clear, however, that Syria's
majority Sunni Arab Muslim population has suffered greatly, both
before and during the four-plus years of the country's terrible civil
war. This is not a human rights crisis that simply comes down to the
majority having brutalized the minority. Virtually everyone has suffered and continues to suffer." The independent United Nations High
Commissioner for Refugees is the best judge of who is the most vulnerable. Yet Harper refused to budge—he wouldn't let UNHCR make
the final call on refugee selection.

On September 2, 2015, the body of little Aylan Kurdi washed up
on the shores of the Mediterranean and stirred the conscience of
the world, including Canada's. With growing national demands that
Canada open its doors, Harper, by now in the middle of the election, tried to stall by playing the security card: "We cannot open the
floodgates and airlift tens of thousands of refugees out of a terrorist
war zone without proper process. That is too great a risk for Canada."
But neither the opposition parties nor refugee advocates were calling him to airlift tens of thousands—let alone without security clearance. Harper was echoing, albeit less crudely, what Donald Trump,

the Republican presidential contender, was saying down south about Syrian refugees: "They could be, listen, they could be ISIS."

Harper's policy came into sharper focus by a *Globe and Mail* revelation that his office had directly intervened in the refugee selection process to screen out both Sunnis and Shiites, and pick out Christians, Yazidis and others, the only exception among Muslims being Ismailis. CTV News followed up with a report that "PMO staff went through the files to ensure that persecuted religious minorities with established communities already in Canada—ones that Conservative Leader Stephen Harper could court for votes—were being accepted. Insiders say PMO actively discouraged the department from accepting applications from Shia and Sunni Muslims."[68]

Misusing free speech

In 2012, the Harper government axed Section 13 of the federal Human Rights Code, a provision that prohibited hate speech on grounds of race, religion, ethnicity, etc. The government did so at the behest of those who demanded the freedom to attack Muslims and Islam without any constraints. The campaign against Sec. 13 had come about in response to four Muslim students filing complaints to the federal as well as three provincial human rights commissions, including Ontario's, against a 4,800-word article in *Maclean's* magazine, published in 2006, asserting that Muslims are prone to violence and pose a demographic, cultural, and security threat to the West, including Canada.[69] While the students' complaint did not meet Ontario's narrow definition of hate speech, the chair of the province's Human Rights Commission, Barbara Hall, condemned the magazine:

> Islamophobia is a form of racism . . . Since September 2001, Islamophobic attitudes are becoming more prevalent and Muslims are increasingly the target of intolerance . . . The *Maclean's* article, and others like it, are examples of this. By portraying Muslims as all sharing the same negative characteristics, including being a threat to "the West," this explicit expression of Islamophobia further perpetuates and

promotes prejudice toward Muslims and others.[70]

She dismissed the free speech argument, noting that the right does not exist in isolation from other rights.

> Freedom of expression is not the only right in the Charter. There is a full set of rights accorded to all members of our society, including freedom from discrimination . . . If you want to stand up and defend the right to freedom of expression, then you must be willing to do the same for the right to freedom from discrimination.[71]

Ironically, within a year of the axing of Sec. 13, the Supreme Court found that section to be valid. Ruling on an earlier case, it unanimously rejected the argument used by defenders of *Maclean's*, including several Harper Conservatives, that unfettered speech helps further public debate.

> Hate speech is antithetical to this objective in that it shuts down dialogue by making it difficult or impossible for members of the vulnerable group to respond, thereby stifling discourse. Speech that has the effect of shutting down public debate cannot dodge prohibition on the basis that it promotes debate.[72]

In yet another irony, the government proceeded in 2014 to restrict free speech.[73] It changed the definition of hate speech in the Criminal Code to include statements made against "national origin," not just race, religion and ethnicity. That was done to "go after the critics of Israel," said Michel Vonn, a lawyer for the British Columbia Civil Liberties Union.[74]

In 2015, the Harper government further curbed free speech, this time in the name of fighting terrorism. Under the aforementioned Anti-Terrorism Act, it criminalized the promotion of terrorism and banned material that could have the effect of radicalization.

So, free speech for Islamophobes but not those whose words the government did not like.

Equating pro-Israel with anti-Muslim

Harper's key foreign policy plank—a blank cheque for Israel[75]—translated into his government ignoring Arab and Muslim Canadians, indeed penalizing those who criticized Israeli actions. The government cut off federal funding to the Canadian Arab Federation as well as Palestine House, alleging that they were anti-Semitic. This was in sharp contrast to the US, where the White House under both Republican and Democratic presidents maintains strong relations with America's Arab and Muslim communities and their representative organizations, even while remaining Israel's staunchest supporter.

The Harper government also targeted Apartheid Week, a movement against the Israeli occupation of Palestinian lands, started in Toronto in 2005, mostly by Arab and Muslim university students but including Jewish activists critical of Israeli policies towards the Palestinians. Minister Kenney called it anti-Semitic and accused universities hosting Apartheid Week of being hostile to Jewish students.[76]

The government barred non-Canadian critics of Israel from entering Canada, such as British MP George Galloway. Yet it allowed pro-Israeli but anti-Muslim bigots, such as the Dutch Geert Wilders, American Pamela Geller, and others to come to Canada and hold anti-Muslim rallies. When Geller came in 2013, it took the Toronto Board of Rabbis to condemn the militant Jewish Defense League of Canada for hosting her. The board, which represents rabbis from all denominations, said it found both her views as well as the invitation extended to her to be "distasteful" and divisive. This was lauded by JSpace Canada, a liberal Jewish group, which said: "A majority of the Jewish community supports the position taken by the rabbis."[77]

The government refused to grant temporary visas for 100 Gaza children, injured and traumatized during the 2014 Israel military onslaught that left more than 2,100 Palestinians dead and 10,000 wounded, 2,700 of them children. The proposal to bring some of those children to Canada for treatment was made by Dr Izzeldin Abuelaish

of Toronto who lost three of his daughters and a niece when Israel
bombed his home in Gaza in 2009 and subsequently moved to
Canada. The idea was wholeheartedly supported by the premier
and health minister of Ontario, the Canadian Medical Association,
Registered Nurses Association of Ontario, and Toronto's major hospitals, among others. But the government wouldn't even meet him.[78]

Writing off Muslim voters

Harper wrote off the one-million-strong Muslim Canadians during
elections, even as he made inroads into various ethnic communities,
including Chinese, Sikh, and Hindu. The Conservatives' 2011 majority was attributed partly to Harper's outreach to South Asians in the
suburban ridings around Toronto. But it was misleading of the media
to have said that the Conservatives had successfully wooed the 1.3
million South Asian Canadians. The Conservatives reached out only
to non-Muslim South Asians.[79]

"South Asian," a Statistics Canada designation, refers to Canadians
from the Indian subcontinent and from the Indian diaspora in
Africa, the Caribbean, the Far East, and Fiji. The Conservatives did
not court Muslim Pakistani Canadians, nor Muslim Bangladeshi
Canadians, nor the Muslims of South Asian origin who came here
from the Caribbean, principally Guyana, nor the Muslim Canadians
who migrated here from India. The Conservatives were seeking votes
among Hindus and Sikhs.

Among the Hindus, the Conservatives have been closest to some
of the more zealous overseas supporters of India's Hindu-nationalist,
Muslim-baiting Bharatiya Janata Party (BJP). Canadian supporters of the BJP had been lobbying Harper for years to lift the visa ban
imposed on BJP leader, Narendra Modi, who had been blacklisted by
the US State Department and several European countries and also
Canada for his alleged role in the 2002 anti-Muslim pogrom in his
state of Gujarat when he was chief minister. While Ottawa maintained the visa ban, it was among the first Western governments to
sponsor Modi's annual pro-business summits in Gujarat. In 2014,

Modi moved to India's federal scene and led the BJP to power nationally, within a year of which Harper invited him to Canada—and shadowed him in Ottawa, Toronto and Vancouver before the Indian, mostly Hindu, diaspora that hero-worships Modi.

There's nothing wrong with Harper, or any politician, appealing to selected segments of the electorate. That's politics. But it is instructive as to whom he studiously avoided and, more crucially, what company he kept.

Attacking the niqab

As far back as 2007, within a year of taking office, the Harper government tried to copy the Quebec separatists in wanting to strip away the voting rights of niqab-wearing women. That attempt was thwarted by Marc Mayrand, chief electoral officer, who pointed out that about 70,000 voters, including inmates, mail their federal election ballots without ever being asked to show their face.

The Harperites, however, found another venue to target the niqab. In 2011, Minister Kenney issued a directive barring niqabi women from obtaining their citizenship while covering their faces. But in February 2015, the Federal Court ruled the policy to be "unlawful."[80] Judge Keith Boswell ruled that Kenney had contravened the government's own rules that instruct citizenship judges to administer the oath of citizenship "with dignity and solemnity, allowing the greatest possible freedom in the religious solemnization or the solemn affirmation thereof." Yet Kenney was forcing citizenship candidates to "violate or renounce a basic tenet of their religion."

Undeterred, the government launched an appeal, with Harper saying that the niqab is "rooted in a culture that is anti-women . . . I think most Canadians believe that it's offensive that someone would hide their identity . . . These are not the views only of the overwhelming majority of Canadians, they are the views of the overwhelming majority of moderate Muslims." So, those who agree with him are moderate, those who don't are obviously extremists, including the non-Muslims who think the government has no business telling women what to wear. It was also strange that Harper would cite public opinion to support his demagoguery, given that his government routinely rationalized some of its most controversial policies as having been guided by principle, not a desire for popularity or to "go along just to get along."

Immigration Minister Alexander and some other Tories were even more incendiary. He associated the niqab with several nefarious practices: "We are concerned about protecting women from violence, protecting women from human smuggling, protecting women from barbaric practices like polygamy, genital mutilation, honour killings." Tory MP Larry Miller told niqab-wearing women to "stay the hell where you came from." He later apologized but the Conservative Party kept using the government's niqab ban in its fund-raising campaign, saying "this is not how we do things here," and Harper, as leader of the Conservative Party, signed Miller's nomination papers for the 2015 election for the Ontario riding of Bruce-Grey-Owen Sound where he was easily re-elected.

In yet another comment on the niqab, the oleaginous Alexander told VICE News, "We've done a lot in the past year to strengthen the value of Canadian citizenship. People take pride in that. They don't want their co-citizens to be terrorists."[81]

This prompted the Liberals to raise the issue in the House of Commons in tandem with the latest Statistics Canada figures on police-reported hate crimes, showing that Muslims were the only religious group to have experienced an increase in hate crimes, as much as 44 per cent in 2013, even as overall hate crimes went down 22 per cent across the country.[82]

John McCallum of the Toronto area riding of Markham-Unionville said: "It is the most predictable thing in Canadian politics. Someone says 'Muslim' and a Conservative minister says 'terrorist.' Yesterday, when asked about rising hate crimes against Muslims, the Minister of Public Safety felt obliged to talk about terrorists. We also saw yesterday that the Minister of Citizenship and Immigration assumes all Muslim women who wear the veil are terrorists, unless proven otherwise. This is simply unacceptable, so will he apologize to all Muslim Canadians?"

Alexander responded: "The Liberals have done nothing to strengthen our measures to fight terrorism, to cancel passports, to take action against ISIL."

McCallum followed up: "It is obvious from the minister's previous statement that he equates terrorism with niqabs. When only Muslims face a rise in hate crimes, it is obvious that the government's toxic anti-Muslim rhetoric is a part of the problem. As when he talks about terrorist plots in mosques, this is the only Prime Minister in my lifetime who sinks to attack a whole community for political gain."[83]

On September 19, 2015, the Federal Court of Appeal rejected the government bid to keep the ban on the niqab.[84] It ordered Ottawa to give Ishaq her citizenship, quickly, so she could vote in the October federal election, as she was keen to. But the government said it would appeal to the Supreme Court. While preparing for that manoeuver, it went back to the Federal Court, asking it to suspend its ruling. That bid failed as well—the third judicial rebuke. The court said that the government had neither proven that there was an important principle at stake nor established that giving Ms Ishaq her citizenship would create "irreparable harm," the two legal tests at play at that stage of the proceedings.[85]

On October 9, Ms Ishaq was sworn in as a citizen—with her niqab on—by a citizenship judge in Mississauga in a private ceremony.[86]

"It was a wonderful moment," her lawyer Lorne Waldman told me later. "The judge made a beautiful speech about what it meant to be a Canadian, and especially mentioned democracy and freedom of religion. Then we all took the oath, including the CBC reporters there, and then Zunera got her certificate and we all sang O'Canada. Very special moment indeed."

Did the government make any last-minute bid to derail the swearing-in? I asked him.

"The government had no choice. We had written to them, and they knew that if they did not give her the citizenship she was entitled to, we would have moved for contempt of court."

A footnote: For all the dust kicked up by Harper as well as Quebec politicians about the niqabis, there were only two women out of 700,000 new citizens since 2011 who wanted to keep their niqab for the citizenship ceremony, and there are only a few dozen niqabis all across Canada.[87]

Two contrary views

It needs to be noted that Harper is a master of wedge politics, and can hold his own with the worst of Republicans in that dark art. He pressed hot buttons to charge his political base, about 30 per cent of the electorate. He "believes in playing politics right up to the edges of the rules," according to his former policy advisor Tom Flanagan, University of Calgary political scientist, who compares Harper to Richard Nixon.[88] The prime minister "can be suspicious, secretive and vindictive, prone to sudden eruptions of white-hot rage over meaningless trivia." Highly partisan, Harper has no adversaries, only enemies—you are either with him or you are with the devil. He called the late Jack Layton, the NDP leader, "Taliban Jack" for suggesting that negotiating with the Taliban was the only long-term solution to the quagmire in Afghanistan. Trudeau was "best friends with Iran, one of the state sponsors of terrorism in the world," for having suggested that dialogue with Tehran on the nuclear issue was a sensible thing to do. Critics of Benjamin Netanyahu's policies were anti-Israeli purveyors of "new anti-Semitism."

So it could be said that Canadian Muslims should wear Harper's hostility towards them with pride. But as a vulnerable minority, subject to much public mistrust and with few institutions and people of power to defend them, they are hardly in a position to laugh off his and the Conservative Party's campaign against them.

Mindful of the charge that it was anti-Muslim, the Harper government trotted out immigration figures showing an increase in the number of Muslims entering Canada: 185,000 during the 2001-06 Liberal years vs. 203,000 during the 2006-10 Conservative years, and

287,000 new permanent residents during 2006-13 with Arabic, Farsi and Urdu as their mother tongues.

It is possible that Harper's attitude and policies regarding Muslims were not a matter of conviction but of simple electoral calculus—Muslim participation rates in elections have been low, and those Muslims who do vote are unlikely to vote Conservative, whereas Muslim-bashing reaped him rich rewards elsewhere. Some statements by Harper lend credence to the view that his approach to Muslims was no more than a political tactic.

Notwithstanding his recent jihad against the niqab, the Prime Minister's Office had this to say in 2009: "In an open and democratic society like Canada, individuals are free to make their own decisions regarding their personal apparel and to adhere to their own customs or traditions of their faith or beliefs."[89]

In the fall of 2014, during a trip to New York, Harper said—contrary to what he had said earlier and what he was to say later—terrorism does not emanate from mosques. Speaking during a question-and-answer session at Goldman Sachs headquarters, he said this of radicalized Muslim youth: "Our experience in Canada has been that their connection to the Muslim community is often extremely tangential. A surprising number of these people have no background in Islam whatsoever. They are individuals who, for whatever reason, drift to these kinds of causes. Even (those with) backgrounds in Islam, they're often people who are not participants in mosques . . . They're off on kind of a radical, political fringe. Our security and intelligence people would tell you that a good relationship with our Muslim community has actually really helped to identify a lot of these threats before they become much more serious."

Kenney had also made the same point earlier: "Our security and police agencies will confirm that potentially violent instances have been prevented, radicalization has been diminished, thanks to the pro-active cooperation of many in the Canadian Muslim communities."[90]

Another example of Harper distinguishing between Muslims

and Muslim terrorists came when he spoke at the opening of the Aga Khan Museum in Toronto in 2014: "The Aga Khan has devoted an extraordinary amount of time, toil and resources to the ideals of Islamic culture and history. In doing so, His Highness has greatly contributed to demystifying Islam, throughout the world, by stressing its social traditions of peace, of tolerance and of pluralism. This is a vision of Islam of which all Canadians can be proud, especially when a contrary and violent distortion of that vision so regularly dominates the news."[91]

Some of Harper's cabinet ministers, too, at times invoked the western formulation that the war on terrorists is not a war on Muslims. Speaking during the 2014 House of Commons debate on Canada joining the American-led war on the Islamic State, Justice Minister Peter MacKay said: "This is not a war against Muslims. This is not a fight between Christianity and Islam." Transport Minister Lisa Raitt: "ISIL's war is not between Muslims and non-Muslims, nor is it between Sunnis and Shiites." Junior cabinet minister, Gary Goodyear: "No god, including Allah, condones this behaviour. No religion, including Islam, supports this behaviour."

In the spring of 2015, Kenney—described by the Canadian Press news agency as being in damage control by that time against growing allegations of playing anti-Muslim politics—noted that Muslims themselves were the biggest victims of Muslim terrorism. Speaking at the Manning Networking Conference, a conservative policy gathering, he said: "The vast majority of the victims of this dystopian vision of the caliphate from Nigeria to the Philippines are innocent, peaceful Muslim people . . . We stand with them, we stand . . . in defence of the vast majority of Muslims who reject this cult of violence. Canadians are in solidarity with them."[92]

Such sensible statements, besides being few and far between, paled into insignificance against the government's and the Conservative Party's overall record, which was arguably even more reprehensible if undertaken merely for propaganda purposes and to raise funds for the party using Muslims as convenient scapegoats. Regardless of motive, one can't shrug off the fact that the Harperites' anti-Muslim drive was far more lethal than that of the separatists in Quebec; while the PQ government mostly talked of targeting Muslims, Harper did for a prolonged period, and how!

Never in the contemporary era has the Government of Canada so systematically sidelined a faith community, leaving the Canadian Muslims bewildered, despondent, angry and alienated.

PROFILE OF CANADIAN MUSLIMS

While they are portrayed as one monolithic whole, Canadian Muslims are highly diverse, by country of origin, language, culture, ethnicity, and race. Nearly a third, 291,000, are Canadian-born, according to the 2011 national census.[93] Of the two-thirds who are immigrants, 145,000 came from Pakistan; 74,000 from Iran; 46,000 from Morocco; 45,000 from Algeria; 40,000 from Afghanistan; 39,000 from Bangladesh; 34,000 from India; 31,000 from Lebanon; 22,000 from Somalia; 22,000 from Iraq; 19,000 from Guyana; and 7,500 from Turkey. As in the Muslim world, the overwhelming majority of Canadian Muslims are Sunni. Among the minority Shi'ites, the most high-profile are the Ismaili Muslims. The latter's imam, the Aga Khan, has been active in Canada, having set up his Global Centre for Pluralism in Ottawa in 2011 and the Aga Khan Museum in Toronto in 2014, both to much-deserved acclaim.

Islam is the fastest growing religion in Canada, as it is in the United States and Europe. The Canadian Muslim population nearly doubled between the 2001 and 2011 census, as it had in the decade before (unlike the United States and France, Canada does collect data by religion, decennially). Canadian Muslims are twice as many as Hindus (497,000) and Lutherans (478,000); more than twice as many as Sikhs (455,000); nearly thrice as many as Buddhists (368,000); and thrice as many as Jewish Canadians (329,000), according to the 2011 census.

Muslims constitute the second youngest demographic in Canada, after aboriginals. Their median age is 28.9 years, compared to the overall Canadian median age of 37.3 years. Proportionately more Muslims are entering the labour force than leaving it—an asset to the economy. Muslims are second only to Jewish Canadians as the most educated of the minorities, with 17 per cent having finished 18 years or more of education. Yet Muslims earn 27 per cent less than Christians, and are disproportionately underemployed. They are also less likely to vote in federal, provincial and municipal elections—partly a function of the fact that a vast majority of them are relatively recent arrivals, starting from the 1970s. But a concerted effort is underway by a nonprofit group, the Canadian-Muslim Vote, to urge Muslims to exercise their franchise. In April 2015, Toronto-area imams used their Friday sermons to urge Muslims to vote in the federal election,[94] in which Muslims could affect the outcome in 23 ridings, 16 in Ontario and five in Quebec, according to the Canadian Press news agency.[95]

CONCLUSION

Xenophobia used to be the preserve of right-wing groups and political parties in Europe and the United States. As they traded their old anti-Semitism and racism for anti-Islamism in the post-9/11 period and gained traction, liberals failed to challenge them, either because of apathy or because of their own creeping anti-Islamic prejudices. Soon, the bigots were leading public opinion and setting the public agenda. It was inevitable that mainstream parties would begin pandering to or partnering with them. In the United States, elements of the Republican Party were getting openly hostile to Muslims. Initially, these developments could be dismissed as populist posturing but when as many as four leading Republican presidential candidates for the 2012 election adopted openly anti-Muslim positions, there was no doubting the mainstreaming of anti-Muslim bigotry—confirmed repeatedly since. Leading GOP candidates for the 2016 presidential election attended a July 2015 retreat to discuss, among other things, "shariah and the Global Jihad movement."[96] In September, one of the candidates, Ben Carson, said that a Muslim should "absolutely" not be president.[97]

In Canada, two successive Liberal leaders felt obliged to go along with public sentiment rather than stand on principle. Michael Ignatieff supported Quebec Premier Jean Charest's abortive attempt in 2010 to ban the burqa and niqab, and Trudeau voted for Harper's odious Barbaric Cultural Practices Act, even while opposing the ban on the niqab for citizenship ceremonies. Both Liberal leaders also supported American-led wars, the main source of homegrown terrorism—Ignatieff backed the 2003 war on Iraq and Trudeau the war on the Islamic State. Trudeau also voted for the Anti-Terrorism Act, a position portrayed by his aides as tactical, to deny Harper an opportunity to paint the Liberals as soft on terrorism. The decisions eroded Trudeau's support among many Canadians, especially Muslims, who began taking a serious look at the NDP, which opposed both the Anti-Terrorism Act and the Canadian involvement in yet another American war in the Middle East.

The saving grace in North America and Europe has been that regardless of what position politicians took in opposition or while campaigning, they refrained from being overtly anti-Muslim once elected and entrusted with power. For example, German Chancellor Angela Merkel ratcheted back part of her anti-Muslim rhetoric and made gestures towards the Muslim citizenry—"I am chancellor of all Germans." In September 2015, she opened the gates to Syrian and other mostly Muslim refugees, agreeing to accept as many as 800,000 by the end of the year and 500,000 a year after that. This at a time when Harper was raising fears in Canada that giving asylum to Syrian and Iraqi refugees posed a security threat, since terrorists could slip in masquerading as refugees. British Prime Minister David Cameron, despite claiming Britain to be "a Christian country," nevertheless made it a point to be inclusive of Muslims, not as much as Obama but enough to portray himself as prime minister of all Britons. But in Canada, of all places, the government of Quebec, the second largest province, and, worse, the national government felt no shame in positioning themselves as guardians against the Muslim hordes—Pauline Marois and Phillipe Couillard in the name of protecting secularism, and Harper in the name of national security. And their policies were backed by a majority of Canadians, especially Quebeckers.

Popular support

Harper's stance on the war on the Islamic State enjoyed the support of two-thirds of Quebeckers,[98] a significant development, considering the province's pacifist history of opposing both World Wars as well as the 2001 invasion of Afghanistan and the 2003 American invasion of Iraq. The public mood in Quebec was no doubt soured in part by the homegrown terrorism of two troubled Quebeckers killing two soldiers in 2014. But the anti-Muslim mood in the province, as catalogued earlier, long preceded the two murders.

A few well-reported incidents of solidarity with Muslims, such as the crowd funding for Alloul,[99] the hijabi Montreal woman thrown out of court by a judge, or such social media campaigns as the hashtag #DressCodePM,[100] by women asking Harper at the height of his anti-niqab campaign whether their own clothing met his approval, made little dent in anti-Muslim hostility in Quebec or across Canada.

Muslims living in the West are among the most law-abiding and hold the same democratic values as a majority of fellow-citizens, according to in-depth attitudinal surveys in North America and Europe by Pew Research Center and Gallup.[101] Yet they are kept under a cloud of suspicion. If Muslims in Iraq, Afghanistan, Yemen and elsewhere are our enemies, Muslims in the West may be suspect as well. If Boko Haram and the Islamic State are barbaric, Muslims here must also harbour such tendencies. If the Taliban are throwing acid in the faces of women, and other groups in far-off lands are mistreating their women, Muslim men in the West may be assumed to be misogynous.

This is the mindset that made it acceptable for national leaders and others in positions of authority to posit their anti-hijab and anti-niqab positions as measures to liberate Muslim women. Hijabi and most certainly niqabi women are to be rescued from their husbands, fathers, and brothers, since such women could not possibly have come to that decision of their own free will. As Trudeau said in March 10, 2015, in a thoughtful Obama-like speech tackling a tough subject: "Cloaking an argument about what women can wear in the language of feminism has to be the most innovative perversion of liberty that conservatives have invented in a while. It is, of course, not the first time the most illiberal of ends has been packaged in the language of liberation." He was speaking of the federal Conservatives. But his criticism applied equally to others, especially Marois and other self-styled "feminists." Trudeau continued: "You can dislike the niqab. You can hold it up it as a symbol of oppression. You can try to convince your fellow citizens that it is a choice they ought not to make. This is a free country. Those are your rights. But those who would use the state's power to restrict women's religious freedom and freedom of expression indulge the very same repressive impulse that they profess to condemn. It is a cruel joke to claim you are liberating people from oppression by dictating in law what they can and cannot wear. We all know what is going on here. It is nothing less than an attempt to play on people's fears and foster prejudice directly toward the Muslim faith."[102]

Twisted thinking

Are Western democracies so spooked by Muslims that they are no longer capable of seeing the illogicality and double standards in their dealings with fellow citizens who are Muslims?

Terrorism is being fought by alienating Muslims who have, time and again, proven to be the best source of tips about home-grown radicals,[103] as Harper and Kenney themselves conceded.

Freedom of speech is being upheld by granting absolute freedom to anti-Muslim bigots, while circumscribing it for others. Free speech is the rallying cry of France in the aftermath of the *Charlie Hebdo* massacres but more than 100 people are charged for not observing a minute of silence for the victims of the massacre or for daring to question France's anti-terrorism policies.[104]

Secularism is being saved by violating one of its fundamental tenets, the right to religion practiced within the secular law of the land. Worse, the secular state is taking sides in internal doctrinal issues—arguing that drawing images of Muhammad may not be sacrilege, that the hijab is not really essential to Islam, or that the niqab is a tribal practice, not Islamic, as Harper argued, while Kenney proudly proclaimed having obtained a fatwa from Sheikh Mohamed Tantawi, Egypt's top Muslim authority, who "clarified for me that people in the West who think this is a religious obligation do not understand (sic) Islam law. So, I am not going to second-guess the most pre-eminent Sharia authority in the Sunni world." But Kenney was second-guessing the Supreme Court of Canada, which has ruled that a religious practice is what the practitioner sincerely believes it to be.[105] The minister was ignoring Canada's top court but taking dictation from a mufti in Cairo!

Harper, Kenney, *et al* were trying to save democratic secularism by playing ayatollah or imitating the practices of authoritarian Muslim regimes that dictate what kind of Islam citizens should practice.[106]

Marois and her feminist supporters were going to liberate hijabi women by firing them from their public service jobs, which gave such women financial and social independence from the fathers, brothers, and husbands who are ostensibly robbing their women of independence.

The absurdity of all this comes into clearer focus when you consider that while in Afghanistan, Iran, and Saudi Arabia, disobedient women are flogged, here in Canada they were deprived of their right to citizenship; made greater victims of violent hate crimes than Muslim men, according to StatCan's 2014 report on crimes;[107] and, in Quebec, are denied public services if they do not wear what they are told to by the government. The Taliban target girls wearing short skirts, while France sends away a fifteen-year-old girl from school, twice, for wearing a skirt too long.[108]

Echoing the extremists

Can there be any greater indictment of our leaders and pundits than that many of them echo the extremists they attack? Those who say that Muslims don't belong in the West are speaking the language of Osama bin Laden, the Taliban, and the Islamic State who say precisely the same thing. Those who concoct new ways to humiliate Muslims are doing what was done during one particular period of Muslim history when infidels were ordered to "remove their turbans, ride bareback and lower their chants to whisper during times of prayer," and officials were instructed to "keep infidels standing at all times, and to rise from divans only when it became necessary to insult the taxpayer concerned or to tug his beard."[109]

It says something when the victim of Harper's anti-niqab policy, Zunera Ishaq of Toronto, denied citizenship for wanting to wear her face covering during a citizenship ceremony, sounded more Canadian than the prime minister. "The beautiful part of Canada is that every person here is free to live in a way in which he or she feels it is right or not," she told the *National Post*, which carried a photo of her doing a very Canadian thing—shovelling snow off her driveway.[110]

All these are signs of a society that has lost its bearings and is blind to the damage it is doing to its democratic foundations. It is a scared society where the majority feels threatened by a tiny minority. We know from history where that can lead.

Muslims cannot be maligned any more than they already have been in recent years. Yet Muslim minorities in the West have remained remarkably calm, perhaps secure in the knowledge that attacks on their faith and their identity dating back to the Crusades have made no difference to the inexorable growth of Islam and Muslims worldwide (which makes Islamophobes madder still). What North Americans and Europeans—Canadians, in particular— should worry about is the steady erosion of their secular democratic principles.

Repeating the mistakes of the past

Opposition leader Thomas Mulcair of the NDP and Liberal leader Trudeau both accused Harper of anti-Muslim bigotry.

"I see that Muslims are often scapegoats for political debate. And that, I find heartbreaking," Mulcair said. He condemned both the Quebec and federal bans on the niqab as "Islamophobic." He termed Harper's accusation that mosques are incubators of terrorism "irresponsible and wrong."[111]

Trudeau, who dilly-dallied on several of these seminal issues, nevertheless got it right when he accused the Harper government of blurring the line between the real threat of terrorism and stoking "simple prejudice" against Muslims. "I believe they have done it deliberately and I believe what they have done is deeply wrong . . . Across Canada and, especially, in my home province, Canadians are being encouraged by their government to be fearful of one another. For me, this is both unconscionable and a real threat to Canadian liberty."[112]

Can anyone recall a time when a sitting prime minister was accused by the leader of the opposition as well as the leader of the third party of leading a campaign of religious discrimination?

Future generations are likely to see this as a dark chapter in our history, not quite as racist or severe as past government's dealings with the aboriginal peoples or Chinese Canadians or Japanese Canadians or Jewish Canadians or Sikh Canadians, but shameful nonetheless— more so because it was orchestrated by the prime minister of the day.

Going to the guru

The final word goes to Professor Charles Taylor, Canada's preeminent philosopher and co-chair of the 2007-08 Quebec commission on pluralism. Author of more than a dozen seminal books on secularism, multiculturalism, and the political culture of modernity, he is much sought after internationally, especially to explain the Canadian model of fostering peaceful coexistence in the most diverse population in human history.

He and I spoke on July 15, 2015 after he had read this essay.

Where would he situate the current national angst about Muslims in comparison to past episodes of mistreating minorities?

"I would situate it in the context of a positive move—the shift to multiculturalism and what Quebec calls *interculturalisme* that got us away from this idea that there was some kind of superiority to the English on one side and the French on the other, and that we didn't really owe anything to the aboriginal peoples and we didn't owe anything to immigrants, some of whom we just didn't want, anyway.

"Multiculturalism gave rise to a new ethic. But you still get perpetuations of former reactions, which are very deeply felt in some quarters—that new people are coming, they are different, they are going to change you, they are gonna endanger your cherished form of life. But you can no longer articulate it in the old way, 'we are much more superior to them, they are culturally inferior to us.' So you have got to moralize it—secularism is this moralization, *laïcité* is the moralization, a respectable front for prejudices and fears.

"In the case of Muslims, this is added to by the geopolitical situation. There's this scary international discourse around it and then there's the Islamophobic discourse, which is sweeping and, as you say, backed by tremendous amounts of money, think tanks and foundations, which is quite frightening.

"And there's the violence.

"So it's easy to moralize your own reactions of not feeling comfortable with these people, by saying, 'they are all actually dangerous.' In Quebec, there's the very obvious mixing up of pious, practising Muslims and dangerous jihadist Muslims . . . If you wear a chador, obviously you are halfway or three-quarters of the way to being a jihadist.

"That's what Harper has also done. And that, of course, to me is the most inexcusable thing leaders can do."

If the Harperites were doing it as a matter of tactics, wasn't it worse than if they actually believed it?

"I don't know which is worse. It's pretty terrible to think that in this day and age you can be educated and still believe in that kind of stuff. There's something very, very sinister."

What do we tell ourselves as Canadians—that we've had episodes of intolerance before and that this, too, shall pass?

"That's how I'd like to see it. We can screw up and it will be more than a passing thing if we do. That really depends on us. If we let them (the Conservatives) drive some of this through, then we move towards the situation in France where you have a really deeply alienated Muslim minority and then they do things that anger the majority, and it goes back and forth like that, and it kind of accelerates. In Canada, we don't need to be totally alarmed about it but we do need to be very, very firm and very, very vigilant and really crack down on the people that are leading us the other way."

What's his message to Canadians at this time?

"We have to see this in the long perspective, and manage to overcome this and create a unified society. We have done it before, and we can do it again. We've overcome this in the past by wise leadership. You can lead people out of it if the leadership is intelligent and sensitive and makes sure that people get to know each other, and that when they do, these fears disappear. If you just go on with that message, I think we could win. We have a good chance in Canada." Unlike France and some other nations, Canada does not have a colonial baggage. "We start off with this tremendous advantage. Don't throw it away."

Was Mr Harper throwing it away?

"Harper is, I think, probably not clear enough on all this to see the full damage he is doing, sacrificing it (national harmony) to his electoral goal. A lot of people don't see it, either. I tried to explain to my friends in the Parti Quebecois that when hijabis walk the streets, suddenly people are shouting at them 'Go back home.' It is terrible in human terms and it is terrible for the country. You can't build a country if you are creating that type of reaction. It is just terrible for my Muslim friends, who say, 'we made a mistake coming to Canada.' I feel like weeping, and saying, 'Hang in there.'"

In the weeks following my conversation with Professor Taylor, the federal election campaign cleared up any lingering doubt over the willingness of the Harper Conservatives to target Muslims in order to win votes. The tactic was widely derided by the opposition parties as well as civic leaders but it did enjoy broad popular support with about 30 per cent of the electorate and even more on specific issues, such as the banning of the niqab. On October 12, I got back to Professor Taylor to ask if he wanted to add anything to our conversation. He said: "Low as my opinion was of Harper, I didn't think that he could sink that low; or especially that he could get away with it. This is pure scapegoating, which is incidentally a barbaric cultural practice with a long and ugly history in human life."

But Harper did not get away with it. On October 19, 2015, his government got turfed out, just as had the Parti Quebecois government in Quebec eighteen months earlier. Canadians may have supported this or that aspect of the cultural warfare on Muslims but at the ballot box they refused to reward the pedlars of bigotry. The challenge ahead is to ensure that the Canadian values of pluralism and equal dignity for all groups are maintained after the elections as well. Justin Trudeau made a good start on election night, October 19, by ending his victory speech with a moving anecdote and a resounding pledge:

> Last week I met a young mom in St. Catharines, Ont. She practises the Muslim faith. She was wearing a hijab. Through the crowd, she handed me her infant daughter. And as she leaned forward, she said something that I will never forget. She said she's voting for us because she wants to make sure that her little girl has the right to make her own choices in life. To her, I say this: 'Your citizens have chosen a new government, a government that believes deeply in the diversity of our country.' We know in our bones that Canada was built by people from all corners of the world who worship every faith, who belong to every culture, who speak every language . . . A Canadian is a Canadian is a Canadian.

—⚏—

I am grateful to Carol Goar, columnist for the Toronto Star and a long-time colleague, as well as Professor James Reilly of the University of Toronto's Department of Near and Middle Eastern Civilizations for reading this chapter more than once and making valuable suggestions. I also thank my nephew Samir Siddiqui of the University of Toronto for his diligent research and editing.

Needless to say, the mistakes and weaknesses here are all mine.

siddiqui.canada@gmail.com

Speaking to Post-secular Society: The Aga Khan's Public Discourse

KARIM H KARIM

Is there a place for religious discourse in secular society? Even though church and state are viewed as being separate in the public sphere, the statements of certain religious figures about the contemporary world are reported widely by journalists. The global media frequently cover the discourses of the Pope and occasionally those of the Dalai Lama and the Archbishop of Canterbury. Canadian media have given the Aga Khan an increased amount of coverage in recent years. This essay examines how this Muslim leader engages discursively with the public sphere.

The Ismaili Imam frequently delivers speeches in "post-secular"[1] contexts on topics that include architecture, civil society, democracy, development, good governance, meritocracy, pluralism, public ethics, and Western-Muslim relations. In addressing non-Muslim audiences, he speaks from a Muslim perspective but expresses himself in discourse that is meant to appeal to broad humanistic interests. He said in a 2006 Columbia University graduation speech:

> A passion for justice, the quest for equality, a respect for tolerance, a dedication to human dignity—these are universal human values which are broadly shared across divisions of class, race, language, faith and geography. They constitute what classical philosophers—in the East and West alike—

have described as human 'virtue'—not merely the absence
of negative restraints on individual freedom, but also a set
of positive responsibilities, moral disciplines which prevent
liberty from turning into license.[2]

Writing in the introduction to a book of the Aga Khan's public
speeches, Adrienne Clarkson, a former Governor General of Canada,
observed that the Ismaili Imam promotes the development of "a universal ethical sensibility."[3]

The Nizari Ismailis (henceforth referred to as Ismailis) are a
branch of Shia Islam. Members of this group have migrated to Canada
from various African countries, South Asia, Afghanistan, Syria, Iran,
Tajikistan and some other locations. The Aga Khan claims descent
from Prophet Muhammad and is accepted by his adherents as the
49th Ismaili Imam in a lineage beginning with the Prophet's son-
in-law Ali ibn Abi Talib. Canada is an important destination in his
travels. Some 100,000 Ismailis reside in the country, with the initial
arrivals coming in the early 1950s.[4] The Aga Khan advised his followers to make Canada their home. Like other Muslims, they have
engaged with Canadian secular society. A number of them have
achieved a relatively high level of success in areas such as academia,
business, journalism, literature, politics, the professions and public
service. Ismaili communal institutions also have a significant degree
of interaction with secular society.

The Ismaili leader has also established non-communal organizations, such as the Aga Khan Foundation Canada, the Global Centre
for Pluralism and the Aga Khan Museum in Canada, which interact
with various Canadian publics. His positioning of institutions vis-à-
vis secular society has been very deliberate as indicated in this quota-
tion from a speech at the foundation ceremony of the Delegation of
the Ismaili Imamat building:

> The Delegation in the city of Ottawa will serve a represen-
> tational role for the Imamat and the non-denominational
> philanthropic and development agencies that constitute the
> Aga Khan Development Network. An open, secular facility,

the Delegation will be a sanctuary for peaceful, quiet diplomacy, informed by the Imamat's outlook of global convergence and the development of civil society.[5]

In announcing the function of a structure named after the "Ismaili
Imamat" as secular the Aga Khan indicated his active engagement
with aspects of public life that are not usually considered to be preoc-
cupations of religious leaders.

Secular and post-secular society

Before proceeding to discuss the Aga Khan's discursive engagement
with post-secular society, it is useful to consider ideas about secu-
larity. They emerged mainly from political developments in the last
few centuries in Western and other societies that have favoured the
separation of church and state. Such leanings towards the secular
generally translate into neutrality towards religious belief. However,
Richard Neuhaus complains that secularism has produced a "naked
public square" in contemporary Western society because religion and
religious values have been systematically excluded from consideration in public life.[6] It is important to point to a distinction between
the terms "secular" and "secularism." In some views, *secular* positions do not necessarily mean the elimination of religion from public
life; on the other hand, *secularism* can stand for strong opposition
towards religion. Aziz Esmail notes that "Secularism in the strong
sense of the term has the characteristics of an ideology, treating religion as a rival to itself, and attempting to offer a total explanation of
its own . . ."[7]

Religion is a basic (although not the only) source of most societies'
concepts of public ethics, morality and values. Fundamental notions
underlying theories of good governance, justice and human rights
are drawn from ideas developed in religious philosophy. Even though
efforts are made to de-sacralise the secular state's structures, a country's culture cannot be completely separated from its spiritual heritage.
Key elements in national constitutions and bodies of legislation come

from ideas that originate in the religion of the majority. Official and unofficial symbols, public ceremonies, common linguistic phrases etc., are often based on religious culture. Even though the spiritual significance of Christmas and Easter may not be acknowledged in official government discourses, these events are commemorated as holidays in the national calendars of Western countries, where Sunday is also the weekly day of rest. This includes France, despite its rigorous application of the policy of *laïcité*. Although India is officially secular, its national days include several Hindu and Muslim festivals, and Indian states with significant populations of Jains, Sikhs, and Christians publicly mark their sacred commemorations.

Canadian governments at various levels have historically engaged with aspects of religion. The *Canadian Charter of Rights and Freedoms* guarantees "freedom of conscience and religion" as a fundamental right.[8] Whereas the federal Charter gives all Canadians the right to hold their own respective beliefs, Christianity, the faith of the majority population, has historically been given a dominant status. The lyrics in French and bilingual versions of the national anthem, "O Canada," proclaim "Il sait porter la croix" ("it is ready to carry the cross") in a clear acknowledgement of the country's Christian heritage. At the formation of the Canadian nation, the Constitution Act of 1867 provided for separate, religious-based schools. Roman Catholicism, the faith of most francophones, was given recognition within the Canadian state in addition to that accorded to the Church of England. By 1967, three other Christian denominations and the Jewish faith had been included in the federal government's Order of Precedence, which determines the seating of individual persons—in this case, religious representatives—at official state ceremonies. In the early 1990s, the religious category in the Order was made inclusive of all religious groups, in acknowledgement of the broadening religious diversity of the population.

However, such entente between religion and state in Canada does not mean that they have not been in periodic conflict with each other. Given that aspects of the national culture are based on the norms of mainstream Christian denominations, the latter's confrontations with the state appear to occur when these norms undergo change—as happened with the legalization of Sunday shopping, abortion and same sex marriage. Recent years have seen an increased discourse about religious identity in the public sphere, mostly due to the growing pluralism of Canadian society. Requests for accommodation have come from a variety of religious groups including Sikhs, Muslims, Jews, Mormons and Mennonites.[9] This has provided for policy challenges at provincial and federal levels in the secular Canadian state.

Quebec's debates on the prohibition of overt religious expression in public spaces were focused in 2014 around a proposed charter that would have strengthened secularism in that province. This tendency appears to draw from the conviction that holds secularism to be integral to modernity. In the middle of the twentieth century, there was a strong belief among social scientists that religion would cease to exist in public life. According to Daniel Lerner's *The Passing of Traditional Society: Modernizing the Middle East* (1958), an influential work of its time, tradition in the form of Muslim cultures and religion had to be surpassed. Modernization involved " . . . the infusion of a rationalist and positivist spirit against which, scholars seem agreed, Islam is absolutely defenceless."[10] The prominent political scientist Donald Eugene Smith speculated that secularism in its "humanistic-pragmatic" form would sweep through Muslim-majority countries.[11] Similar views were also embraced by leading Arab social scientists such as Hisham Sharabi, who wrote in 1966 that "in the contemporary Arab world Islam has simply been bypassed."[12] Needless to say, such thinking has had to be significantly reassessed in the light of the last few decades' developments.

Jürgen Habermas points to the increasing influence of churches and other religious organizations in shaping Western public opinion and public policy.[13] He also notes the impact on Europe of the contemporary intensification of religious discourse in majority-Muslim countries and the growing presence of non-Christian religious communities resulting from large-scale immigration. These developments, according to Habermas, have led to the emergence of "post-secular society" in which the Western Self has become a complex conglomeration of secular and religious, indigenous and immigrant. No longer can the supporters of secularism take for granted that religious considerations will have no bearing on public life. Even though religious faith does not have the role that it did in Western societies some three hundred years ago, what has been called the "return of religion" has changed the socio-political dynamics of the contemporary public sphere. The idea of post-secular society is a new and evolving concept which is being shaped by influential academic, political, and religious actors. The Aga Khan appears to be one of the individuals whose work and discourse are giving particular nuances to this concept.

A Muslim leader's public discourse

Public discourse in most Western states tends dominantly to be secular. There is a general sense of a universal framework of public discourse that is non-religious and in which all members of society can potentially participate. Nevertheless, it takes for granted the religious heritage of Christianity and, by extension, Judaism. The narratives of the Old and New Testaments underlie Western consciousness, as Northrop Frye has demonstrated.[14] This does not necessarily imply a religious adherence, but usually a cultural one. Even those members of society who do not have a Christian or Jewish background are implicitly expected to understand some cultural allusions which originate in the Bible but have become interwoven into everyday language.

It seems to be such a discourse in which the Aga Khan appeared to participate in referring to the "the Good Samaritan" in a speech in Germany in 2006. The term is part of common parlance in many Western societies. However, the Aga Khan's use of this term drew on both the public knowledge about this figure as well as its origins in the New Testament. The nature of the event—the ceremony of the awarding of the Tolerance Prize to the Aga Khan at the Tutzing

Evangelical Academy—seemed to call for such a two-fold discursive approach. In the course of his acceptance speech, he spoke about Islamic ideals regarding the unity of the human race and their resonance in Biblical teachings.

> Despite the long history of religious conflict, there is a long counter-history of religious focus on tolerance as a central virtue—on welcoming the stranger and loving one's neighbour, "Who is my neighbour?" one of the central Christian narratives asks. Jesus responds by telling the story of the Good Samaritan—a foreigner, a representative of the Other, who reaches out sympathetically, across ethnic and cultural divides, to show mercy to the fallen stranger at the side of the road.[15]

This discourse operated at two levels: in an interfaith context and a secular one that drew on the broader cultural familiarity with the figure of the Good Samaritan. Beyond the actual context of the religious education institution in which the address was delivered, its publication in a book of the Aga Khan's speeches made it available to a wider readership. Its contents are understandable in Christian, secular and post-secular settings.

In order to explain the dual nature of his office, the Ismaili Imam often refers to the dyadic Islamic concepts of *din* and *dunya*, which are variously translated as faith and world, religion and society, or spirit and matter.

> One of the central elements of the Islamic faith is the inseparable nature of faith and world. The two are so deeply intertwined that one cannot imagine their separation. They constitute a "way of life." The role and responsibility of an Imam, therefore, is both to interpret the faith to the community and also to do all within his means to improve the quality and security of people's daily lives.[16]

Speaking from a position legitimized by Islamic tradition, the Ismaili Imam is able to deal with secular matters in a manner that would seem anomalous to those who believe that faith leaders do not involve themselves extensively in worldly affairs. Such a platform provides for a breadth, dynamism and flexibility through which matters such as culture, economics, institutional development and organizational management can be addressed at considerable depth by the Imam. The Aga Khan Development Network[17] includes organizations that work in areas such as aviation, banking, education, health, heritage conservation, infrastructure construction, industry, insurance, media, and rural development. This broad range of endeavours is explained by "the inseparable nature of faith and world."

In speaking to various publics, the Aga Khan situates himself as a religious leader as well as the head of a conglomeration of transnational institutions which he has founded and led for over fifty years. This experience provides him with authority on two substantial grounds. Though a Muslim leader who is not a head of state, he can speak with credibility to high-level government leaders in gatherings where he is frequently invited. In an address to the Canadian parliament in 2014 he said,

> I will comment, as a faith leader, on the crisis of governance in so much of the world today, before concluding with some thoughts about the values that can assist countries of crisis to develop into countries of opportunity, and how Canada can help shape that process.[18]

It might seem out of place for the head of a relatively small Muslim group to comment on international matters of governance to a G-8 government. Yet audiences in Western and other countries seem keen to hear the Ismaili Imam's insights.

A convergence of values

A combination of several factors has enabled the Aga Khan to be in a position to conduct his public discourse. The close relationship with the British government fostered by the present Ismaili Imam's predecessors provided for favourable conditions under colonial rule to build a transnational institutional network.[19] During his own

Imamat, the current Aga Khan has developed an international presence through sustained engagement with a number of states and international organizations; these efforts have been complemented by those of Ismaili communities in Africa, Asia, Australasia, Europe, and North America. A rigorous organization of Ismaili communal and "non-denominational" bodies along contemporary lines has provided for a measure of success that has raised the credibility of the Ismaili Imamat internationally. The growing presence of Muslims in Western countries and the emergence of the conditions of post-secular society have provided for a more welcoming environment for an Islamic leader like the Ismaili Imam. Additionally, the threat of militancy exhibited by certain Muslims has also made the Aga Khan's discourses on pluralism and partnership more attractive.

A significant discursive approach of the Aga Khan is to draw on commonalities between Muslim and Western societies. He builds his arguments around the perceived universality of concepts such as ethics, democracy, human dignity and pluralism. At the ceremony to mark the agreement between the Ismaili Imamat with the Canadian government to establish the Global Centre for Pluralism, he spoke of "This successful collaboration . . . [which is] deeply rooted in a remarkable convergence of values."[20] However, unlike the Aga Khan, a previous Parti Quebecois-led government of Quebec saw a strong divergence between the values derived from religious and secular societies when it proposed a charter to strengthen secularism.[21] In this environment, the Ismaili Imam's discourse appears to provide strong support for the emergence of post-secular society in which values drawn from religious bases, including Islam, find a place in public debates.

The Aga Khan appears to have found that the language of ethics is one in which he can communicate his views to non-Muslim audiences. This is a topic that has a strong relationship with a religious outlook and is at the same time firmly embedded in secular philosophy. In addressing students at a University of Alberta graduation ceremony, he gave illustrative examples from various walks of life to which a diverse audience could relate:

> When we talk about the ethical realm, when we attack cor-
> ruption, we are inclined to think primarily about govern-
> ment and politics. I am one, however, who believes that cor-
> ruption is just as acute, and perhaps even more damaging,
> when the ethics of the civil and private sectors deteriorate.
> We know from recent headlines about scoundrels from the
> American financial scene to the halls of European parlia-
> ments—and we can certainly do without either. But the
> problem extends into every area of human enterprise. When
> a construction company cheats on the quality of materi-
> als for a school or a bridge, when a teacher skimps on class
> work in order to sell his time privately, when a doctor rec-
> ommends a drug because of incentives from a pharmaceuti-
> cal company, when a bank loan is skewed by kickbacks, or
> a student paper is plagiarized from the internet—when the
> norms of fairness and decency are violated in any way, then
> the foundations of society are undermined. And the damage
> is felt most immediately in the most vulnerable societies,
> where fraud is often neither reported nor corrected, but
> simply accepted as an inevitable condition of life.[22]

In speaking about these real-life situations he invokes the universal
concern for the importance of ethics in society. The Islamic leader
presents this discourse that is based on religious sensibilities but he
does it without mentioning religion or quoting scripture.

Indeed, he has suggested that certain types of behaviour based on
religious precepts can sometimes become an obstacle to the broader
interests of humanity.

> There are several forms of proselytism and, in several reli-
> gions, proselytism is demanded. Therefore, it is necessary to
> develop the principle of a cosmopolitan ethic, which is not
> an ethic oriented by faith, or for a society. I speak of an ethic
> under which all people can live within a same society, and
> not of a society that reflects the ethic of solely one faith. I
> would call that ethic, quality of life.

> I have serious doubts about the ecumenical discourse, and
> about what it can reach, but I do not have any doubts about
> cosmopolitan ethics. I believe that people share the same
> basic worries, joys, and sadness. If we can reach a consen-
> sus in terms of cosmopolitan ethics, we will have attained
> something, which is very important.[23]

This is an intriguing statement by a religious leader: it seems to be
promoting the idea that people rise above particular religious interests to a universal cosmopolitanism that is of benefit to everyone.

Conclusion

Despite the Ismaili Imam's vigorous engagement with secular ideas,
his frequent references to the value of faith make it clear that he is not
diminishing the place of religion in the public sphere. The Aga Khan
asserts that even though he holds ideas such as democracy to be vital
for contemporary society, "as a Muslim, I am a democrat not because
of Greek or French thought but primarily because of principles that
go back 1,400 years, directly to the death of Prophet Muhammad
(peace be upon him)."[24] He ensures that his audiences know that he is
"a faith leader."[25] The Ismaili Imam frequently begins his speeches by
reciting "Bismillah-ir-Rahman-ir-Rahim" ("In the name of Allah, the
Most Compassionate, the Most Merciful"), which is the first phrase
of most Qur'anic chapters.

The Aga Khan's two-fold discursive approach simultaneously
addresses the spiritual and the worldly. He does not make direct
religious references in many of his speeches, but ideas of the sacred
underlie his discourses. The Islamic leader presents the concepts of
ethics, democracy, development, meritocracy, pluralism and quality of life as some of the "bridges that unite"[26] ways of understanding
that are religious and secular. He has been able to speak effectively to
a post-secular society that is dealing with rapidly-changing local and
global conditions. The apparent success of the Aga Khan's model of
inter-civilizational communication is especially significant given the
often troubled relationship between Western and Muslim societies.

Who I Really Am: Communicating Islam Across Generations

ASMA SAYED

On a quiet December afternoon several years ago, my five-year-old daughter burst into the house in tears. She had been at Sunday school at the local mosque in Edmonton, where my kids learn Arabic and the basics of Islamic history. She had been chatting excitedly with a classmate, talking about her letter to Santa Claus. She was very happy, anticipating Santa's visit and all the gifts he would bring. Her zealous Sunday-school teacher overheard the conversation and reprimanded her. She told my daughter that Santa did not exist, and even if he were real, he would not visit Muslim homes, and further that as a Muslim, my daughter should not be talking about such "Christian" practices at the mosque. My daughter came home, confused about Christian and Muslim identities, and worried that Santa Claus would not bring her a gift.

My husband and I had made the choice to expose our children to both religious and secular traditions. This was the way we had both been raised in India, and we were confident that as our children grew up they would be better situated to make their own choices and follow their own paths. Therefore we sent them to the Sunday school at the local mosque, and we allowed for the possibility of Santa. However, this particular incident got us thinking—were we doing the right thing? Or were we confusing our children? Should we expose them to religious practices or not? If we didn't, would they grow up and tell us that we had not fulfilled our duties as parents? And then, what about culture? What other way was there for us to introduce them to our ancestral culture? If they didn't attend mosque, how would they understand their grandmothers' faiths? How would they understand their heritage and themselves? How would they understand the cultural and ancestral identity reflected in their names—identities that others would expect of them, to varying degrees, for better or worse? Now, more than a decade later, the kids are almost grown and we still don't have the answers to these questions. One incident at a time, we have simply done our best to navigate sometimes smooth and sometimes rough waters. At the time, we convinced our daughter that Santa Claus did not discriminate. She was reassured. And, lo and behold, he did make a stop at our house that year.

Nonetheless, incidents such as this one raise many questions about living at the intersections of multiple identities. Add to that the complexity of raising the next generation in a multicultural Canadian society. What does it mean to be a first-generation Canadian with an Islamic identity? What does it mean to my second-generation children raised in a family that is all at once Shia, Sunni, agnostic, and secular, as well as Indian and Canadian? What is an Islamic identity? Can one be secular while being part of an Islamic community? This essay, more than answering these questions, is about confronting them, tackling them, and in the process, exposing even more difficult topics. These issues have been raised before, by a chorus of voices. But if Muslim voices are not to be reduced to the representations provided by a few select members of our communities, then we must all dare to speak out and interject with our personal stories.

—⚭—

Canada is a multicultural country, yes. But so too is India where I spent the earlier years of my life. Thinking about the relevance of an Islamic identity in Canada rerouted me from the present and sent me on a trip down memory lane to reflect on what it meant in my childhood to be a secular Muslim in India. I have a very powerful memory about a seemingly insignificant moment, when I was in grade 10, studying at a Christian convent school. One afternoon right before Eid, one of my classmates, who was already in the holiday spirit knowing that the next day was a holiday in recognition of Eid, happily wished me Eid Mubarak. My science teacher overheard the greeting. She sharply inquired why my friend had wished *me* a happy Eid. My maiden last name is porous enough not to give me any particular religious identity, and my first name was taken for a "fashionable" poetic name. I could have been Hindu. What I realized in that moment, as a fourteen-year-old was that our identities are not only personal, but political—a simple greeting from my friend had shattered my teacher's perception of who I was. Of course, neither what the teacher had assumed about me, nor what she may have thought afterward, is any closer to capturing who I really am.

I was raised by a Sunni mother, who was once a devout young woman but whose attitudes and beliefs have inevitably been influenced by almost fifty years of marriage to a staunch atheist rationalist. When I find myself needing to explain myself, I simply say I was raised in an atheist-Sunni household. All of this, of course, in the context of a predominantly Hindu society in Gujarat. I visited more temples than mosques, celebrated Diwali, Holi, and Dussehra with more pomp than Eid. In fact, my siblings and I were happy to wake up early on the Hindu New Year—the day after Diwali—excited to visit all our friends to wish them Happy New Year. By contrast, on the day of Eid, despite my mother's insistence that we wake up early and say our prayers, we slept in. Yes, it was a public holiday but we had no Muslim friends or family in town to visit and celebrate with. But we did look forward to the special sweets my mother would make— Dudhpak and Puri—and the new clothes she would have bought for us to wear. And of course, later in the day our Hindu friends would visit and enjoy my mother's cooking. The phone would be ringing off the hook with well-wishes from relatives around the country.

Occasionally, Eid fell during summer months when school was out. At those times, we would be at our grandparents' house in Upleta, a small town with a much larger Muslim population relative to Rajkot, my hometown. The atmosphere in Upleta on Eid was much different from the one in Rajkot; there was more pomp and show, more variety of food, and girls put henna on their hands—my favourite part of the festival. At those times, I was provided more insights into the religious aspects of the holiday. All the men and boys went to the mosque in the morning to say their namaaz, and all the women and girls said their prayers at home. I was expected to know how to behave in this context, but it was a very different reality from what I experienced in Rajkot. Growing up in this way—between urban and rural life, between Hindu and Muslim cultures, between Christian and Hindu friends, between my atheist father and my Sunni mother—meant continuously negotiating my way across a range of identities. Perhaps it follows that I eventually married a Shia Muslim I had met at university. Somehow, it didn't seem that complicated, until I moved to Canada, when the very cosmopolitan aspect of my youthful multicultural interfaith life suddenly became a barrier to belongings.

Migration, language, history, and xenophobia all mark us in different ways. I came to Canada from India in 1998. I knew little about the country on a practical level. I had studied Canadian literature briefly and thought that I knew enough to be able to live here. I was introduced to the local Shia Ithna-Asheri community, many of its members from East Africa, but speaking Gujarati and Kutchi, languages I knew. The community at large is also highly religious with many members following and expecting strictly religious edicts. At times much of it was driven by the fear of losing children to an "alien" White culture. I was, and remain, somewhat a misfit in the community. I remember that a few weeks after my arrival, a group of women from the community came to greet me at my house. At the end of a short afternoon together, just as they were leaving, they told me that I should consider wearing hijab. Then, looking for other communities to belong to, and being from Gujarat, I hoped to connect with the local Gujarati community, which was predominantly Hindu. It was Navratri and I went to celebrate the festival. But despite the fact that I had lived my entire life in Gujarat, here in the West, when I said my identifiably Muslim married name, I felt the subtle rejection as a question invariably followed: "But, didn't you just say you are a Gujarati?" Gujarati identity was conflated with Hindu identity. The question lurking in their eyes: what business did I, a non-Hindu Gujarati, have standing in solidarity with this group of Gujarati Canadians and singing hymns to a Hindu goddess? How was it that I found myself a misfit within the community with which I felt perhaps the most affinity: my ethnic cultural community?

And then came 9/11. The world was talking about Islam all over again. Muslims were being profiled—at airports, in schools, in universities, and certainly in the North American media. All over again, I was compelled to look at my immediate world, my upbringing, my adopted country, the country that I had left behind—all from a new perspective.

One would like to think that Islamic identity does not have any relevance in an increasingly globalized world, and that one would not need to identify oneself as Muslim or of Islamic heritage, or for that matter of any other religious or secular tradition. And yet our identities are always up for dissection. Our names are the first markers of belonging—or exclusion. If one has a first name such as mine (in Canada, especially post-9/11, I often get addressed as Asama, Osama or a variant of those names), or the name Mohammed, Aisha, Ali, or Karim, or if one has a last name such as Sayed, one is immediately assumed to be a practising Muslim. The question of identity gets further complicated when linked to language. I grew up speaking Kutchi at home, English at school, Gujarati with friends. I learned Hindi and Sanskrit at school, and learned to read Arabic from my mother who wanted me to be able to read the Quran. I absorbed Urdu through continuous exposure to the old Hindi cinema, given my father's passion for it. My husband grew up speaking Urdu at home, and I now speak Urdu mixed with Hindi, Gujarati, and English to our children. Language too comes with identity tags. When I speak Urdu, people think I am from Pakistan. When I speak or mention Kutchi and Gujarati, I am instantly (mis)taken for Ismaili. Arabic makes people wonder if I am Arab. Along with each of these languages, identities are assumed and expectations are imposed.

—〰—

I have lived in two multicultural countries: India and Canada. The question of the relevance of an Islamic identity applies in both. I am part of what is considered a minority culture in each of these countries. However, identity politics lends itself differently to each of these situations. In the last few years, both countries have increasingly, and unfortunately, become antagonistic to liberal and secular voices. Currently both India and Canada have conservative governments that tend to scapegoat Muslim communities for political leveraging. The constitutions of both the countries promise secularism, and yet Canadian Prime Minister Stephen Harper time and again, in his public talks, asks God to bless Canada; the Indian Prime Minister Narendra Modi climbed the political ladder by inciting sectarian violence. And it comes as no surprise, then, that after Modi took office in 2014, Harper provided him a king's welcome regardless of the fact that formerly, as the chief minister (premier) of Gujarat province and on his path to becoming leader of the country, he did little to control the Gujarat pogrom of 2002 (and may even have orchestrated it, according to numerous human rights activists and government officials who have now either been murdered or bullied into retracting). That massacre of 2002 left more than a thousand Muslims dead and tens of thousands displaced. Now his government and Stephen Harper's work together, solidifying ties around nuclear energy, itself hardly a neutral issue.

India's relationship to Muslims is complicated. Muslims make up the largest minority group in the country. Muslims do hold many important positions in the public and private sector, but they are also discriminated against both socially and politically. India's Partition of 1947 still haunts it. Communal riots, which have continued to erupt sporadically since independence render the minorities vulnerable. Post-Babri right-wing politics in the country has made life generally more difficult.

In Canada, Islamophobia has been on the rise post-9/11. The state itself is complicit—as witness the recent Bill C-51, inspired by xenophobia and exaggerated fear of Muslims. The government's treatment of Maher Arar, its intransigence in the case of Omar Khadr, and its stand on Egyptian Canadian journalist Mohamed Fahmy are three further examples of official attitudes that push us to ask: What does it mean to be a Muslim in multicultural Canada, in this first part of the twenty-first century? Media only aggravates this situation with its ignorance and hype. Many of my students at university, who will become leaders in tomorrow's Canada, tend to have opinions about Islam, but the majority know very few Muslims and know even less about the Quran. More often than not, they form their opinions about Muslims based on what they learn from the media.

Essentializing Muslim communities is not helpful. First, we have to understand clearly the difference between Islam as a religion and Islamic culture. At the same time, we cannot deny the need for communication and understanding between various faith groups and the need for dialogue between various Islamic communities. Unless we inform ourselves and others about the secular values of Islam and the heterogeneity of Muslims, we will continue to perpetuate what Edward Said has called "the clash of ignorance." We are living in times when Muslims are saddled with the responsibility to "educate" people about Islam and, often, to apologize for the deeds of a few. But on that last count, I refuse. I draw a line. While I condemn all violations of human rights, I will not apologize for the deeds of the Bin Ladens, the ISIS, or any other organization becuase they do not represent me or the Muslims I know. A heterogeneous, diverse, and multi-ethnic community of nearly two billion people cannot be held to account for the deeds of a few bad apples.

Yet, despite all these political problems, if Islam can thrive anywhere, perhaps it is in a secular multicultural democracy such as Canada. Given the variety of sects and beliefs within Islam that broadly include Shia and Sunni, and further sections within those—Ahmadiyya, Ismaili, Baha'i, and Sufi, to name a few—we can all agree that there is no single Islam. Under "Islamic" governance or any theocratic political system, there is always the risk of the persecution of not only the non-state-sanctioned beliefs but also of other religious minorities—a cursory look at global politics provides ample examples of such situations. In Canada, Muslims are able to coexist not only with their own *ummah*, but also with followers of other belief systems and agnostics and atheists. In Canada, Muslims enjoy the freedom to practice whichever version of Islam they wish, in whichever language. A small town such as Edmonton, with a population of under a million, has many mosques and Islamic study centres. The Shia Ithna-Asheri community alone has five centres catering to the multiple cultural and linguistic communities: the East African Indian community has a centre that operates predominantly in Gujarati (with occasional nods to Swahili); the Pakistani centre in Urdu; the Afghan community in Pashto; the Iraqis in Arabic; and the Iranians in Persian. There are also many Sunni mosques and Ismaili Jamatkhanas. And of course there are also Muslims who, like me, are raised in multiple communities and do not fit comfortably within any rigid definition of any of these communities: Muslims for whom Islam represents a culture and a space of belonging more than a religion.

—⚋—

Tariq Ali reminds us that there have been many secular Muslim intellectuals and artists: "The last century alone produced Nazim

Hikmet, Faiz Ahmed Faiz, Abdelrehman Munif, Mahmud Darwish, Fazil Iskander, Naguib Mahfouz, Nizar Qabbani, Pramoeda Annanta Toer, Djibril Diop Mambety among others" (5). Interestingly, many of these writers suffered the consequences of identifying themselves as secular. It seems that secular Muslims (and secular people from other traditions as well) pay a price in many ways, receiving overt and covert threats, and many times being shunned by their own communities. Ali, a secular intellectual himself, writes that he at times refers to himself as "a non-Muslim Muslim," but this doesn't always work because "the appellation doesn't quite fit. It has an awkward ring to it" (5). Similarly, as much as I identify myself as secular or agnostic, I cannot completely shed my Muslim identity.

Who can really explain why or how we become who we are? Perhaps I cannot shed my Muslim identity because that is what others see in me. Perhaps it has something to do with a sense of self I developed a long time ago. All I can do is intellectualize what at the end of the day is partly driven by affect, partly by nostalgia, and partly because of a desire for some kind of genealogical continuity to my story and that of my children's. Olivier Roy writes,

> [T]here is no abstract process of secularization: what you are after you have left religion is clearly marked by the particular religion you have left, and the forms and spaces of secularization are defined by reference to each particular religion. These spaces are the product of a history and also of a religious history. Religion inhabits society: religion has shaped society, and it returns either in a secularised form or, on the contrary, in outbreaks of fundamentalism.

My upbringing was both intercultural, interfaith, and yet secular all the way. My grandmothers were Muslims. I grew up listening to them, and to my mother, reciting the Quran and telling stories of the Prophet. I don't pray, or fast during Ramadhan, but I celebrate Eid. Neither can I shed my Hindu self. When I lived in India, I took part in Navratri garbas and sang aarti; during Diwali I drew rangoli (to commemorate the return of Lord Rama after fourteen years in exile) in my yard, lighted diyas, stayed up late at night enjoying the firecrackers, and rejoiced as we ritualistically set fire to the effigy of Ravana, symbolically proclaiming the triumph of good over evil. But I don't identify myself as Hindu. Nor can I shed my Christian self. At my convent school we celebrated Christmas. I grew up singing psalms and learning about Jesus although such activities were never imposed on us. I set up a Christmas tree in my home in Canada. I don't identify as Christian. The beauty of a multicultural secular society is that we can celebrate many cultural experiences and interfaith expressions as acts of community belonging and as our acceptance of our neighbours, which over time become part of who we are.

My children's heritage is Shia, Sunni, Hindu, Christian, atheist, and agnostic; hopefully, they are learning to embrace these all, growing up in a multicultural Canada, learning about the beliefs and nonbeliefs of others. Most of all, I want them to grow up as global citizens grounded by an understanding that what matters the most is human dignity and human rights. I hope they will embody plurality and embrace intercultural dialogue. And when in doubt about their heritage, when dominant Western discourses perpetuated by mainstream media tell them otherwise, I hope that they will remind themselves of the intellectual history of Islam and the contributions that Muslim—religious and secular—intellectuals have made. And hopefully they will understand that Canadian society is what we collectively make it, therefore we all have a responsibility to transform Canada into a more intercultural space. If we don't wish multiculturalism to be reduced merely to festivals and adventures in "ethnic" foods, we must make genuine attempts to understand cultural practices, learn languages, study customs and traditions, and engage meaningfully with different communities. If we are all guided by a respect for the human rights of all, we will have little to worry about. If we must live together, why not live in peace? A simplistic proposition, but what is the alternative?

Married to a Believer

MAYANK BHATT

Toronto, June 18, 2015: the Muslim holy month of Ramzan has commenced. During this hot summer period, when the days are long, my wife Mahrukh will fast for nearly seventeen hours every day.

Annually, over the last two decades since we've been married, Ramzan is the time when I'm at once confounded by the rigidity of rituals and the beauty of belief. Having alternated between atheism and agnosticism for all of my adult life, I've always had a problem reconciling to practices borne out of faith. And through these years, Mahrukh has patiently but resolutely prevented me from interfering with what she believes her religion requires her to do.

The ritual of day-long fasting, I argue with her, was conceived and meant for places where day and night are almost equally divided, not for the summers of the northern hemisphere. Therefore, fasting for nearly two-thirds of a day for thirty days couldn't possibly be what Allah ordained, it is quite unnecessary. Such arguments don't move her; and if I persist, she glares at me with a finality that implies that if I know what's good for me, I'd better shut up.

Even now, I cannot resist having that discussion with her at least once every year, before the Ramzan fasting begins. Over the years, however, I've noticed that my resistance has gradually transformed into tolerance and, as we age together, into acceptance.

She is pragmatic and doesn't let her belief totally govern her life. So she prefers halal both at home and when eating out, but will also dine where halal is not served. She'd want to pray five times a day, but will be satisfied if she's able to do it at least once, preferably at dawn. She has never worn a burqa, or a hijab, and finds the practice irrelevant to a woman's existence. But she covers her head when she prays.

I have come to admire the rootedness and certitude that her belief gives her, and I often wonder whether these are the benefit of belief—solace, peace, and the ability to live in the moment, accept life for what it is. I had seen this in my late grandmother Harvilas, a devout Hindu. Religion gave her a sense of self-assurance that was at once enviable and intimidating. For the last two decades of her long life she lived in a predominantly Muslim milieu, with a masjid opposite our home, and the azaan flowing through the speakers five times a day. Adjusting rather remarkably to her new environment, Harvilas created an exclusive world of her own, looking for and perhaps finding inner peace in her puja.

For Mahrukh, religion is deeply personal, as it was for Harvilas, and the only external and physical manifestation of their belief is the ritual of prayer—the namaaz for Mahrukh and the puja for Harvilas. My lifelong disappointment has been that Harvilas died about a year before Mahrukh and I got married. They would have found many similarities between them, many experiences to share.

Rarely, if ever, does Mahrukh proclaim her belief to the world, but just as equally she never disguises or hides it. In many ways, and perhaps without realizing it, she has matured into a person who is a strange combination of her parents—mother Shakera and father Aga Vaqar. Growing up in cosmopolitan Bombay, she had friends who spoke different languages and had different beliefs. Her decision to get married to a non-Muslim didn't overtly dismay her family perhaps because of her father's distinctly Marxist views.

For Aga Vaqar, being a Muslim in India was not so much about faith as it was about identity. Despite our similar views on many aspects (or perhaps because of them) my relationship with him remained uneasy till he died. On the other hand, Mahrukh's mother Shakera, who is a deeply religious person, has little in common with me; and yet on several occasions, she steadied our rocking marriage in the initial years, because of her affection for and trust in me. I don't talk to her often, but merely knowing that she is there in this world makes me feel secure and gives me strength.

Living together has transformed both of us gradually, and as with all couples who live together, the process of adjustment has been fraught with friction. In the early years, I often thought that religion was instrumental in whatever problems we faced in our marriage, but over the years I've realized that what to outsiders may seem like an unending television soap opera of quarrels with all-too-brief interludes of togetherness is perhaps true of most marriages. Mahrukh and I don't make any attempts to hide our differences. And yet we are together and will be together because we love each other, and because we want to be together.

Immigrating to Canada has made me more appreciative of my wife. We talk of assimilation for newcomers to Canada, and what has struck me about cultural assimilation is that while most of us would willingly change our lives to become part of the mainstream, the biggest challenge (at least for me) is adapting to a different cuisine. I have singularly failed in adapting to "Canadian" food, and prefer my vegetarian Gujarati diet. My rigid inability to adjust has made me appreciate Mahrukh's sacrifice two decades ago when she came to live with me after our marriage. It must have been an immense challenge for her to leave behind her dietary habits, her lifestyle—which at many levels was so completely different from mine—and quickly and willingly adjust to a new life.

Mahrukh prepares Gujarati cuisine with consummate ease; every day, she packs my lunchbox with simple, basic Gujarati food. I can't think of anyone who can quite make the karela nu shaak like she does. Her adad ni daal tastes exactly like my grandmother made, and she even attempts the saat paadi (a Surati version of the bhakhri); her daal is almost as good as my mother's. I have to constantly remind myself that she is not a Gujarati. Her transformation has been imperceptible, unannounced, and without any accompanying drama that is generally associated with such life-changing journeys.

Mahrukh's vivacious personality helped her in gaining acceptance in my family, including extended members of the family, with most of whom I have maintained little or no connection. She is connected to them all or at least most of them on social media, and is my source of information for all that happens in my family. Also, given my generally depressing state of dispensation, she has also become the sole contact point for my immediately family (mother, sister) who are never quite sure how I would respond to their queries.

She has transformed me too, but gradually, and not in the manner that she'd have wanted. One of the biggest changes has been to acknowledge the relevance of religion. My father was a lifelong socialist, influenced in equal measure by Jawaharlal Nehru (India's first prime minister, a Fabian socialist) and Ram Manohar Lohia (a socialist leader), and had little patience with God or godliness. He absolutely refused to perform the janoi (the sacred thread) ceremony for me, much to my disappointment because all my cousins had great fun tonsuring their heads and putting on the sacred thread amidst the chanting of holy mantras. "The only use of a janoi is to circle it around your ear when you piss," he said dismissively. My mother has turned religious as she has aged, but her religion encompasses all belief systems, she finds peace in the Siddhivinayak mandir as much as in the Haji Ali dargah.

Once I outgrew my grandmother's influence, I turned an agnostic and have remained so since. I called myself an atheist earlier but have stopped doing so; I don't think I am (or was) an atheist, because I respect those who believe, even if I don't share their beliefs, and I think that transformation has occurred because of Mahrukh's influence on me. She has made me aware of religion's many dimensions. I had grown up seeing my grandmother perform puja, and go to the mandir every day. I associated religion with older people. My wife's religiosity began a process of questioning in me.

Why was a person who was not dissimilar to me in most ways be so completely different in one crucial aspect, and be so committed to a belief system? It led me to explore religion—not just Islam, but also Hinduism, Christianity, and other religions of India. It made me understand India and Indians better. It made me more tolerant, better equipped to accept differences, develop an ability to find commonalities even with people who are completely different from me, and who preferred to revel in that difference. And it has helped me better adjust to Canada's multicultural society.

When our son was born, we agreed to name him Che, after the Argentinian revolutionary. It was a momentous event in our lives, and even though I have never been a diarist, I recorded it. This is what I wrote then:

When he will ask me why I named him Che:

Monday, September 8, 1997, 21.48 hrs: A baby boy is born to Mahrukh. And my world has changed. This is my single biggest achievement. The 7 lbs baby will be called Che, after Ernesto Che Guevara, the Argentine revolutionary, who fought alongside Fidel Castro in Cuba (and who was killed in Bolivia). His remains were found earlier this year. Che Guevara is the only revolutionary of this century who, after having succeeded in ushering in a new order in a country, did not sit down permanently to rule the country. He went on fighting in other countries for the cause which he felt was right.

Che essentially means "my". But it is not just that. "For the residents of the pampas, Che can express, depending on intonation and context, the entire spectrum of human passions—surprise, exhilaration, sorrow, tenderness, approval or protest" (quoted from *Ernesto Che Guevara*, a biography by I Lavretsky)... I know Meghnad (my father, who died about four months before my son was born) would have liked the name, Durga (my mother) will, too, and Mahrukh has begun to like the name (though I suspect this has more to do with her fear that her son may otherwise be named with a Sanskrit word). More importantly, if I succeed in making him a decent human being, I am sure, even my son will like his name.

Che was conceived just before the month of Ramzan in 1997 (I think it was during a trip to Aurangabad in December 1996) and was born during the Ganapati festival of 1997. The nurses at the Holy Family Hospital, Bandra, told us that September 8 was also the feast of the Virgin Mary. Che's date of birth also coincided with the holy month of the Jains—Paryushan.

Fairly early on, I decided that I would not decide what religion my son would follow. It wasn't a tough decision for me. It may have been a bit challenging for Mahrukh, but even she has never made any overt attempts to force her views on him. One of the reasons for our decision to immigrate to Canada was to make it possible for Che to grow up in a society where his identity would not be restricted merely to his religion. I believe that Canadian society is generally open and fair, and doesn't judge a person by his or her faith, although many recent events have severely challenged this belief.

Over the last eighteen years, I have consciously avoided influencing my son's mind, and not merely about religion, but even about other matters. I believe that a child is influenced by what he sees his elders do rather than what his elders tell him to do. I realize that because of his mother's faith, my son is more exposed to it. It was my experience, too, growing up in a household where though my parents weren't religious my grandmother's religiosity influenced me especially during my adolescence. But I quickly abandoned the narrow confines of religion once I was exposed to different experiences.

What helped was the multi-faith milieu of Teli Gali, a narrow lane in Andheri, where I grew up. My friends and neighbours belonged to different religions, different castes; we happily celebrated all festivals, and participated in rituals of all faiths. Opposite my home to the south was a masjid, and to the north a Swaminarayan mandir; a church, another Ganapati mandir, four movie studios, and eight cinemas were within walking distance. Teli Gali made me who I am

today. In the same way, I'm sure Canadian multiculturalism will help
Che develop his own ideas about himself, his identity, and his place
in the world.

As a family, we don't often discuss these matters. But much to
my consternation, I have realized that it is a major concern for the
people we know, and often even for people we don't know. Everyone
wants to know if religion is a source of friction between Mahrukh
and me, and I joke that we have many other important reasons to
quarrel. People want to know if it would become a cause for friction
if Che were to decide one way or the other, and I'm at pains to explain
that it wouldn't really matter, and that why should he have just two
options—he could choose from many that are available, or like most
rational human beings these days, choose none.

I remember one particular incident that rankles even after many
years. In my struggle to find a proper job after I came to this country
in 2008 (at the ripe age of 46), and upon realizing that finding one
was next to impossible, I enrolled in a short program in flash anima-
tion at the Yorkdale Adult Education Centre in Toronto. I also wrote
a column for *Canadian Immigrant*, and wrote about this experience.
I want to share this here because it is the sort of response that I regularly encounter, and which I find extremely annoying.

In the column titled *Questions of Identity*, I wrote,

> Once, while I was waiting in the corridor for the class to
> commence, two of my classmates also arrived. They were
> immigrants, too, but they were in Canada for more than
> two decades. After a brief discussion about our course, the
> subject veered to our children.
>
> "I have one son," I said, "He's 12 and he would be able to
> do this course better than me."
>
> Both the women nodded their heads in agreement. To
> become a student when you're middle-aged poses peculiar
> challenges. One of the two women was a Tamil from Sri
> Lanka and had come to Toronto soon after she completed
> her education in Madurai (India) in 1988. The other woman
> was from Somalia and had come to Toronto in 1986. The

Tamil woman has two sons—the elder is 17 and the younger 13; the Somali woman's elder daughter is 18 and she has two other children aged 6 and 4.

I have often wondered why is it that we have a tendency to know the other person's faith and religion. I can live with ethnicity. But questions about my religion are something that I find deeply disturbing; not because I feel defensive answering them, but because I know my answers disturb the people who ask them. The Tamil woman wanted to know my country of origin.

"India," I replied.

She asked, "Are you a Hindu?"

"By birth," I said.

"I'm also a Hindu," she said.

I nodded.

"You pray to Krishna?" she asked again.

"I don't pray at all," I said, and quickly added, "But I respect those who do."

"Your wife also doesn't pray?" she asked.

"My wife is a Muslim," I answered.

The woman from Sri Lanka looked at me with a sense of disquiet. But the Somali woman perked up.

"Your wife is a Muslim?" she asked.

"Yes."

"She prays five times a day?"

"Not five times, but at least once early morning," I said.

"I can't get up early every morning," the Somali woman sighed, and then added with unconcealed pride, "But my elder daughter does."

In five minutes of conversation we had discovered not what united us—our visible minority status and our lower-income status—but what differentiated us. We weren't three immigrants in Toronto. We were now a Muslim, a Hindu and an agnostic.

"Didn't your parents object (to your marriage)?" the Tamil woman asked.

"No," I said.

"Even your wife's parents," the Somali woman asked.

"Not really," I said.

"What religion will your son practice?" the Somali

woman asked.

"I don't know," I said, "I'd rather that he decides what he wants to be when he is mature enough to take such decisions on his own."

"Have you given him a Hindu name or a Muslim name?" the Tamil woman asked.

"Neither. I've named him Che. It means 'my'."

I don't want to create the impression that my wife and I don't have differences. We differ on many issues, and constantly. The *Charlie Hebdo* massacre was a recent instance when we had different views; the annual memorial in New York for the victims of 9/11 is another. I've learned—sometimes with great difficulty—to accept as valid those of her opinions that are diametrically different from mine; and she has acquired the confidence to express her views without the fear of being labeled. We understand that we can express our views to each other and be understood even when the other person does not share our opinion. We have become patient with each other.

The Performing Identities of Muslims

ZAINUB VERJEE

Their story begins on ground level, with footsteps. They are myriad, but do not compose a series. They cannot be counted because each unit has a qualitative character: a style of tactile apprehension and kinesthetic appropriation. Their swarming mass is an innumerable collection of singularities. Their intertwined paths give their shape to spaces. They weave places together.
— Michel de Certeau, in *The Practice of Everyday Life.*

I am collecting my things to leave the hotel room to attend the Toronto International Film Festival. The phone rings. As I pick it up, I wonder if I am running late and see that it is past 9:00 a.m. My colleague from Quebec who's on the line says, "*vite* . . . turn on the television," and hangs up. It is not part of my morning rhythm, even when I am traveling, to switch on the television. But I hear an urgency in her voice and wonder what it could be. I follow through though, not sure what I am tuning into. The sound and image on the TV are simultaneous, a plane crashing into a building. It was September 11, 2001.

Later, upon my return to Ottawa, I was informed about the memorial ceremony that would be held on Parliament Hill. I asked my boss whether he would attend. He was a bit perplexed, both by my question and the sense of urgency that it carried. There was a pause. I did not wait for him to say anything. "I want to attend the memorial and you need to be with me. I can't go alone." He was even more perplexed by my utterance, which was very uncharacteristic of me. He did not understand my state of mind. "I am afraid. I fear for myself," I quipped.

That was the moment when I experienced my Muslim identity, foregrounded in an accentuated form. It was my subjective moment and experience telling me that I too was a Muslim.

From the 1970s to the turn of the century, I was at the forefront of identity politics, influenced by the decolonization and postcolonial movements that emerged out of the postwar liberation of countries in Asia and Africa. I was impacted by the major economic recessions during the reign of Thatcher in Britain and their violent outcomes such as the 1981 Brixton race riots. Race and ethnicity were at the centre of my existence. I witnessed the rise of the British Black Artists' movement, which contributed enormously to the discourse in the arts around race and identity. Gender issues were brought to the fore and added to this mix. In Canada, Trudeau's mosaic theory, heralding the concept and policy of multiculturalism, had effectively whitewashed the cultural landscape, and in the late eighties and early nineties Canada had only seen a handful of events by people of colour such as InVisible Colours, Asian New World, Race to the Screen, Yellow Peril Reconsidered, and *Desh Pardesh*. Identity politics and the tensions therein were debilitating, where appropriation of any kind was condemned almost to the point of reaching essentialist proportions.

In the subsequent weeks, months, and years after 9/11 my Muslim identity became foregrounded. I wanted to know more, learn more, talk more, and share more about what it was to be a Muslim in Canada.

The manufacturing of Muslim identity

"What is Islam?" or "What constitutes a Muslim identity?" is no longer restricted to the rationalities of the outsiders, meaning the

Western nations. On the contrary, it has emerged as a cornerstone of all revivalist Islamic movements. In these debates, the disjuncture that is articulated is pegged onto the difference between what is Islamic and what is not. And further, with a shift to the study of Muslim modernities, including social movements, religious discourses, popular culture, social practices that characterize the everyday life of Muslims. These Muslim modernities also take place with reference to social imaginaries.

How do we imagine our social reality? What constitutes this social imagination? The answers to these obvious questions lie in the understanding of modernity. Canadian philosopher Charles Taylor has grappled with the central tenets of modernity, especially its Western experience and manifestation. In *Modern Social Imaginaries*, Taylor lays out the mutation of a new moral order into our social imaginary that led to the formation of certain social forms such as "ways of living (eg. secularization, rationality, individualism), new institutional forms (eg. industrial production, urbanization, role of technology), and forms of malaise (eg. meaninglessness, alienation). In explaining the seemingly amplified contestations on the primary constituent ideas of our social selves, Taylor talks about the need to make way for the idea of multiple modernities—more than the dominant Western modernity.

In *Orientalism*, Edward Said offers a critique of the West's essentialized image of Islam that is rooted in its modernity. Islam is seen as a static, monolithic, backward doctrine that both explains and determines Muslim behavior. This implies that for the non-Western world the notion of progress is imperative for the evolution of Western-style institutions and its modernity. Similarly, democratic politics is closely linked with the cardinal ideas of constructing meaningful modern selfhoods. Remember George W Bush's clarion call for bringing democracy to the Muslim world!

On the other hand, a "Muslim" society, in the cultural and sociological sense, is not an "Islamic" society *per se* for the Islamic fundamentalist and conservative revivalists, implying that it is not a society

based on principles of Islam. Therefore, it is necessary to reformu-
late what it means to be a Muslim, to define this identity in keeping
with the globalization-induced deterritorialization and acculturation
manifesting as re-Islamization in the West. Writing on political Islam,
the Arabist and political scientist François Burgat argues that "the pervasive movement of re-Islamization or Islamic revivalism has been
explained in terms of identity protest or as a way to reconcile modernity, self-affirmation and authenticity" (as manifested in the return of
the hijab among many Western-educated women) (Burgat 2003).

In everyday experience, a Muslim feels compelled to explain what
it means to be a Muslim. It is the everyday Muslim who takes this
call to publicly state his or her identity as if it were a civic duty. The
everyday modality of being a Muslim comes into play through a set of
collective expressions shaping and appropriating a collective meaning. Further, it is not only imperative to understand the everyday life
of a Muslim and the production of Muslim identity but also there is
an urgency because of the growing Muslim population in Canadian
cities. According to the Pew Research Centre's report on *The Future
of Global Muslim Population Report*, the Muslim population in
Canada in 2010 was 940,000 and is estimated to triple in twenty years
to almost 2.7 million.

Over the last decade and a half many studies have grappled with
the challenges of being a Muslim in Canada. What they have been
able to identify is that the dominant site of this crisis is witnessed
largely on the body of Muslim women. Feminist scholars like Sunera
Thobani and Yasmin Jiwani argue how the historical narrative has
focused on the figure of the Muslim woman, who has become the
cause for particular national consternation, her body the site of the
clash of civilizations (Thobani 2007, 238; Jiwani 2010). The wearing
of the chador, or the headscarf, often destabilizes the assumed notion
of the superiority and alleged universality of Western values (Bullock
1999, Zine 2012).

The post-9/11 narrative has been a major signifier of the fundamental understanding of a Muslim/Islamic identity in Canada.

Muslim identity has been cast either as a "securitized identity," or a "veiled identity," or in terms of "discursive citizenship," each concept essentially problematizing being a Muslim in the context of the dominant framework of multiculturalism and highlighting the challenges of diversity that affect Muslims in Canada.

In Canada, like its other colonial cousins, the larger attempt to understand the construction of identity is based on difference. Under the rubric of multiculturalism, such identity formation has been described as a "governmentality of tolerance" by political scientist Wendy Brown. She argues that this process valorizes liberalism, which "emerges as the only political rationality that can produce the individual, societal, and governmental practice of tolerance, and, at the same time, liberal societies become the broker of what is tolerable and intolerable (Brown 2006, p. 166)." Multiculturalism is nothing short of a redeployment of a new technology, argues Sunera Thobani, wherein whiteness is recast as part of a more benevolent process of national identity formation (Thobani 2007, pp.152-155). This allows new narratives of the nation to be constructed around diversity that reconstructed whiteness as tolerance.

Unveiling implies modernity?

The 2015 niqab debate in Canada has made inroads into the electoral campaign and points to the the complexity as well as the nuance required to understand the issue at hand while balancing it with a fundamental articulation of Muslim identity.

What is it about the status of women in Islam that invites special remedial attention? Why has the veil been singled out as an icon of the intolerable difference of Muslims? How has the insistence on the political significance of the veil obscured other anxieties and concerns of those obsessed with it? How has the veil become a way of addressing broad issues of ethnicity and integration in Canada and in Western Europe?

In August 2010 in Mississauga, Ontario, Inas Kadri, a veiled Muslim woman shopping with her two young children at a mall was assaulted. A white woman from the nearby city of Brampton swore at her, her religion, and her veil and ripped the veil off Inas's face. In November 2011 the woman pleaded guilty to the assault and was given a suspended sentence. It was considered to be a serious enough crime to merit a criminal record and she was asked to do community service at a mosque and learn about Muslims and the Islamic faith.

The following is the Canadian Broadcasting Corporation (CBC 2011) reportage of the event, continuing with the premise of modernity:

> A Muslim woman from Mississauga, Ontario, who had her niqab pulled from her face at a local mall, says her young children no longer feel secure with only her nearby.
>
> Inas Kadri, whose assault at Sheridan Centre in Mississauga was caught on a security camera, spoke to CBC News on Tuesday as she awaits the sentencing of the woman who attacked her.
>
> Kadri was shopping with her three-year-old son and two-year-old daughter when she was approached by two women. One of the women began swearing at her, about her religion and her veil, telling her, "Leave our country. Go back to your country," Kadri said.
>
> The woman can be seen in the video grabbing Kadri's veil and pulling her off-camera. The attacker walked away while Kadri ran for help. "Being attacked for no reason—for no reason—that's something difficult," she said.
>
> Kadri's victim impact statement reads, in part, that, "My kids don't feel secure with me alone, and always prefer to have someone bigger in size than me to feel safe." The accused, Rosemarie Creswell, pleaded guilty after the video was played in court.
>
> When CBC News spoke to Creswell on the phone, she admitted to pulling off the veil but insisted it was all just a misunderstanding, before hanging up mid-interview. Kadri believes the attack was motivated by hate, which could bring a stiffer sentence.
>
> York University law professor Faisal Kutty, who is Muslim, will watch for the judge's sentencing Friday with

interest. "As Canadians in a multicultural, liberal, democratic society, I think we need to send a clear message and I hope the judge does so," he said.

Kadri said she won't stop wearing her face veil no matter what anyone else says or does. "Not my father, not my husband, not no one at all," she said. " It's me, and it's my choice."

In *Politics of the Veil*, as Joan Scott (2007) suggests, simply responding to dichotomies offered by people who are against the veil and for its ban, as in pluralism versus national unity, identity versus equality, church versus state, particular versus universal, fundamentalism versus secularism, private versus public will not enable us to address the complexities of the relationship between Islam and the West and the making of Muslim identity in the West. Often we see that such an attempt to simplify the problem into dichotomies leads to polemics like Samuel Huntington's thesis of the clash of civilizations.

Muslim as a border

In September 2015 a photograph of a dead toddler on a Turkish beach shattered the settled torpor of most Canadians, much as it poked the mood of lassitude reigning the world. In a sudden thrust, the corporealness of the Syrian refugee crisis was laid bare. All previous cries for help had been lost amidst the drumbeat of the "war on terror," to defeat the "barbaric Islamic State." In March 2015, Prime Minister Harper declared, "Canada will fight ISIS threat as long as it is there," and he continues to bombard this message at every pit stop in his election campaign. Political campaigns are getting bruised as the mood of the nation dictates embracing more refugees. The narrative of the incumbent government continues to peddle the plight of the Syrian refugees as an outcome of the war in the Middle East and connected to a possible threat to Canadian security.

A defining marker of the twenty-first century, *War on Terror* was the term coined by US President George W Bush on September 20,

2001 to focus efforts to combat militant Islamist terrorist organizations and Al-Qaeda. The War on Terror has successfully defined the
interrelationship between war, citizenship, and territory as a project
of modernity. It is in the nexus of war, citizenship, and territory that
the monumental and the mundane of political life are produced. The
nation-state has strengthened its control of juridical power over its
border through securitization. Citizenship, in times of globalization,
has posed a more peculiar problem. In normative terms, this national
subjectivity plays the central role in *othering* through a discursive
process to form new intersubjectivities. Implicit in this process, of
othering and formation of new intersubjectivities, is the production
of fear and anxiety and the idea of nationalism, which can be defined
as a territorial form of ideology.

In the post 9/11 phase, Canada mirrored strategies and arrange-
ments to respond to the heightened sense of threat. Like US's new
Department of Homeland Security, Canada in 2003 formed a new
department, the Ministry of Public Safety, to ensure coordination
across all federal departments and agencies responsible for national
security and the safety of Canadians. It had a clear mandate to keep
Canadians safe from threats ranging from natural disasters to crime
and terrorism.

The relationship between security and borders is juxtaposed with
the openness of Canadian society and the reliance on the notion of
diversity. The agenda set by the national policy on security is important to note for the response of the Canadian government to newcomers and immigrants, and in terms of the nation's commitment
to multiculturalism. This ideological use of multiculturalism in the
security policy document offers an insight into how diversity is perceived and managed through citizenship. The outline of the policy's
strategic framework reveals the centrality of multiculturalism in the
management of the nation's differences in the policy of security and
policing.

This policy reveals the "tough on terror" attitude of the
Conservative government and clearly identifies the threat as located

within the nation's borders. Chiefly, it identifies violent Islamist extremism as the leading threat to Canada's national security. Several Islamist extremist groups have in fact identified Canada as a legitimate target. Violent "homegrown" Sunni Islamist extremists pose additional threats. According to this policy, counter-terrorism activities are guided by the principles of respect for human rights and the rule of law, the treatment of terrorism as a crime, proportionality, and adaptability. The successful execution of such a strategy confirms the French philosopher Étienne Balibar's position that *borders are everywhere* and explains how bordering occurs. The strategy is dependent on external as well as internal partners and includes collaboration between security intelligence, federal, provincial and municipal law-enforcement agencies, and all levels of government and civil society. In particular, the relationship between security intelligence and law-enforcement has strengthened over time and demonstrates the extent of bordering. This seamless cooperation, critical to addressing the terrorist threat, indicates how well entrenched is the process of securitization.

Borders are everywhere, so are bordering practices. As the Canadian theorist Brian Massumi has established, much of the border work is often premised on the politics of everyday fear. They take the form of inclusion/exclusion discourse, racial profiling, data gathering, etc. to create differentiated and racialized categories. Securitization of *others* is not a new feature of political and social life. It is necessary to identify securitization of *others* for what it is: a discursive tool aimed at gaining more powers with the purpose of furthering a party's interests under the pretext of protecting an identity, often resulting in an exaltation of *self*. This process is complicated further by the overlap of securitization with racism and discrimination. Islamophobia is a case in point that demonstrates how, without an appropriate referent, the media and popular discourse usually employ a racial or an ethnic lens to portray a minority or to describe any harassment rooted in prejudice against the minority.

Instead of it being a clear example of a "constructed threat of

Muslims," the national subjectivity often deflects and gets cast in the multicultural policy of the state. Nandita Sharma, an exponent of open borders states: "It is the nationalization of identity, and of society itself through juridical legal state practices and the everyday social practices [,] that produce certain people as national subjects and others as foreign objects within the same territorial and legal landscape (Sharma 2006, p.141)."

In the War on Terror, bordering has produced a securitized Muslim identity. This Muslim identity in an increasingly plural society is faced with a paradox: on one hand, "Muslims are a risk" and subject to surveillance and policing, on the other hand, they have to constantly defend themselves and affirm to being part of Canadian society and representing its values. Exclusionary narratives in media and popular cultures get built through entrenched Islamophobia and racial profiling.

Fear is a powerful weapon when it comes to the securitization of an identity. Neoliberal governance goes hand in hand with a culture of risk, knowing when and how much to intervene. The key is to hold back, because government intervention is itself a risk; the most important thing a government can know is when not to act. The more successful government policy is, the farther it moves towards the longed-for horizon of non-doing. The inertia and refusal to act in the cases of Omar Khadr, Maher Arar, and the Syrian Refugees by the government of Canada stems out of this rootedness of neoliberal governance. Be it the case of the Syrian Refugees or Omar Khadr, a Muslim has become a border. This is in stark contrast to the wholesale disruption of borders in Europe with millions of Syrian refugees, mostly Muslims, fleeing the civil war.

The narrative of difference is emphasized in the post 9/11 scenario, in the fundamental understanding of Muslim identity in Canada. Muslim identity is constructed as disruptive, and religiously and culturally overdetermined, whose ways are fundamentally irreconcilable with the demands of secular modernity, argues Canadian academic Jasmine Zine (Zine 2012, 24). Such talk has turned the primary notion of religious experience into a political category whereby differentiating "good Muslims" from "bad Muslims." In his epigrammatically titled book *Good Muslim, Bad Muslim*, Mahmood Mamdani, the Ugandan scholar, captured the very essence of this Western narrative, and one can see its ramifications closer to home. A quick clue: the idea of the Model Minority.

Performing Muslim at the Muslim Festival

In their everyday life, Muslims feel compelled to explain what it means to be a Muslim. I was very keen to unpack this subjective process, and understand how in the public sphere Muslims collectively engage with the larger Canadian society. Such public enactments are often seen during a Mayoral poll or when contentious issues arise, such as mosque-building. Each of these are poignant spaces as well as opportunities to make sense of the fears and aspirations of the community. Here I would like to draw attention to another interesting manifestation—the Muslim Festival of Mississauga (www.muslimfest.com).

I came across this festival in 2007 when I worked at the City of Mississauga as its inaugural Director for Culture. Every edition of the festival has consumed me in some form or another. Over a period of time, I began to take a closer look at the festival to see how it fits within my larger intellectual preoccupation with the making of Muslim identity in Canada.

Launched in 2004 as a bridge-building organization, the Muslim Festival of Mississauga states on its website: "In post 9/11 world filled with violent images, we at Muslim Fest believe it is imperative to hold bridge-building events that positively engage young Canadians." Apparently, though the Muslim Festival of Mississauga is an annual summer event, it is contingent upon the everyday life of a Muslim. This event is held at the City's Celebration Square, which plays a central role in representing an order that is both symbolically and visually persuasive, bound up with a larger and more substantive socio-spatial ordering project. Representations of such order are increasingly filtered through discourses of safety, quality of life, and multiculturalism, which are central to the power and practice of neoliberal urbanism.

The Festival offers the usual fare: a bazaar with a variety of offerings—food stalls, clothing (hijabs, burqas, abayas, headgear for men), accessories for rituals (perfumes, rosaries, prayer-time clocks), toys, religious literature, and therapy and counselling booths for new converts. On the central stage are performances (religious songs and dances) while the adjoining auditorium and library spaces feature an art exhibition, film screenings, and lectures. Prayer times and spaces are well defined and are punctiliously followed. Thousands flock from the Greater Toronto Area, at ease in their attire, demonstrating a sense of solidarity and community. Strategically placed are writings, on posters at the stalls and on T-shirts, airing opinions and drawing attention on the hot issues: Middle East politics, Toronto 18, Free Syria, Burma's Rohingya Muslims Genocide, anti-racism, and Islamophobia. Despite being local the fair is at once connected to the larger Muslim world.

It visually invokes an essentialized meaning of public space, and of safety and a certain quality of life for the people of Mississauga. However, this urban storytelling has more than a scalar significance. The responsible citizenry, and the examples of tolerance and diversity that are presented mirror a vernacular of power shaping the form and functioning of cities across Canada and the larger global north. The Muslim Festival is a meaning-making event for the visitors as well as the organizers. Collectively it creates an understanding that is premised upon concepts, arguments, beliefs, and judgements that cannot be attributed to individuals. Rather, they are the shared ideas of groups in society and are rooted in everyday practice.

From a layman's perspective it is the framing of the festival as "multicultural" that enables an unproblematic representation of communal identity. Mississauga's diversity is displayed as a healthy play of cultures, yet this is often the source of criticism of multicultural policy, that it is simply a superficial take on the complexities of difference. If we focus on the more visual aspects of such a "multicultural festival," the emphasis of the festival as a site of social cohesion leads to a relatively straightforward and untroubled interpretation of communal identity. This illustrates the ways in which performative strategies are used to create a sense of identity and belonging. The way in which such a "multicultural" identity is created and enacted within the festival framework encompasses the performances in everyday life in which the self is expressed through a repertoire of performances appropriate to its social and geographical setting. At a deeper level, it offers a kind of performative text, where the everyday modality of being a Muslim comes into play through a set of collective expressions shaping and appropriating into a collective meaning.

The concept of *performative* was developed by Judith Butler, whose work has been central to debates around identity politics and cultural recognition. While analyzing the Muslim Festival, Butler's concept of performativity allows us to see the Muslim as an embodied agent and to ask the question, how does a Muslim identity perform at the Muslim Festival of Mississauga? How can the concepts of the *Other* and *Otherness* be rethought outside of established cultural frameworks? In her book *Gender Trouble*, Butler argues that "there is no gender identity behind expressions of gender; that identity is performatively constituted by the very 'expressions' that are said to be its results" (1990:25). Identification is an enacted fantasy in which the subject attempts to create a coherent, whole self where its internal core is expressed through the external body. The assertion of this coherent self is produced through words, acts, and gestures, so the body does not confer identity on to the subject, rather identity is attributed to the subject through signifying practices that create identity. The body is a "variable boundary, a surface whose permeability is politically regulated" (Butler 1990: 139). Drawing on Butler's work, we might then think of the Muslim self within the festival framework as an expression of identity created out of speech, rituals, gestures, clothing, food, and prayers. In keeping with Butler, these are not the elements of one essential identity, rather it is a response to other selves.

However, the everyday interactions and negotiations that, in the aggregate, shape power dynamics over time have yet to receive a thorough interrogation. In my estimation the Muslim Festival as an event offers two reasons for the understanding of a Muslim identity. First, it enables investigation into the ways in which social relations and institutionalized forms of power interact to produce changes within the built environment. Also, it enables research into how opposing symbolic constructions of space are contested and shaped within the deliberative process of urban planning. Second, such an approach allows one to examine the agency of religious groups who through their engagement with planning procedures and programs have influenced the processes through which the built environment is experienced, used, and materially (re)configured.

The performance of Muslims at the Festival uses Celebration Square (a public space or commons) in a subversive way to create a dissenting narrative and takes a central role to counter the Western discourses such as that of securitized identities and niqab issues.

The Framing of Canadian Muslims

IHSAAN GARDEE & AMIRA EL-GHAWABY

"Not the way we do things here."[1]

This is how the Conservative Party of Canada describes its view of the wardrobe choice of the minority of Muslim women who wear the *niqab* or face veil. In that one simple, seemingly innocuous line, an entire faith community was framed as being alien, out of touch with modern society and, worst of all—un-Canadian.

Narratives can be used for good or for ill. Narratives, and more specifically frames, can be used for a number of purposes including emphasizing our common humanity and the values we share and cherish, or conversely they can be used to stoke fear and suspicion about the "Other" in order to help further particular political or personal agendas. That's why it is critical that we understand how these frames can be used, and at times even manipulated. As an illustration of the deliberate framing of Canadian Muslims we will be examining and analyzing the public discourse around two particular issues: the wearing of the face veil and issues generally affecting Muslim women, and the challenge of confronting a particular strain of terrorism.

Manufactured hysteria

The recent controversy around the decision by a Toronto woman named Zunera Ishaq to take her citizenship oath wearing the *niqab* was not the first time when Canadians witnessed such manufactured and disproportionate hysteria around the issue. Despite the reality that only a small minority of Canadian Muslim women wear face veils,[2] this issue is continuously brought forward by various political parties and elected officials at various times, for various aims.

We first saw formal attempts at legislating against the right of women to wear the face veil in the proposal of Bill 94.[3] This bill proposed banning the *niqab* in the province of Quebec for those giving or receiving certain services in the public sector. While face veils have always been generally unpopular in Canada, many Canadians still opposed the bill and even campaigned against it.[4] There was an inherent understanding that to prevent Muslim women from practicing their faith freely was to contradict the Canadian Charter of Rights and Freedoms as well as federal and provincial human rights codes. The Charter and our codes guarantee religious freedoms for all, regardless of how popular or unpopular a personal religious practice may be.

Bill 94 died on the order paper when an election was called in Quebec. But this wouldn't be the last we'd hear about the topic. Several years later, in 2013, the pro-separatist governing party, Parti Québécois (PQ), proposed Bill 60, the so-called Charter of Values.[5] Its official title was much longer: "Charter affirming the values of State secularism and religious neutrality and of equality between women and men, and providing a framework for accommodation requests."

The bill would have erased most religious clothing or "ostentatious religious symbols" from the public sector, and quite possibly from the private sector as well.[6] In the end with the defeat of the PQ in the 2013 provincial election, this proposal also went nowhere. However, the current governing Liberal Party in Quebec has advanced what's been dubbed as "Charter Lite."[7] This bill once again proposes banning services to women who wear the face veil.[8]

At the time of this writing, the federal government is also weighing in, appealing a Federal Court judgement in a case brought by Ms Ishaq that a regulation banning the *niqab* from citizenships oaths violated the Citizenship Act.

At first glance it seems strange. Not that a woman wants to veil herself at the moment she is "joining the Canadian family," as Prime Minister Stephen Harper put it at a campaign-style rally in a Quebec town.[9] What's strange is why anyone, let alone political leaders, would challenge this right given that the Supreme Court of Canada famously concluded in 2012 that no Canadian should be asked to check their religion at the door of any institution.[10] In other words, our courts have definitively concluded that so long as there is no harm done to anyone else's Charter rights and no law is being broken, Canadian men and women are free to practice their faith in this country. This decision also reaffirms other precedent-setting cases such as *Multani v Commission scolaire Marguerite-Bourgeoys,*[11] in which a Sikh Canadian student was permitted to wear his kirpan to school. That's the democracy we're all proud of.

So the question remains: Why have elected leaders continued to kick around the issue of *niqab*, a proverbial political football, which has deep and real impact on the lived experiences of Canadian Muslim women and, by extension on an entire faith community?

Impacts

We know that Canadian Muslim women often bear the brunt of discrimination and attacks. Professor Barbara Perry at the University of Ontario Institute of Technology (UOIT) documented this observation in one of the few academic studies initiated about Islamophobia in Canada.[12] At the National Council of Canadian Muslims (NCCM), where we work, we regularly receive reports about Canadian Muslim women being told they aren't employable because of their clothing, and equally devastating, women report physical and verbal harassment for being visibly Muslim.[13]

Recently, in a case that made national headlines, a Canadian Muslim woman, Rania El-Alloul, was denied her right to appear in a Quebec courtroom because she wore the *hijab*, the headscarf.[14] Not only was she denied access to justice, a fundamental human right, because of her choice of religious clothing, but also her choice was belittled by the judge, who likened it to the wearing of a hat or sunglasses. It is difficult to imagine the kind of uproar that would have ensued had she made a similar comment about a Jewish kippa or Sikh turban.

The question arises: is the debate really about the *niqab*?

Chris Alexander, the Minister of Citizenship and Immigration, once tweeted his opposition not only against the *niqab*, but also against the *hijab*.[15] He should know the difference. Not only is he an Oxford scholar but he spent years as Canada's ambassador to Afghanistan. Was this an attempt to make it seem that the choices of Canadian Muslim women were outside the norm of what it meant to be a Canadian? Alexander went so far as to suggest that someone taking the citizenship oath might worry that they were standing next to a possible terrorist if a woman concealed her face.[16]

This rhetoric does not exist in a bubble. It is systemic, as Edward Said observed.[17] Even before 9/11, Karim H Karim of Carleton University had analyzed Canadian newspapers, confirming that the dominant images of Muslims there align with what Jack Shaheen, in his book *The TV Arab,* had identified as the four primary stereotypes of Arabs: "they are all fabulously wealthy; they are barbaric and uncultured; they are sex maniacs with a penchant for White slavery; and they revel in acts of terrorism."[18]

As a song in the Disney cartoon *Aladdin* says, "Oh I come from a land, from a faraway place, Where the caravan camels roam; Where it's flat and immense, and the heat is intense; It's barbaric, but hey, it's home."[19]

In Canada, the "Protecting Canadians from Barbaric Cultural Practices" bill was passed into law in 2015.[20] Even women's groups advocating for the safety and well being of all women took issue with the way the bill was framed.[21]

Murder is murder

Let's examine the term *honour killings,* one of the crimes re-criminalized in the new Act.

Critics oppose the deliberate attempt at framing the issue as emerging from communities regularly portrayed or perceived as foreign, often those from Muslim-majority countries. Labelling such violence against women as honour crimes needlessly separates women and girls into groups based on race, culture, and religion.

Using terminology like *honour*, or *barbaric*, implies that this particular violence against women is unique and the sole purview of those of "other" cultures. The frame is set: these foreigners bring their barbarism to Canada, whereas we in the cultured West have long since moved beyond misogyny in all its manifestations.

Alia Hogben, executive director of the Canadian Council of Muslim Women (CCMW), refuses even to use the term *honour killing*, choosing instead femicide.[22] This isn't a question of semantics alone. It has a real impact in how the state chooses to spend taxpayer money. Status of Women Canada, a federal government agency charged with promoting gender equality and women's rights, spent almost five times more money to specifically address "honour crimes" or "harmful cultural practices" than it did addressing violence against Aboriginal women, when the number of murdered and missing Aboriginal women far exceeds the number of cases of femicide.

This isn't about political correctness or hiding truths, it's about acknowledging and contextualizing truths, even if and when they challenge and shatter stereotypes. A 2010 report commissioned by the Canadian Department of Justice concluded that "honour killings are not associated with particular religions or religious practice: they have been recorded across Christian, Jewish, Sikh, Hindu and Muslim communities."[23]

Frames as mental pictures

According to the cognitive scientist George Lakoff, frames are mental pictures that are formed unconsciously in the brain to shape the way we see the world and help shape the goals we seek, the plans we make, the way we act.[24] Frames are activated unconsciously thanks to the language used. The very title of his recent book, *Don't think of an elephant!* demonstrates that even when you negate a frame, you activate it. Like a muscle in the body it becomes stronger the more it is activated. The lesson for political and even public discourse is clear: When you argue against someone on the other side of an issue using terms they choose, you are strengthening those terms and those frames and undermining your own point. Put another way, you should say what you believe, using your own language, your own terms.

As we know, Canadian Muslims and Islam have been framed as communities and a religion which inherently support terrorism. How does that happen? Knowingly or unknowingly, the linguistic appropriation of terms like *jihad* by both violent extremists and those who do not care to understand the true religious nature of the term leads to a misrepresentation and misunderstanding of how Canadian Muslims view extremist violence.

As Marie-Danielle Smith wrote recently in *Embassy News*,

> Prime Minister Stephen Harper has consistently character-ized terrorist threats facing Canada as coming from a single category: Islamic extremism or "jihadism". In a January 30 speech introducing the controversial Anti-Terrorism Act, or Bill C-51, Mr Harper said: "Jihadi terrorism is not a human right; it is an act of war."

> That exact phrase has been repeated, verbatim, ten times in the House of Commons by 10 different Conservative MPs in the last couple of months, according to Open Parliament, largely in defence of Bill C-51.[25]

Not only does this language tar minority communities with a single brush, it neglects even to acknowledge the existence of other terrorist threats—never mind their scope and scale. Most Canadians would be surprised to learn that law enforcement agencies categorize violence motivated by White supremacist and extreme right-wing ideology as a much more significant threat than religiously motivated terrorism.[26]

And so the new anti-terror legislation, which introduces a swath of new powers for Canada's spy agencies, was passed in a climate of fear.[27] Four former prime ministers, several former Supreme Court justices, and several other prominent Canadians expressed deep concerns about it, as did a variety of legal experts and civil society representatives.[28] As more and more Canadians learned about the actual contents of the legislation, it became less and less popular.[29] The bill is now the subject of a charter challenge by two groups—the Canadian Civil Liberties Association and the Canadian Journalists for Free Expression.[30] Yet rather than engage in the law's actual merits, the government has chosen political rhetoric to suggest that those who oppose it support *jihadi* terrorism.[31]

At the same time the criminal plot uncovered in Halifax involving young Canadians hoping to kill scores of people at a shopping mall on St Valentines Day wasn't considered as terrorism because the plotters weren't "culturally" motivated and were simply "murderous misfits," according to Justice Minister Peter MacKay.[32]

Not only does the use of these terms serve to further stereotypes about Muslims and Islam based on simplistic interpretations and understandings, it may actually be counter-productive from the standpoint of preventing the radicalization and recruitment of young and vulnerable people by actual terrorists.

University of Ottawa Law Professor Errol Mendes echoes this same point in a commentary he wrote in *iPolitics*. "Giving them titles of practitioners of war or even jihadists is giving them credibility and a legitimacy that they may actually crave and which could attract others."[33]

Both CSIS and the RCMP acknowledge this phenomenon. "Terms like 'Islamic terrorism,' 'Jihadism,' and 'Islamofascism' succeed only in conflating terrorism with mainstream Islam, thereby casting all Muslims as terrorists or potential terrorists," note the authors of a 2010 RCMP report titled "Words make worlds."[34] And according to internal documents obtained by the *Toronto Star*, CSIS noted that: "[i]nternational terrorist groups place a high priority on radicalizing

Westerners who can be used to carry out terrorist attacks in their home countries. The narrative that the West is at war with Islam continues to exert a very powerful influence in radicalizing individuals and spreads quickly through social media and online fora."[35]

Using the terminology employed by terrorists means we accept as true their religious claims. Why should we not assume the opposite, that in fact terrorists are sinister and exploit religion to justify their violence, much in the same manner that groups like the KKK cite biblical scripture to support their ideologies of hate? Very few Westerners would accept that KKK beliefs are representative of Christianity.

Reframing

Canadian Muslim women and men need to reclaim their identities and reframe harmful narratives.

Canadian scholar Imam Dr Zijad Delic states in his book *Canadian Islam: Belonging and Identity*:

> There is no single reality that would adequately express Islam in Canada. Canadian Muslims do not constitute a monolithic bloc, but are in fact abundantly diverse[. . .] If Muslims are to settle successfully in Canada and constructively integrate, participate, and contribute to the well-being of their community and to all of Canadian society, they need to build a clearly defined place in this country for themselves and for future generations. [36]

It is important to understand who we're talking about when we speak of Canadian Muslims.

According to researcher Daood Hamdani, the first Muslim born in Canada was the child of Scottish immigrant Agnes Love, thirteen years before confederation. The first mosque in Canada was the Al Rashid mosque built in 1938 in Edmonton. Unlike the monolith that it is portrayed as, the Canadian Muslim population comes from a wide variety of ethnic, national, and linguistic backgrounds. It is also growing faster than any other faith group and includes Canadians identifying themselves as having no religion.

Canadian Muslims are highly educated, with forty-five percent holding a university degree as compared to thirty-three percent of their fellow citizens.

Canadian Muslim women are more educated than the general Canadian female population—1 in 3 hold a postsecondary degree, compared to 1 in 5 for the general population. Muslim women, points out professor and author Katherine Bullock, are highly educated, professional, urban, and culturally diverse. They are highly likely to possess the skills, finances, opportunities, and time to become activists in both the informal and formal political sectors.[37]

In 2011, Canadian Muslims comprised 3.2 percent of the population, or just over one million people. According to projections from the Washington-based Pew Forum on Religion & Public Life, they are set to increase both in number and proportion to 2.7 million, or 6.6% of the Canadian population, by 2030.

This is important data because it can help all Canadians, and in particular politicians and the media, to gain a better understanding about who they are speaking of when they talk about Canadian Muslims. It ensures that we question the frames within which Canadian Muslim communities are placed.

How do we move forward from here? It is necessary to change the way Canadians in general see Canadian Muslims, to reframe the public discourse, and what has come to be conventional wisdom.

"Because language activates frames, new language is required for new frames" writes Professor Lakoff.[38]

> Thinking differently requires speaking differently. Reframing is not easy or simple. It is not a matter of finding some magic words. Frames are ideas, not slogans. Reframing is more a matter of accessing what we and like-minded others already believe unconsciously, making it conscious, and repeating it till it enters normal public discourse. It doesn't happen overnight. It is an ongoing process. It requires repetition and focus and dedication.[39]

Reframing is actually the opposite of spin and manipulation:

> It is about bringing to consciousness the deepest of our
> beliefs and our modes of understanding. It is about learn-
> ing to express what we really believe in a way that will allow
> those who share our beliefs to understand what they most
> deeply believe and to act on those beliefs.[40]

To those who argue that removing religious labels when describing violent extremism is political correctness gone too far, that we have to "name it in order to tame it," we would say, yes, we have to name it. But the faith-based labels used are imprecise and do not accurately identify the perpetrators of violent extremism. Better terms would identify the perpetrator or ideology, for example "Al-Qaeda or ISIS-inspired terrorism."

As Daniel Kahneman argues in his seminal book, *Thinking Fast and Slow*: "Ultimately, a richer language is essential to the skill of constructive criticism. Much like medicine, the identification of judgement errors is a diagnostic task, which requires a precise vocabulary."

For politicians and decision-makers, Kahneman notes, "There is a direct link from more precise gossip at the watercooler to better decisions. Decision makers are sometimes better able to imagine the voices of present gossipers and future critics than to hear the hesitant voice of their own doubts. They will make better choices when they trust their critics to be sophisticated and fair, and when they expect their decision to be judged by how it was made, not only by how it turned out."[41]

All of this is critical if we are to move away from frames which seek to divide and instead look for ways to bring Canadians together. For Canadian Muslims, the responsibility to demand a more accurate and nuanced representation in the country's political and popular discourse has taken on new urgency, given geopolitical realities that have brought Islam and Muslims into sharp and often negative focus.

As Peter Morey and Amina Yaqin conclude in their book, *Framing Muslims*: "So there is no neat conclusion to the story of the framing of Muslims."

Until the day when politicians see the advantage in seriously addressing all the aspects—social, political, economic, and international—that lead to alienation and injustice Muslims are likely to remain in the frame. Both sides in the so-called clash of civilizations fetishize a "pure" (and entirely fanciful) idea of who they are and where they come from. At the same time, the media have a duty to deal seriously with the sometimes unappealing complexity of Muslim identity claims, not to dismiss them out of hand or make them the object of ridicule. We move forward by inches when we move forward at all. A greater diversity of voices must be brought to the table, allowed to speak and be seriously listened to, before any progress can be made to unpick stereotypes and allow Muslims as they are to walk out of the frame and into the political life of the twenty-first century.[42]

This is what many of us are working for, and must continue to work for.

The Future of Islam in North America[1]

MOHAMED ABUALY ALIBHAI

What is your aim in philosophy?—To shew the fly the way out of the fly-bottle.

—Ludwig Wittgenstein[2]

INTRODUCTION[3]

The American constitutional principle of liberty of conscience is destined to exert the most fateful influence on the long-term evolution of Islam in North America.[4] This fundamental principle of the American system of government is the fount of the political, social, economic, and cultural currents that are steering the immigrant Muslim community inexorably towards an unforeseen destination: a conscience-based reconceptualization of the Quran and its institutional embodiment in a new gender-equal denomination[5] reflecting a new Muslim self-understanding.

In spite of attempts to reform Shariah Islam[6] for the modern world, there are built-in limits to its ability to serve the needs of North American immigrant Muslims who are enjoying unprecedented personal freedoms. Among contemporary Muslim reformers no one wields as much respect and influence within the European and North

American Muslim communities as does Tariq Ramadan.[7] European Muslims seek his guidance on how "to be a European Muslim."[8] His proposals for "radical reform"[9] constitute the most comprehensive and systematic reconceptualization of the foundations (*usūl al-fiqh*) of the Shariah since the time of the founding fathers of the Shariah.

This essay attempts to discern the long-term prospects for Shariah Islam in Europe and North America through a consideration of Ramadan's innovative reform proposals, a task that makes it necessary to compare Europe and North America as political entities. This essay contends that the American principle of liberty of conscience will inevitably compel conscientious Muslims in Canada and America to question their belief in the verbal revelation of the Quran, and that this questioning will prompt them to conceptualize and build a new denomination drawing inspiration from the hitherto neglected conscience-based enlightenment traditions of Islam.[10]

Liberty of conscience

Liberty of conscience is the bedrock commitment driving the argument, eloquently articulated by Thomas Jefferson in the Declaration of Independence, that a new set of political principles, hitherto unknown to humanity, is necessary if humans are to order their affairs in a way that recognizes, respects, accommodates, and protects each individual's liberty of conscience while at the same time balancing this liberty with the liberty of conscience of other individuals. Whereas the Declaration offers a vision of this new political order, the American Constitution defines the system of government and its ground rules that delimit the scope of the government's authority and at the same time serve as the framework upon which Americans would create the political order envisioned in the Declaration.

The Protestant understanding of conscience as a fundamentally embattled entity persecuted by religious authority and constantly striving to liberate itself from its clutches began its career with Martin Luther (d. 1546). Luther claimed that faith was a private and inviolable relation between the believer and God. Justification of faith came from God alone, not from the Church or from anyone else. The Pilgrim Puritans brought this understanding of conscience with them to America. But they quickly forgot why they had sought religious freedom in the new land. Fearful in a new, unfamiliar, and hostile country, they proceeded to establish a rigid religious orthodoxy and a theocratic government that suppressed, punished, or banished members for disobedience or dissent. In banishing Roger Williams (d. 1683) from Massachusetts they unwittingly set into motion events that would lead to a distinctive American constitutional and political philosophy.

On Rhode Island, where he settled and established his colony in 1636,[11] Roger Williams was struck by the kindnesses shown to him by the island's Native Americans. Their exemplary conduct prompted him to subject his theological understanding of conscience to a searching examination. He came to realize that conscience was not just something that only Christians possessed: all humans, including pagans and atheists, possessed conscience that was their private and inalienable link with God (or the Supreme Being, the Great Spirit, or some impersonal cosmic principle). Williams argued that conscience was innate to the human makeup and was therefore separate from religion, even though individuals acquired their understanding of conscience through their respective religious beliefs.

Williams concluded that no established religion, supported and promoted by the state, was capable of giving equal treatment to the consciences of nonestablishment individuals, and that this unequal treatment by the state, based on religious grounds, would constitute unequal treatment of individuals as civil subjects of the state. To order the relations among them in a way that protects the freedom of each individual conscience to worship and believe as it sees fit, citizens would need to acknowledge that civil peace can only come about if they respected each other's different conscientious commitments. It would be necessary to make conscience a constitutional principle of a political system that protects and guarantees its freedom.[12] The Rhode Island Royal Charter granted by King Charles II in 1663 was the first on American soil to enshrine liberty of conscience as an inalienable right that neither the state nor the church could violate.[13]

Learning from the evolution of Judaism in North America

The evolution of Judaism in North America[14] offers an exceptionally instructive example that enables Muslims to foresee with reasonable assurance the evolution of Islam under the influence of forces rooted in the principle of liberty of conscience. Judaism and Islam are not only sibling faiths within the Abrahamic family; they are also law-governed faiths in which the lives of the believers are governed in detail by divine laws—*halakhah* (rooted in the Torah) for Jews and *sharī'ah* (rooted in the Quran) for Muslims.

The powerful individual-centric North American environment led to the emergence of a spectrum of Jewish denominations, with the Orthodox (including the *Hasidim* and *Haredim*) at one end, and the strongly individual-centric liberal Reform Judaism at the other.[15] The Reform movement today centres its liberalism conspicuously on the principle of liberty of conscience. Women rabbis are now a regular feature in all but the Orthodox denominations (the Reform movement blazed the trail as far back as 1972[16]). The emergence of these non-Orthodox denominations shows that the individual-centric forces in North American society will inevitably challenge orthodox Shariah Islam and lead to the emergence of a non-legalist conscience-centered Muslim denomination comparable, if not identical, to Reform Judaism.

TARIQ RAMADAN'S PROPOSALS FOR RADICAL REFORM

Contemporary Muslim reformist thought

Muslim reformers who concentrate their reform efforts on the religious system of Islam[17] fall into two main categories: those whose principal focus is on the Quran and those whose principal focus is on the Shariah.

Reformers in the first group seek new ways of studying and interpreting the Quran from a variety of modernist perspectives. They focus on two sets of verses in the Quran: (1) those that can be interpreted through these new perspectives to show that the Quran teaches the same liberal and progressive values as those of the West; and (2) those that constitute the explicit legislative content of the Quran (including the punishments known as *hudūd*). Some of the Quranic laws regarding women are proving particularly intractable for Islamic feminists because, as the direct unadulterated words and commandments of God for all time and contexts, no believer may disobey or change them.

Reformers in the second group focus on the Shariah. Here their aim is to find ways in which the Shariah can provide legal rulings (*fatwā*) for areas of modern life that the traditional Shariah does not cover, for example medical ethics, banking, investment and finance, environment, and cosmetics. For the most part, they direct their reform proposals towards the Muslim-majority governments, which they hope will turn these proposals into state laws. So-called Shariah-compliant Islamic finance is perhaps the fastest growing part of this reform activity. Islamic feminists and some progressive male reformers focus on family and personal status laws of the Shariah. Their main aim is to show that these laws and the massive historical corpus of legal rulings reflect and codify the gender inequalities of their contexts and cannot be binding on Muslim women today.

Leading reformist intellectuals like the late Mohamed Arkoun and Nasr Hamid Abu Zayd and the contemporary Abdolkarim Soroush have given less attention to Islam as a worship-centered faith (*īmān*) and religious tradition (*dīn*) than they have to Islam as a predominantly intellectual tradition. The system of worship (*'ibādah*), especially its core elements—the sermon (*khutbah*) and the prayer (*salāt*)—is the heart of Islam for the ordinary believer—illiterate farmer, factory worker, elderly grandmother, street vendor, restaurant waiter, cab driver, and so on—for whom the Quran is first and foremost a recitation rather than a text.[18] Recitation of the Quran is central to

Muslim piety. It is the moment in which the believer is closest to God, for in reciting God's words the believer allows God's words to enter into and take over the heart and mind and address the believer from within. And the believer, in turn, addresses God by using the Quran's own words for addressing God.[19] Through life's ups and downs, beset with anxieties about the future, the Quran has offered guidance, comfort, confidence, courage, and hope that no amount of sophisticated literary interpretive stratagems can ever replace.

The reformist thinkers have not been mindful of these "constituencies" when they write their jargon-filled hermeneutics of the Quran. They do not appreciate fully that the believer looks to the imam and the legal scholar for knowledge and understanding about Islamic faith and how to deal with the ethical choices posed by everyday social transactions. The reformers do not write for the imams and legal scholars, for if they did, they would write books of the sort that Rabbi Harold Kushner writes.[20] Rabbi Kushner writes in a very accessible language, but the topics he writes about—for example, how to live according to the dictates of one's conscience—are fundamental to Conservative and Reform Judaism.

The future of Islam rests with the ordinary believer, and this future is not being secured when the ordinary believer is ignored or disrespected because he or she lacks competence in the intricacies of Quranic hermeneutics based on the turgid and obfuscating language and lexicon of Jacques Derrida, Michel Foucault, Paul Ricouer, and other thinkers. The reformists view the Quran almost exclusively as a text and study it in isolation from the Quran's central role as audible recitation and a direct-speech "face-to-face" conversation that is governed by its own aesthetic attuned to the psychology of devotion and worship. They have adopted the models for textual and literary analysis from the humanities without recognizing that these models are "secular" texts, not scriptural texts that have vital nontextual functions in a believer's life. They have also unwittingly adopted the model used in Biblical studies, in which academics study the Biblical text in isolation from its function in worship and the religious life of the believer.[21]

Tariq Ramadan's reform proposals

Tariq Ramadan is the exception. Motivated by the demands of ordinary Muslims in Europe and North America for a more responsive religious legal system in a non-Muslim environment that lacks the traditional support systems of Muslim-majority states, Ramadan has subjected the classical foundations of Shariah[22] to a thoroughgoing examination. This examination has led him to redefine these foundations and to propose a new class of peer-level scholars to complement the scope of the traditional legal scholars.

The new foundations and new class of scholars would strengthen the religious system's capacity to provide legal rulings (*fatwā*) in response to issues faced by Muslims living in the West. Thus Ramadan, in conspicuous contrast to the entire spectrum of reformers, is heavily invested in the traditional scholar as the centre of religious authority for the faithful, and he wants to increase and strengthen this authority; he does not view himself as a rival and replacement for it, as do the other reformers. Again in contrast to other reformers, Ramadan's reform ideas are principally targeted at the Western Muslims and not at the Muslim-majority states. His experiences in Europe[23] attest to the continuing relevance and greatly increased demand for legal rulings, especially among young Muslim men and women.

According to Ramadan,[24] the dramatically transformed realities of the modern world have opened up a huge gap between, on the one hand, the traditional religious sciences based on the scriptural sources (Quran and Hadith) and, on the other hand, the rapidly expanding "other sciences" (human and natural sciences). This gap has paralyzed Muslim thought and created a crisis in which the faithful discover to their dismay that the traditional scholars lack command over the new forms of knowledge and are therefore incapable of formulating ethically correct legal rulings.

Ramadan contends that it is not possible today for the traditional legal scholar to acquire mastery over the vast, complex, and rapidly changing world of knowledge produced by the human and natural sciences.[25] Consequently, "We can no longer leave it to scholarly circles and text specialists to determine norms" to address scientific, social, economic, or cultural issues.[26] Ramadan's key suggestion is that Muslims must henceforth treat the human and natural sciences as a "source of law on their own"[27] on a par with scripture, and they should rely on the expertise of specialists in these sciences for their understanding of social, physical, and biological realities. Ramadan calls the traditional experts in the scriptural texts *'ulamā' al-nusūs* (scholars of the texts) and the modern experts in the sciences and the humanities *'ulamā' al-wāqi'* (scholars of the context).[28]

Ramadan proposes that the specialists in the human and natural sciences, instead of imparting knowledge about their respective disciplines to the traditional scholars, should participate in the *fatwā* councils and collaborate with the traditional scholars to analyze the ethics of issues arising in their specialized fields. "We need to widen the circle of expertise and call on context specialists to formulate judgments."[29] The specialists "must be integrated into the circles of text scholars during their debates and deliberations to formulate legal rulings about specific issues."[30] Rulings formulated in this manner would be the most appropriate ethical responses to these context-specific issues.

Although Ramadan insists that the role of the "context scholars" in his scheme is different from the role they play today in the *fatwā* councils of many Muslim-majority states, this difference is not readily apparent from his writings. The traditional text scholars today are typically at the mercy of the context scholars. This is already evident, for example, in the rapidly growing number of so-called "Shariah compliant" legal rulings dealing with finance and medical issues. Shariah scholars typically rubber-stamp what the context scholars (and the interest groups they represent) want.

EUROPE AND NORTH AMERICA: THE FUNDAMENTAL
DIFFERENCES

Ramadan's "radical reforms" constitute the first major reconceptual-ization and reformulation of Islamic (Sunni) jurisprudence (*usūl al fiqh*) since the age of the classical founders in the eighth and ninth centuries; and precisely because these proposals represent the fur-thest development of legalist Islam today, they serve as a litmus test for exploring the scope and limits of the legalist conception of Islam in North America. Ramadan has assured North American Muslims that his ideas, which have been developed principally with the European context in mind, are equally applicable to their con-text. This assumption unfortunately obscures from his view the fun-damental ways in which Europe and North America differ in their political philosophies and systems of government.

Reconceptualizing the European nation-state: the "proprietor state" model

A striking feature of the countries of Europe is that, almost with-out exception,[31] they are nation-states that bear the names of their respective dominant ethnic group, the "nation." The nation-state is the result of the powerful forces of ethnic nationalism that midwifed the emergence of modern Europe. It is a *proprietor state*,[32] owned and run by its *proprietor nation* (Germany for the Germans, France for the French, Denmark for the Danes, etc.). The new nation-states minted from the meltdown of the Soviet Union—Serbia, Slovakia, Kazakhstan, etc.—show that ethnic nationalism remains, and prom-ises to remain, a powerful force in post-War Europe.[33]

Several key consequences of the nation-state model are crucial for understanding why Europeans have been unable to form a political union, why they seem unable to integrate their immigrant popula-tions, and why they are grappling with a "Muslim Question."[34]

> ➤ **Ethnic nationalism.** Ethnic nationalism is fueled by
> the belief in ethnic/cultural purity and uniqueness, and
> this belief in turn fuels the drive for a separate territory

created exclusively for the ethnic group (the "nation"). The ideal nation-state is a monoethnic and monocultural state; it cannot be multiethnic and multicultural. The nation-state cannot equally serve the interests of other ethnic groups because these ethnic groups are not proprietors of the state. Ethnic nationalism is different from patriotism: it is the belief held by the proprietor nation that it is the rightful owner of the state and its resources.[35]

➤ **Political identity.** Political identity (citizenship) is derived from, and remains subservient to, ethnic/national identity (nationality). Because the same word stands for political and national identity, an ethnic/national French person, to take one example, interprets the statement "I am French" to be a statement not about citizenship but about ethnic/national identity and his proprietorship of the state. Nationality, not citizenship, constitutes the fundamental identity of the nation-state.

➤ **Weak Supreme Court and lack of First Amendment tradition.** The nation-state is inherently collectivist. The state is the executive and legislative arm of the proprietor nation. Loyalty to the nation overrides liberty of conscience. An American-style independent judiciary, headed by the Supreme Court, to protect individual conscience from the encroachments of the state is a concept that is foreign to the nation-state model. Whereas legislation in the American system can be declared unconstitutional by the Supreme Court, in the European nation-state what the state legislates is by definition constitutional. The First Amendment prevents the majority from discriminating against and persecuting the minority. It provided the constitutional grounds for the Civil Rights Act of 1964 that recognizes and protects the inalienable right of American citizens to be different from fellow Americans. Such checks on the majority do not exist in European nation-states with their weak courts.

➤ **Democracy.** The spread of democracy has strengthened

representative government in the nation-state by widening the circle of citizens empowered to choose their representatives, but since the overwhelming majority of the citizens are also members of the proprietor nation, democracy has paradoxically strengthened the control of the proprietor nation over the state. The collectivism inherent in ethnic nationalism has combined with ideas of representative government to produce *social* democracy rather than the individual-centric *liberal* democracy characteristic of American and Canadian polities.

➤ **Enlightenment ideas.** As Enlightenment ideas spread across Europe, each proprietor nation absorbed these ideas into its ethnic nationalism and used them to strengthen its hold over the state. Enlightenment values, far from eliminating ethnic nationalism, were themselves ethnicized and conflated with ethnic nationalism. For example, the anomalous French principle of secularism, *laïcité*, is the outcome of an anti-clerical French ethnic nationalism absorbing into itself Enlightenment ideas about Reason and declaring that French republicanism is the political expression of Reason.

➤ **Religion.** Religion is a key determinant of the proprietor nation's identity, cultural values, and social cohesion.[36] Far from wanting the state to remain separate from and indifferent to religion, the proprietor nation, through democratic control of the state, uses the resources of the state to support its denominations and churches. Nearly all European nation-states have officially recognized churches—the so-called "established" denominations prohibited by the American Constitution—that are granted taxpayer-funded support and privileges (for example, exclusive control of cemeteries and burial procedures, and theology programs to train clergy at state universities) that unrecognized denominations such as Islam do not enjoy.

➤ **Secularism.** The growth of individualism and humanism within the proprietor nation, while not strong enough to overcome its ethnic nationalism, has weakened the direct punitive authority of the church over the private morality of its members. Paradoxically, then, the *individual* is increasingly secular (nonreligious), whereas the *state* continues to support and—as in France—covertly regulates the churches.[37] A strict separation of church and state on the American model is foreign to the European nation-state. In the American and Canadian[38] models, it is the state that is neutral with respect to religion while the majority of the population is religious. The word "secularism" obscures these fundamental differences between the European nation-state and North America.

The immigrant as "citizen-alien"

When an Arab citizen of France says, "I am French," the proprietor French person retorts, "No, you are not. You are a *citizen* of France, but you are not a French *national*." The Arab citizen is invoking political identity (citizenship), whereas the proprietor French national is invoking national/ethnic identity (nationality). Both identities have the same name or label ("I am French"). The proprietor French person believes that the label is pointing to his *nationality* (ethnic/national identity) and to his joint ownership of the state (with fellow French nationals). The Arab, on the other hand, is referring to his *citizenship* (political identity). The Arab is a *French* citizen but an *Arab* national, whereas the ethnic French person is a French citizen as well as a French national. Consequently, even though the Arab is a citizen, he is an alien and is therefore a legitimate target of discrimination by the state. He is French (he is a citizen), but not fully *French* (because he is an Arab national). The proprietor citizen is a *citizen-national*; the immigrant citizen is a *citizen-alien*. Nationality, not citizenship, is the fundamental identity in the nation-state.[39]

The subservience of political identity to proprietor national identity means that *nationality* (ethnic/cultural identity[40]) supersedes *citizenship* (political identity). That is why the label "Irish-English,"

"Welsh-Scottish," "Danish-French," are unknown and incomprehensible, for these composite names combine two ethnic/cultural identities that are exclusive of each other: an individual is Scottish or English by nationality but not both.[41] In sharp and significant contrast, Canadian and American political identity is a supra identity separate from ethnic/cultural identity. It subsumes a wide range of ethnic and cultural (including religious) identities and their often mutually conflicting value systems, all of them enjoying the political rights and protections granted by political identity. The independence and supremacy of political identity over cultural identity is reflected in composite names like Italian Americans, Irish Americans, and Muslim Americans. These composite names are meaningful and comprehensible because they combine two different types of identities, a political identity (American) and a cultural/religious identity (Italian, Irish, Muslim).[42]

Europeans fail to see these fundamental distinctions between Europe and North America because they have grown up as members of a proprietor nation in which their national identity absorbs their political identity—their political identity is simply their national identity democratically exercising political power through its ownership of the state. Consequently they comprehend and view their political life through the conceptual lens of their national/cultural identity. The notion that political identity can be separate from and sovereign over national/cultural identity is foreign to their conceptions and experience.

Canada and the United States are not nation-states. They are not proprietor states[43] constitutionally designed for and controlled by some proprietor nation or ethnic group that claims to own the state. Of course, some groups—for example, Anglo-Saxons, of whom Samuel Huntington was the most prominent ideologue, Christian movements that claim that "the Bible should be the Constitution," and White supremacists who claim that America is a European nation—claim to be proprietors of America. Unfortunately for them, they cannot find support for these claims in the American

Constitution, which deliberately defines political identity in such a way as to accommodate multiple, even mutually incompatible, ethnic, cultural, and religious identities and values (Ayn Rand libertarians and anti-religion humanists at one end of the spectrum, Orthodox Jews and Muslims, polygamous Mormons, and the Amish at the other end). American political identity is defined by the Constitution and is independent of religious, ethnic, or cultural identity. It is not the product of centuries of historical processes, nor is it a Christian nation, as Benjamin Franklin clarified,[44] but is created *ex nihilo* by the Constitution.

French laïcité

The concepts "proprietor nation,"[45] "proprietor state," "political identity," "national identity," "citizen-national," and "citizen-alien" constitute the core concepts of the Proprietor State model that enable us to see why France is experiencing major problems that remain dishearteningly intractable—for example, cultural pluralism, immigration, and religious freedom. Of all the states of Europe, France's extreme form of church-state relations—*laïcité*—presents the strongest test case to Ramadan's reform proposals. An analysis of *laïcité* based on the Proprietor State model will lead us to a different understanding of France as a nation-state and, by extension, to a different understanding of the European nation-state as such.

Laïcité was not introduced as a constitutional principle until 1905, more than a century after the French Revolution.[46] The *laïcité* law of 1905 was the culmination of several steps taken by the state in the late nineteenth century to chip away at the influence of religion in public life.[47] The core of the 1905 law concerned state funding of religion. Prior to this law, the state had used taxpayer funds to build religious buildings such as churches. The 1905 law abolished this funding program and transferred such buildings to local government or retained them for the national government but allowed religious organizations to use these properties free of charge. *Laïcité* is not about protecting religion from encroachments by the state (as in the United States and

anglophone Canada), but of constitutionally entrenching the power
of the state to impose its will on the exercise of religion and justify
its actions as defensive measures to protect the state and society from
religion.

Nothing reveals more clearly the fraudulent nature of France's
laïcité than the shadowy existence[48] of the Constitutional Council
(France's "Supreme Court"). This body is charged with deciding
the constitutionality of decisions made by state institutions, which
submit their decisions to the Council for review; however, it cannot
strike down legislation, a power that the French political class,
from the days of the revolution, has been unwilling to give it. The
Constitutional Council does not protect fundamental rights. Most
significantly, the twelve-member Council is appointed by the officers
of the executive branch.

The relative weakness of the French "Supreme Court"—France is
not the only case: all European states have weak "Supreme Courts"—
is a predictable and logical consequence of the proprietor state. One
of the foremost champions of the proprietor nation, Jean-Jacques
Rousseau (d. 1778), considered the state to be an expression of the
"General Will"[49] of the nation and cannot tolerate any constitutional body with the authority to overrule its decisions. Indeed, he
cannot tolerate any citizen who does not believe in the "dogmas of
civil religion" as he envisions them.[50] That the French Constitutional
Council is appointed by the executive branch, and includes former
presidents of the Republic and other heads of the executive and legislative branches, is so glaringly at odds with American and Canadian
constitutional philosophy that it is disheartening to find that, apart
from Martha Nussbaum, American intellectuals and constitutional
scholars have not unmasked this fundamental deficiency that has
been cloaked by proprietor-nation rhetoric about French *laïcité* as the
political expression of Reason.[51]

The logic of the Proprietor State model predicts that the proprietor
nation will seek cultural homogeneity. At the political level it "solves"
the problem of culturally different citizens (immigrants, Muslims) by

intervening[52] and manipulating their evolution (through institutional frameworks such as church-state liaison committees; associations; taxpayer-funded imam-training programs at state universities; etc.) along a path designed to produce a compliant religion[53] that does not challenge the hegemony of the proprietor nation.

The French have added to this general European approach the principle of difference-blindness. The idea here is that France must create a homogeneous society in which cultural and religious differences do not exist. Underlying this principle is the assumption that there is a normative ("orthodox") culture against which other cultural values and practices are measured and found to be "heterodox" and therefore unacceptable—they must be erased, not accommodated (as in the American and Canadian systems).The proprietor nation demands that non-French cultural groups erase their respective cultures so as to produce this difference-blindness (for example, prohibiting, through legislation, Muslim school girls from wearing the hijab). Failure to comply with this policy risks punishment by state-legislated discriminatory laws (as the hijab law illustrates). The principle of difference-blindness translates into a policy of *unequal* treatment under the law. American scholars of *laïcité*, with the notable exception of Martha Nussbaum, Joan Scott, Naomi Davidson, and Mayanthi L Fernando,[54] are content to point out this extreme discriminatory secularism but rarely criticize it from the perspective of the American experience with cultural difference.

The American and Canadian approach looks past religious and cultural differences to the common humanity of all American and Canadian citizens and accords them all equal treatment under the law. No religious/cultural group is privileged as the normative religious/cultural group against which the rest are measured. They all share the same political identity, and this political identity includes the principle of accommodation of difference—rooted in individual conscience—that Roger Williams introduced into American political philosophy. The French conception is uncompromising and does not allow for the principle of accommodation. Indeed, the logic of the proprietor nation-state, which reserves political identity to the proprietor nation, entails that citizen-aliens be subjected to unequal treatment under its jurisprudence. In sharp contrast, the principle of equal treatment under the law is a cornerstone of American constitutional philosophy. Sadly, Canadian constitutional philosophy has not fully eliminated anglophone and French proprietarist thinking and consequently does not—indeed, cannot—commit itself as unflinchingly and as formally to this principle as does American constitutional philosophy.

France was, and remains, a Roman Catholic society. Historically, French Catholicism was doctrine-centred. Its principle of orthodoxy was implemented in officially formulated homogeneous beliefs that all believers had to accept. Any other belief was not simply heterodox but was an act against the Church (and God) and a threat to the established clergy-laity order. This sharp orthodox-heterodox binary is deeply etched into the cognitive structure of the traditional Catholic believer.

The French Revolution may have destroyed Catholicism as an institutional force in French social and political life, but mental structures are not erased that easily. The revolutionaries could not help but continue to view and comprehend society and politics through the cognitive lens of this orthodox-heterodox binary.[55] Where, before the revolution, the clerics had ruled the laity, now, after the revolution, the laity would rule the clerics. Where homogeneity of belief (orthodoxy) had been the guarantor of peace and social order, now homogeneity of culture (orthopraxis) would guarantee these results. And just as the old dispensation viewed heterodoxy with horror and uncompromising rejection, so the new dispensation would view "heteropraxis" (religious/cultural differences or pluralism: for example, the hijab) with horror and uncompromising rejection.

Europe exerts centripetal forces on Muslims

The inherently collectivist proprietary character of the European state exerts an array of *centripetal* political and cultural forces acting on Muslims from all sides aimed at demanding from them that they abandon their values and adopt those of the proprietor nation as precondition for full—that is, nondiscriminatory—acceptance into the proprietor nation. They demand *conversion*, not *integration*. Expediently ignoring their commitment to secularism, European states have legislated policies and have set up programs (imam-training programs, state-appointed Muslim councils, etc.) to deliberately intervene and direct, with collusion from their respective "supreme courts," the development of Islamic religious thought and practice towards state-defined ends. The Muslim leaders they have appointed to these committees are typically legal (Shariah) scholars. These policies and programs will invariably reinforce Shariah Islam and steer young Muslims towards legal scholars like Tariq Ramadan in search of legal (Shariah) rulings for their problems.

All these centripetal forces converge to push the Muslims inward and circle their wagons in defense of their religious/cultural identity, dignity, and self-respect. Such responses are in their nature conservative, and they tend to reinforce religious law (Shariah) as the identity-bestowing norm system governing relations among Muslims—and it will inadvertently strengthen the authority of the legal scholars over the internal life of their communities.

Individual Muslims in Europe who wish to follow the dictates of their consciences within the confines of a behaviour-prescribing Shariah Islam may therefore find it hard to do so. They may come to feel that they can gain acceptance in proprietor-nation European society by leaving the Muslim community and "converting" to proprietor-nation values by trading in their Shariah-based Islamic identity for an assimilationist identity as "secular" or "cultural" Muslims, or simply as atheists. While they may find personal empowerment on the outside, from the perspective of the Muslim community they would constitute a "brain drain" that would unwittingly confirm the claims of proprietor-nation Europeans that Islamic values are alien to European society and incapable of reconciling with the propietor nation's value system.

When Europe's Muslims are asked, "Can you be European and Muslim at the same time?" they search for answers that they hope will convince Europeans. But Europeans will not be convinced as long as they conceptualize themselves through the lens of the Proprietor State model. This is the fundamental truth about Europe that Tariq Ramadan and his fellow Muslims need to recognize. For all Ramadan's valiant effort to show that one can be European and Muslim at the same time (an issue that does not arise in Canada and the US), it is in vain, for his thought operates within the confines of the Proprietor State model that blinds him to the reality that he is a *citizen-alien* who can never hope to convert this status into that of *citizen-national* as long as the proprietor nation continues to own and run the political system.[56] French *laïcité* is the most extreme European example of the proprietor state, and it makes the sharpest discriminatory distinction between citizen-national and citizen-alien.

Hemmed in from all sides by these centripetal forces, Europe's Muslims, especially young Muslims, will be psychologically hard-pressed to identify with the proprietor-controlled political system and feel that they have a stake in it. Conversely, the proprietor nation's elites, from the political class to the journalistic class that vents and shapes proprietor-nation feelings and opinions, will be unwilling to acknowledge the impact of these centripetal forces on the Muslims so long as these elites remain mired in their proprietor-nation mindset. An escalating feedback loop, in which each side blames the other for the exacerbation of tensions and misunderstandings between them, is therefore inevitable.

The fundamental dilemma facing European proprietor states as they grapple with their citizen-aliens is that they will have to relinquish their proprietorship of the state and accept the principle of liberty of conscience protected by a strong supreme court that can prevent the majority (proprietor nation) from democratically discriminating against the minority. It is not enough for the European state to be a republic or a monarchy with a parliamentary system of government. Europe will need to accept the idea of a constitutional republic on the American model.[57] Europeans must find a way to replace the hierarchical binary of citizen-national/citizen-alien with a single category: citizen as a culturally (and religiously) neutral and sovereign political category.

North America exerts centrifugal forces on Muslims

The powerful individual-centric North American environment, in sharp contrast to Europe, exerts *centrifugal* forces on Muslims. It offers the Muslim individual vast possibilities for individual empowerment, economically viable independent existence and define-your-own-lifestyle constitutional space and protections. Active throughout the political and social sphere, and rooted in the constitutional principle of liberty of conscience, these centrifugal forces pull the Muslim individual, especially young men and women, away from the authority of family, community, and religious leaders. This privileging of individual conscience over scriptural or cultural tradition militates against a legalist (Shariah) conception of Islamic faith, for it is of the essence of this legalist conception that its practice be prescribed through divine sanction that overrides individual conscience.

However, unlike Europe where the secular public space is hostile to the exercise of a religiously mediated conscience (for example, when a Muslim woman conscientiously chooses to wear the hijab at school or work), the North American public space offers individual Muslims a constitution-protected space in which they can exercise this religiously mediated conscience, an option not presently available within the constricting confines of behaviour-prescribing Shariah Islam that dominates North American masjids today. Already, in much of what they do today, North American Muslims are disregarding—conscientiously or expediently (knowingly disobeying Quranic commandments)—a wide range of Quranic laws and Shariah rules: they earn interest from banks; they do not observe the penal laws; they do not practice polygamy; they no longer subscribe to the Quran's acceptance of slavery and armed violence;[58] they ignore its inheritance laws, eat non-halal meat, drink alcoholic beverages, do not observe Shariah-defined marriage laws, etc.

Muslim women, in particular, are the most strongly impacted by these individual-centric forces rooted in the principle of liberty of conscience. They increasingly enjoy greater freedoms to choose their careers, to run their own lives, and to make individual lifestyle and moral choices affecting sexuality, relationships and marriage, dressing and appearance.[59] Their menfolk increasingly support women's rights and the education of their daughters, who enjoy freedoms at school and workplace that exposes them to new ideas and anything-is-possible economic and social opportunities for advancement and empowerment—for example, merit-based performance evaluation, respect, managerial and executive authority, working alongside men, and running for public office.

Conscience and scripture (Quran and Shariah) do not necessarily have to be in conflict, but what is a Muslim to do when they are in conflict? Behavior-prescribing Shariah Islam classifies acts according to a "permissibility index" ranging from "compulsory" at one end to "prohibited" at the other end. For example, a Muslim woman may wear the hijab as an act of free exercise of her conscience, in which case all is fine; or she may wear it because her parents, peers, community, or Shariah scholars insist that it is a "compulsory" requirement, in which case her conscience comes into conflict with the Shariah. The constitution-protected space of North American polities offers her the opportunity to ground her Islamic identity in alternative conscience-supporting traditions of Islam that do not require her to wear the hijab.

Thus Muslim women, more than Muslim men, will recognize much at stake for them in the individual-centric centrifugal dynamic of Canadian and American society, and we may safely expect them to be heavily vested in supporting and strengthening the principle of liberty of conscience that is the root of the two polities.

The Canadian context and the challenge of Quebec

The powerful conscience-rooted centrifugal forces in the American polity are also active in the Canadian polity, and just as they press upon Shariah Islam in the US, so they also press upon it in Canada. However, the relative weakness of Canadian political identity and of its Supreme Court[60] in protecting the liberty of conscience as an unalienable right, coupled with the Charter's provision allowing for limits to be placed on the exercise of these rights and for provincial legislatures to temporarily override them, has the potential to be exploited by political opportunists (as the Parti Quebecois in Quebec attempted to do with its Charter of Values). The controversy during 2003-2005 that engulfed and doomed the proposals for a Shariah arbitration mechanism within the framework of the Ontario Arbitration Act testifies to the weakness of the Canadian Supreme Court (relative to the American Supreme Court) in protecting and accommodating religious freedom and cultural differences.[61]

The exceptional constitutional conundrum posed by Quebec carries different implications for the future of Islam in the province than in anglophone Canada. The essential tension in Canada's constitutional thought and practice is between, on the one hand, the two-nation theory that acknowledges the French nation as an equal partner of the English nation in Canada's founding—conveniently ignoring the fact that the First Nations are the dispossessed original proprietors[62] of the land—and, on the other hand, the status of Quebec as just one peer-level province among the rest of the (overwhelmingly English and Protestant) provinces in the federal system. Quebec's anomalous situation as a "nation within a nation" is exacerbated by the multiple immigrant "nations" within it. Its obsession with the survival of French culture (the locus of French nationality) in Canada goes all the way back to its incorporation into the British Empire by the Treaty of Paris (1763). As a proprietor state, it conforms to the Proprietor State model for European proprietor states and reflects European anxieties about immigration. French influence in Quebec political life increased sharply in the 1950s and reached blatant levels when French president Charles de Gaulle cried out "Vive le Québec libre!" during a visit to Quebec in 1967. Separatist aspirations may have weakened today, but they can flare up again if the French come to believe that their culture is facing dire existential threats. Defenders of Quebec's *laïcité*[63] seek philosophical credentials and moral endorsement from France's own anti-multicultural *laïcité* so that they can proceed with impunity to impose discriminatory policies on Quebec's non-French citizen-aliens.

The future of Islam in Canada will be shaped by two subcontexts, Quebec and anglophone Canada. As long as the French in Quebec remain obsessed about their cultural heritage—within Canada or outside as an independent nation-state—they will harden their already strong proprietor-nation mindset and will continue to view non-French culture as a threat to their hegemonic "national" culture. Should they feel dissatisfied with the assimilation "performance" of the non-French cultural groups (especially Muslims), they may be expected to resort to draconian discriminatory actions of the sort envisaged in the defeated Charter of Values (which had been shrewdly worded to target the Muslims in the province). It will prove extremely difficult, if not impossible, for the principle of liberty of conscience to take root among Shariah-based Muslims in the province.

RECONCEPTUALIZING THE QURAN

The American and Canadian constitutions support and protect the right of Shariah Islam to flourish, much as Orthodox Judaism and the Amish are flourishing under their protection. The dilemma confronting Islam in North America is not whether Shariah Islam will survive—it will survive—but how it will respond to the needs of the Muslim who enjoys freedoms unknown to the Islamic tradition but who wants to be guided by his or her faith in using these freedoms in conscientious ways.

Unless Muslims evolve a conscience-based individual-centric conception and practice of their faith, the brain drain from Shariah Islam that is taking place today will continue and will confirm the fears of individual-centric Muslims (and non-Muslims too) that

Islam is inherently incapable of empowering the individual to heed the dictates of his or her conscience for fear that an autonomous subjective ethics will lead to what the traditional scholars condemn as *bid'ah* (innovation), causing anarchy and breakdown of the social order.

There is a fine line between conscientious and licentious uses of individual freedoms. Some American Muslims invoke the juristic principle of *ijtihād*[64] to justify their rejection of Quranic commandments and Shariah rules, but as long as they believe that the Quran is the direct Word of God they are taking morally inconsistent expedient liberties with scripture. The few, like Aminah Wadud, who have conscientiously rejected some Quranic commands, deserve to be included among Americans who have struggled with the "scripture versus conscience" tension inaugurated in American religious history by Roger Williams.

At the root of the dilemma that Muslim reformist thinkers have struggled unsuccessfully to solve for nearly two hundred years is the paradigm that has governed Shariah Islam ever since the Quran was compiled under the direction of the third Caliph, 'Uthmān (d. 656), soon after the death of the Prophet. This paradigm rests on two bedrock beliefs: (1) the belief that the words that make up the Quran are the words of God, conveyed to humanity by Muhammad who did not tamper with them in any way; and (2) the belief that these words of God include commandments that believers must obey. It is a cornerstone of Muslim belief that the Quran is God's guidance for all humanity in all cultures for all time to come. No individual can ever have the authority to change or ignore the words of God or place conditions on their authority over his or her life. To appreciate the square-the-circle consequences of this paradigm when it is applied to the realities of the modern world, consider the two examples below.

Islamic finance and Shariah-compliance stratagems: the notorious hiyal

Islamic finance is a rapidly growing area that includes banking, insurance, investment, and taxation (*zakāt*). The field is left to specialists in the banking and investment industry who create new financial instruments that are incomprehensible to nonspecialists and whose provenance in the classical texts of the Shariah cannot be easily investigated by old-school "orientalist" scholars who disdain, or lack competence in, financial subjects.

N J Coulson, the prominent scholar of Islamic law, describes how the classical legal scholars circumvented unambiguous Quranic prohibitions through the concept of *hiyal*[65] (tricks) that allowed them to comply with the literal statement of the divine law but completely undermine its ethical intent. The trillion-dollar windfall being reaped today by the giant financial establishments, aided, on one side, by the stamp of approval from Wall Street and, on the other, by Shariah scholars who issue legal rulings attesting to these contrivances as "Shariah compliant," shows starkly that Shariah Islam's focus on behavior compliance and the immutability of Quranic laws tempts believers to subvert the ethical intent these laws express.

Tariq Ramadan insists that his new class of experts, the "context scholars," among whom will be experts from the financial sector, should be trusted to determine the ethics that should guide their professional activity and decisions. To be fair to Ramadan, he has not fully worked through this issue—for example, can the context scholars (say, evolutionary biologists) issue legal rulings (*fatwā*)?—and we must wait for him to clarify the ambiguities in his positions. The American experience has shown time and again (but most dramatically in the market crash of 2008) that Congress is at the mercy of the financial sector, dominated by the likes of JP Morgan and Goldman Sachs, who form a revolving door into and out of the executive branch of the government and whose staff write technically abstruse legislation for Congress. If this is the case with the world's foremost democratic legislature, how will Muslims judge the claims of the Muslim investment bankers—the context scholars—that their decisions meet the ethical objectives (*maqāsid*) of the Shariah?

Islamic feminism

There are at least three main categories of feminism among contemporary Muslim women. Secular Muslim feminists promote the agenda for empowering women on secular humanist principles, without resorting to the Quran or the Shariah for justifications. A second group consists of Muslim women who remain personally devout but who choose to live their lives without seeking legal rulings from the legal scholars. They anchor their gender-equality work in the Quran's egalitarian teachings and do not give further intellectual attention to the Quran's inequality verses. Modern social media technology offers them a platform and social space to express their ideas in personal blogs and websites, or through online networks for like-minded women to share their experiences and seek support from fellow sisters.[66] The third group, one that concerns us here, consists of Muslim women who argue for women's rights on scriptural grounds by promoting an egalitarian woman's-point-of-view interpretation of the Quran and the Shariah. This group can properly be termed "Islamic feminists."

Islamic feminists accept that the Quran is the Word of God. They have studied the Quran and have become convinced that God supports gender equality. But they are torn by some verses that seem to support gender inequality and that have been consistently interpreted throughout Islamic history by the full spectrum of male elites in Muslim society as supporting male privilege and dominance. Of all the "difficult" texts in the Quran, verse 4:34[67] has challenged their faith the most because, taken at face value, it commands a patriarchal, hierarchical, unequal and punitive treatment of women. Ever since the first publication of the landmark and deservedly influential book by Aminah Wadud, *Qur'an and Woman*,[68] Islamic feminists have concentrated great creative intellectual effort in an anguished attempt to demonstrate, in effect, that this verse only *appears* to be advocating a patriarchal position but in *reality* is advocating its opposite. Wadud herself, after more than twenty years of struggling with her conscience, finally decided to reject verse 4:34: "There is no getting around this one. I have tried through different methods for two decades . . . I have finally come to say 'no' outright to the literal implementation of this passage."[69]

Wadud and her colleagues have developed a theological semantics of the Quranic concepts of equality and justice. But they, along with male Muslim progressives, have not shown how these concepts would translate into practical legislation in Muslim societies. In what ways would these practical implementations differ from the practical implementation of the Western concepts of equality and justice in Western society?

Consider first the concept of equality. When Islamic feminists think of the practical aspects of the principle of gender equality that they believe the Quran teaches, how do these practices differ from Western practices? In Western practice gender equality translates into laws for equal political and civil rights (voting, nondiscrimination in the workplace, etc.); equal pay for equal work; the right to one's body (reproductive rights), to pursue one's lifestyle, to education, to choose one's partner, to rent or purchase an apartment and own property, etc. Neither the feminists nor the male progressives have shown that the legislation based on Quranic understanding of gender equality would be different from Western practices.

Consider now the second major concept for which Islamic feminists (and male progressives) are fighting: justice. In what ways does its practical implementation differ from Western practices? In Western practice it is to the state that citizens turn for justice when they feel they have been wronged or injured by another citizen (or by legal persons such as corporations). Where justice in the Western conception is a *political* and *legal* relation between state and citizen, grounded in nontheological premises, and is delivered by the power of the state, in the Quranic conception justice is an *ethical* relation between an individual and another individual, grounded in theological premises, and is "delivered" by the conscience of the individual. If it is not "delivered," then injustice has occurred that will be set right in the next world where God will deliver final justice on the Day of

Judgement. Thus, in the Quranic conception "judicial proceedings" continue until the Day of Judgement, when God will bring them to a close. If the practical implementation of the Quranic understanding of justice will be adopted from Western practices—for example, presumption of innocence, courtroom protocols, trial by jury, criminal versus civil trials, admissibility of evidence obtained under torture, due process—can Islamic feminists and their fellow male progressives really claim that these practices are Quranic?

  One may ask: Why is it necessary for Islamic feminists to undertake this tortuous and tortured expenditure of semantic energy when the end result—adoption of Western practices—is the same as that produced by secular Muslim feminists who argue their case on straightforward humanistic grounds? It may be comforting for them to stamp Western practices with a "Made in Islam" label insinuated by this theological semantics, but then they are unwittingly reinforcing the belief held by Islam's detractors that contemporary Muslims are incapable of inventing Quran-inspired practical solutions that are better than Western practices and that benefit all of humanity, not just Muslims. Tariq Ramadan has decried this type of reform activity as *adaptation reform* that is forever playing catch up to Western thought and practices. Instead, he argues, Muslims need to engage in *transformation reform* that is inventive rather than imitative. Ramadan contends that his *radical reform* of the foundations of the Shariah will produce transformation reform.[70]

Thinking the unthinkable: abandoning verbal revelation

The two examples above may be construed as extreme end-points of the range of problems that can arise when the Quran is taken to be the Word of God and its laws applied to modern realities. In one case, that of Islamic finance, the believer is tempted to circumvent God's commandments by stratagems (*hiyal*) designed, in effect, to hoodwink God into thinking that the believer is obeying His commands. In the second case, that of Islamic feminism, it can cause great spiritual torment to conscientious believing women to summon the courage to defy God's words, as Wadud's poignant personal testimony regarding verse 4:34 shows.

Although Wadud herself does not go so far as to question the doctrine of verbal revelation of the Quran, it is only a matter of time before Muslims recognize that this assumption is creating insurmountable problems for Muslims today and has brought the legalist paradigm to a dead end.

One example of insurmountable problems caused by the legalist paradigm is the scriptural justifications offered by jihadist and other violent Muslim movements. They claim that they are obeying God's commands.[71] The Quran indeed contains verses in which God commands Muslims to take up arms against their enemies. It is irrelevant for our purposes here whether these Quranic commands are defensive or offensive. The key point here is that these verses are part of the text of the Quran, and as long as the Quran exists it will be possible for someone to lift its words out of context and use them to justify actions of the sort exemplified by contemporary jihadist groups.

The experience of Judaism is once again helpful here. Most Jews today ignore the problematic contents of their scriptures that conflict with modern values. This is especially true of the individual-centric denominations (Reconstructionist, Conservative, and Reform) who reject the principle of verbal revelation of the Torah and can therefore reject its laws as nonbinding on them. And just as some Muslims lift Quranic verses out of context, so some contemporary Jews lift passages from the Torah out of context to justify their actions.[72]

The time may have finally arrived when North American Muslims will not be able to avoid thinking the unthinkable with respect to verbal revelation. The experience of American Jews teaches us that once the question is raised it is difficult to put the genie back in the bottle. The only way forward is to abandon the belief in the verbal revelation of the Quran and to adopt an alternative understanding—for example, that the words of the Quran are words that Muhammad uttered and authored in a divinely inspired involuntary and creative cognitive-emotional state.

The idea that the words, verses, and syntax of the Quran are the work of Muhammad acting under the shaping authority of (divine) inspiration is not new to Islamic tradition. The philosophers Abu Nasr al-Farabi (d. 950) and Abu Ali ibn Sina (Avicenna, d. 1037) were inquisitive theoreticians by disposition, interested not just in Islam but in religion as such and the beliefs and rules that govern each religion. Al-Farabi's *Kitāb al-Millah* (Book of Religion) develops a humanistic—nontheological, nonethnic and nonracial—general theory about religion that is in principle applicable to any religion in the world. According to it, the founder of the religion (*wādi' al-sharī'ah*, lawgiver) translates the inspiration from the cosmic source of all things into culturally comprehensible linguistic formulation. The Fatimid Ismaili philosophers also developed cognitive theories to explain Muhammad's authorial contribution to the linguistic composition of the Quran. These conceptualizations were marginalized in the subsequent intellectual history of Islam as Shariah Islam gained ascendancy throughout the Muslim world.

Other religious traditions typically regard their scripture as the involuntary product of divine inspiration: the guru or sage does not, in the manner of the contriving artful wordsmith, sculpt the words and their organization; they spring from an internal "transcendental" place that lies beyond the guru's consciousness and will.

In the case of Muhammad, the inspirational mode in which the words came to him ready-made calls to mind some poets who describe their respective creative processes: they "see" the lines of the poem on some mental "screen" and write them down. Brewster Ghiselin collected personal testimonies about their respective creative processes from leading scientists and artists in his book, *The Creative Process: Reflections on Invention in the Arts and Sciences* (1952).[73]

Two contributors on poetry are particularly relevant here: A E Housman and Brewster Ghiselin. Housman attests to his moment of "verbal revelation" in the following way: He would be on a walk when

[There] would flow into my mind, with sudden and unac-
countable emotion, sometimes a line or two of verse, sometimes a whole stanza at once, accompanied, not preceded,
by a vague notion of the poem of which they were destined
to play a part . . . When I got home I wrote them down,
leaving gaps, and hoping that further inspiration might be
forthcoming another day . . . Two of the stanzas . . . came
into my head, just as they are printed . . . One more was
needed, but it did not come: I had to turn to and compose it
myself. It was a laborious business.[74]

The second example is Brewster Ghiselin. Describing his creative
process, he writes:

One morning weeks later, some words came to my mind
and I wrote them down . . . The lines flew into my mind as
casually and effortlessly as the shore birds of the coast fly
across one's vision out of the light and foam mist . . . [In] the
same instant I had the lines . . . Because the creation of a
poem involves a reordering of consciousness, its development cannot be forced and regulated wholly by an effort of
conscious authority.[75]

Ghiselin's comment, that the poem's "development cannot be forced
and regulated wholly by an effort of conscious authority," can be construed as a suggestive explanation of how the Quran was composed
from words in Muhammad's culture-specific cognitive system without Muhammad's "conscious authority" but under the "authority" of
an inspiration that Muslims would regard as "divine."

This reconceptualization of the Quran leads to a second "unthinkable" for Muslims, namely that the Quran is therefore the linguistic expression of Muhammad's personal understanding and interpretation[76] of the preverbal and prestructured inspiration that was
"refracted" through Muhammad's cognitive/emotional systems
and linguistic repertoire before he uttered the words that form the
Quran.[77]

The history of astronomy teaches us that a new paradigm emerges after the unwieldy attempts to solve the "anomalies" faced by the old paradigm make things worse and create more anomalies so that at some point someone wonders if the problem may not lie with the paradigm itself. The new paradigm of inspiration, if adopted by Muslims, would reveal the "difficulty" of verses such as 4:34 as falsely construed problems created by the inappropriate old paradigm of verbal revelation. One would not need to prove that the inequality teachings of verse 4:34 are in fact equality teachings—to prove, in effect, that the circle is a square. Instead, the new paradigm would simply discard such verses as intended specifically for the seventh-century Muslims of Mecca and Medina with no binding force on subsequent generations of culturally diverse Muslims. The new paradigm immediately opens up the Quran to a contextual analysis through which the entire legislative content can be discarded as having no authority over Muslims today.

The new paradigm would liberate Muslim minds from the captivity of the legislative content of the Quran and enable them to rediscover and re-engage with those verses[78] that speak to individual conscience as the wellspring of enlightened subjective ethics. But it would do more than that: it would draw out the diverse enlightenment traditions that have been obscured by Muslim and non-Muslim Manichean discourse on "liberal/moderate" Islam locked in mortal combat with "political/fundamentalist" Islam.

There is as yet no typology of the enlightenment traditions in Islam that defines criteria upon which a classification of these traditions might be built. All enlightenment traditions of Islam assume, explicitly or implicitly, in one form or another, the soul-body or mind-body duality along with a corresponding assumption of a soul-body or mind-body duality in the universe, and they direct their enlightenment agenda at the soul or mind (or soul and mind together) of the individual rather than at his body (the regulation of whose behavior is the "portfolio" of the Shariah). There are two main types of goals these traditions seek to attain. Traditions that stress fellowship or companionship (*suhbah*) seek to draw ever closer to

God in intimacy (*qurbah*) and ultimately to attain union (*fanā'*) or face-to-face encounter with God. On the other hand, traditions that stress knowledge (*ma'rifah*) seek access to the spiritual and intellectual realities (*haqā'iq*) of the universe that lie beyond the reach of the five bodily senses and the mental capacities grounded in these senses. Sufism, more than any other tradition in Islam, was predicated on the crucial role of conscience in the individual's spiritual, intellectual, and ethical enlightenment.

A new Islamic denomination for North America

Muslims who wish for a conscience-rooted faith that supports personal ethical decision-making will need to acknowledge that it is futile to attempt to transform legalist Shariah Islam into a subjectivist personal faith. Instead, they should seek inspiration and courage from the individual-centric movements in American Judaism—Reconstructionist, Conservative, and Reform—and create their own separate denomination and incorporate individual-centric and gender-equal values into its founding principles. Immigrant Muslims may also be well-served by the example of African American Imam Warith Deen Mohammed and his conscience-based understanding of the Quran and the Prophet's career.[79] The new denomination would place the enlightenment traditions of Islam at the center of its life and programs.

But while all the enlightenment traditions of Islam rest ultimately on the concept of conscience, in practice they all adhere in their conceptions and practices of social life to the behavior-prescribing laws of Shariah Islam. Enlightenment did not lead men to question the patriarchy, androcentrism, and other inequalities in the Shariah and to develop a liberal and progressive social theory aimed at eliminating them—they were heavily vested in the gender privileges granted to them by the Shariah.

This acceptance of the gender inequalities in the Shariah and lack of engagement with the dominant political, legislative, economic, social, and cultural issues facing fellow American and Canadian citizens characterizes even those North American Sufi groups whose spiritual masters and members are predominantly of Western European extraction. They withdraw from society and hold their retreats away from "materialist" civilization deep in the woods, by lakeside lodges amidst pristine forests, or in remote semidesert locations. Their overriding ethos of antimaterialism as a necessary precondition for spiritual advancement militates against remaining in the political and social realm and seeking to infuse it with enlightened ethics for the benefit of all citizens. In sum, conscience remains severely constricted within the lexicon, semantics, and practices of these enlightenment traditions. This imprisonment of conscience parallels the imprisonment of conscience within the theological lexicon and semantics of Puritan scripture that Roger Williams rebelled against and from which he sought to liberate conscience. The new denomination, impelled by the principle of liberty of conscience, would undertake a similar liberation project to emancipate conscience from the traditional concepts, vocabulary, and practices of the enlightenment traditions of Islam. Only when conscience is freed from this captivity can it discharge its proper function as the internal ethical guide for the individual who cherishes the personal decision-making freedoms guaranteed by the American and Canadian constitutions.

Muslim women would be the biggest and immediate beneficiaries of the new gender-equal denomination. In order to ensure that the new denomination is fully gender-equal, women would find it opportune to be involved at its creation as co-founders and later as equal partners of men across all levels of the religious and administrative organization of the new denomination. They would be launching the new denomination with all their present reform aspirations and demands built into it "at creation time." In particular, they would be able to serve as imams, lead prayers, and deliver sermons to mixed congregations. They would be able to officiate at religious ceremonies and conduct rites of passages and in general perform all other religious and organizational duties that have been the traditional preserve of men.

Although it is outside the scope of this essay to address the practical aspects of founding and building the new denomination, we may venture a glimpse into the denomination's core principles and institutional components towards which the principle of liberty is steering the immigrant Muslim community.

Perhaps the most important practical consequence of abandoning the belief in the verbal revelation of the Quran is the corresponding abandonment of the legalist conception of Islam. The new denomination would be premised on the principle that it is possible to practice Islam without the Shariah. Islam as a religious system did not exist in the Meccan phase of the Prophet's mission; there was no Shariah before the migration to Medina. This is true also of the system of worship that Muslims observe to this day: it was established in Medina. The "first Muslims"[80] in Mecca had a nonlegal conception of Islamic faith and its practice. They had to draw on their personal consciences and understandings of faith, guided by Muhammad's example, for judging the ethics of a situation.[81]

In addition to adopting a nonlegalist conception of Islam, we may expect the new denomination to adopt two other core principles. The first is the strong commitment to the principle of separation of church and state that is at the heart of the American and Canadian systems of government. The second is the new denomination's strong endorsement of science as the only trustworthy method of inquiry into physical reality.[82] Among the core institutional components of the new denomination, we may anticipate masjids, a special-purpose college to train the denomination's imams and scholars, and chapters at college campuses.

CONCLUSION

In the foregoing pages the principle of the liberty of conscience has served as a conceptual analytical thread weaving through and linking together the major components of this essay: Ramadan's reform proposals, the Proprietor State model, the differences between the political systems of Europe and North America, the limits of Shariah Islam in North America, the need to rethink the belief in verbal revelation and reconceptualize the Quran, and the conceptual vision and institutional framework for a new denomination rooted in this principle.

The Proprietor State model presented above is a novel approach for understanding features of the modern European nation-state that bear directly on the "Muslim Question" in Europe. It clarifies the distinction and relationship between the proprietor nation's political identity and its national/cultural identity, and the conditions under which, in the one case, political identity is subservient to national/cultural identity and, in the other case, national/cultural identity is subservient to political identity.

In the proprietor states of Europe and Quebec, political identity remains absorbed in national/cultural identity because the numerically overwhelming proprietor nation exploits the democratic process to control the state and marshal its resources to advance and protect its interests—political identity is nothing other than national/cultural identity taking over the political system. In contrast, the United States (and to a lesser extent anglophone Canada) is perhaps the only state in the world in which political identity is strictly separated from national/cultural identity and is anchored solely in the Constitution, thereby making it possible for mutually incompatible and antagonistic sets of cultural identities and value systems—Amish, Orthodox Jews, polygamous Latter-Day Saints, atheists, LGBTQ communities, white supremacists, etc.—to share the same Constitution-defined political identity.

The Proprietor State model suggests that Tariq Ramadan's proposals for the "radical reform" of Shariah Islam is an understandable response to the alienating and discriminatory centripetal forces directed towards Muslims by the European proprietor state. In North America, however, Ramadan's proposals will be less successful. This is so because the powerful individual-centric centrifugal forces, rooted in the principle of liberty of conscience, offer dissatisfied Muslims an alternative and constitutionally protected space into which they can "migrate"[83] and practice a conscience-based faith drawing upon Islam's diverse enlightenment traditions.

As the experience of Orthodox Judaism shows, the individual-centric centrifugal forces in North American civilization have steadily enticed Jews away from Orthodoxy towards other denominations that reinterpreted Judaism in individual-centric terms. These Jewish denominations reconceptualized the Torah as words authored by Moses under divine inspiration. In the same way, these same centrifugal forces are pressing Muslims to reconceptualize the Quran as words authored by Muhammad under divine inspiration and to abandon the doctrine of verbal revelation and its contingent legalist conception of Islam.

Roger Williams transformed what had been a purely theological concept of conscience in Protestant Christianity into a humanistic constitutional principle upon which different religious communities might coexist peacefully. The new denomination, in fusing the Quranic conception of conscience with the conception of conscience articulated by Roger Williams, would offer North American Muslims an Islamic life rooted simultaneously in the Quran (cultural/religious identity) and the American Constitution (political identity), for it is the same conscience within the individual that is the seat of political identity as well as cultural/religious identity.[84]

Contemporary thought about Islam remains trapped inside the "clash of civilizations" paradigm and cannot therefore imagine an alternative relevance of Islamic identity for North America. But as this essay has argued, a conscience-based Islamic denomination, engendering a Muslim self whose political and cultural/religious components are equally grounded in conscience, promises to be an unwavering champion and defender of the principle of liberty of conscience, working in concert with like-minded individuals, movements, denominations, and organizations to form a bulwark against forces that would weaken, corrode, or eliminate altogether this bedrock principle of the Canadian and American systems of government.

The conscience-based Islamic denomination envisioned here is the "unthought" that lies beyond the universe of thought spawned by the "clash of civilizations" paradigm, and for that reason its very possibility, let alone its eventuality, may seem counterintuitive to contemporary Muslims and non-Muslims alike. Yet its inevitable emergence will have demonstrated not only the continuing vitality of Roger Williams's principle of liberty of conscience but also the relevance of Islamic identity for nourishing this vitality and ensuring that the Canadian and American constitutions and polities remain firmly anchored in the principle of liberty of conscience.

Notes

Reexamining Relations Between Men and Women

1. Abu'l Faraj Ibn al-Jawzi, *Ahkam al-Nisa'* (Cairo: Maktabat al-Turath al-Islamic, 1984).

2. Amira El-Azhary Sonbol, Yvonne Yazbeck Haddad, and John L Esposito, "Rethinking Women and Islam" in *Daughters of Abraham: Feminist thought in Judaism, Christianity, and Islam* (Gainesville, FL: University Press of Florida, 2001).

3. http://www.asma-lamrabet.com/articles/l-emergence-de-nouvelles-voies-de-liberation-pour-les-femmes-en-islam/

4. Qur'an 6:101 ("Cattle")

5. A few examples of verses in which God uses the words "companion" and "associate": 10:35: "Say: Are there among your ascribed associates with God ones who guide to the Truth?" 25:2: "He to Whom belongs the dominion of the heaves and the earth and takes to Himself not a son." 72:3: "Truly He, exalted be the grandeur of our Lord, He has taken no companion to Himself nor a son."

6. *The Oxford Universal Dictionary on Historical Principles*, 3rd Edition (Oxford: Clarendon Press, 1955); The Free Dictionary, http://www.thefreedictionary.com/companion.

7. The professions of other prophets are examined in Ibn Katheer, *Stories of the Prophets from Adam to Muhammad*, translated by Sayed Gad, Tamir Abu As-Su'ood, and Muhammad A M Abu Sheishaa, nmusba.wordpress.com.

8. For more detailed presentations of the types of commercial contracts in Islam, see Muhammad Ayub, *Understanding Islamic Finance* (Hoboken, NJ: John Wiley & Sons, 2007).

9. Ibid.

10. El-Azhary Sonbol, op. cit., p. 138-139

11. 30:21: "... He created for you wives from among yourselves that you may rest in them and He has made affection and mercy among you ... "

12. http://www.unesco.org/new/en/education/themes/leading-the-international-agenda/efareport/reports/2012-skills/

13. See Yvonne Yazbeck Haddad, "Islam and Gender: Dilemma in the Changing Arab World," in *Islam, Gender and Social Change*. In it, she mentions the position of Rashid al-Ghannushi in his *al-Mar'ah bayn al-Qu'ran wa-Waqi`al Muslimin* (Tunis: Matba`at Tunis Qurtaj al Sharqiyah, n.d.), which, she argues, insists on competence and not gender as a selection criterion in hiring practices.

14. http://ccmw.com/wp-content/uploads/2014/09/Canadian-Muslim-Women.pdf

15. http://www.ispu.org/pdfs/ISPU%20Report_Marriage%20II_Macfarlane_WEB.pdf

16. Approximately 75% of the data was collected from respondents in the United States, and 25% from Canada. No pervasive differences were noted between the two jurisdictions, and the analysis presented here does not distinguish between the United States and Canada.

17. More than 95% of Muslim women live in metropolitan areas.

18. See note 14.

19. See note 14.

20. See note 14.

21. See note 14: 56.7% of Muslim girls and women 15 years and older possess postsecondary diplomas and degrees. The employment rate among Canadian Muslims is 65.6% compared to 70.8% for other women. According to the National Household Survey 2011, 50% of Muslim women who had or were looking for a job had preschool and school-age children. This rate includes divorced and separated women as well.

Anti-Muslim Bigotry Goes Official

1. "Spiegel Interview with Aga Khan," Spiegel Online, October 12, 2006.

2. Wajahat Ali, Eli Clifton, Matthew Duss, Lee Fang, Scott Keyes and Faiz Shakir, *Fear, Inc.: The Roots of the Islamophobia Network in America*, Center for American Progress, August 26, 2011.

3. Aziz Z Huq, "The Rise of the Anti-Muslim Fringe," *Boston Review*, April 17, 2015.

4. Matthew Duss, Yasmine Taeb, Ken Gude and Ken Sofer, *Fear, Inc. 2.0: The Islamophobia Network's Efforts to Manufacture Hate in America*, Center for American Progress, February 11, 2015.

5. Tariq Ramadan, *Western Muslims and the Future of Islam* (New York: Oxford University Press, 2004), 94.

6. M M Pickthall, *The Glorious Qur'an* (New Delhi: Goodword, 2002), 4:3.

7. *The Glorious Qur'an*, 4:129.

8. *The Glorious Qur'an*, 4:97.

9. *The Glorious Qur'an*, 18:29.

10. *The Glorious Qur'an*, 49:13.

11. "The Last Sermon (Khutabul Wada) of Prophet Muhammad," *Sound Vision*. http://www.soundvision.com/article/the-last-sermon-khutabul-wada-of-prophet-muhammad.

12. Abdullah Yusuf Ali, translation of *The Holy Qur'an* (Brentwood: Amana Corporation, 1989), 96:1 and 96:4.

13. "This Charter shall be interpreted in a manner consistent with the preservation and advancement of the multicultural heritage of Canadians," *Canadian Charter of Rights and Freedoms*, s. 27.

14. Individual equality before and under the law "does not preclude any law, program or activity that has as its object the amelioration of conditions of disadvantaged individuals or groups," *Canadian Charter of Rights and Freedoms*, s. 15(2).

15. Marion Boyd, *Dispute Resolution in Family Law: Protecting Choice, Promoting Inclusion*, December 2004. http://www.attorneygeneral.jus.gov.on.ca/english/about/pubs/boyd/fullreport.pdf.

16. "Racism alive and well in Canada," Forum Research Inc., September 18, 2013. https://www.forumresearch.com/forms/News%20Archives/News%20Releases/12124_Fed_Racism_(18092013)_Forum_Research.pdf.

17. Louise Leduc, "Le Malaise Musulman," *La Presse*, March 16, 2014.

18. "Canadians view non-Christian religions with uncertainty, dislike," Angus Reid Global, October 2, 2013. http://angusreidglobal.com/wp-content/uploads/2013/10/Canadians-view-non-Christian-religions-with-uncertainty-dislike.pdf.

19. Randy Boswell, "Muslims face negative perception in Canada: Study," *Postmedia News*, October 15, 2011.

20. Gerard Bouchard and Charles Taylor, *Building the Future: A Time for Reconciliation*, Gouvernement du Quebec, 2008.

21. Terence McKenna, "The political strategy behind Quebec's values charter," CBC News, website, November 7, 2013.

22. Steve Rukavina, "Rania El-Alloul, kicked out of Quebec court for wearing hijab, fights back," CBC News, website, March 27, 2015.

23. Michelle Lalonde, "Concordia library to help Muslim students cull 'inappropriate' books," *Montreal Gazette*, March 5, 2015.

24. Les Perreaux, "Quebec to give police, courts new tools to fight extremism," *National Post*, June 8, 2015.

25. "Quebec tables new religious neutrality bill banning face coverings," CBC News, website, June 10, 2015.

26. Haroon Siddiqui, "Warped standards on terror," *Toronto Star*, July 27, 2011.

27. Glen McGregor, "The Gargoyle—Kenney tweets misleading photos of Muslim women in chains," *Ottawa Citizen*, March 10, 2015.

28. "Official transcript of Stephen Harper's remarks after parliament dissolved," *The Canadian Press*, August 2, 2015.

29. Faisal Bhabha, "Does Stephen Harper Care About Muslims," *The Harper Decade*, May 21, 2015.

30. In January 2015, Prime Minister Harper said he would crack down on terrorist ideas hatched "in a basement or a mosque," Siddiqui, "Being stupid in the endless war on terror," *Toronto Star*, February 25, 2015.

31. Siddiqui, "Harper senators hold McCarthyesque hearings," *Toronto Star*, March 4, 2015.

32. Kashef A Ahmed, "Senate committee a witch hunt," *Toronto Star*, March 2, 2015.

33. Siddiqui, "Conservative senators hold kangaroo court on security," *Toronto Star*, March 7, 2015.

34. Frank Gaffney, "The Muslim Brotherhood in America," Center for Security Policy. https://www.centerforsecuritypolicy.org/the-muslim-brotherhood-in-america/.

35. Mohammed Azhar Ali Khan, "The business of Muslim-bashing in Canada," *Saudi Gazette*, June 5, 2015.

36. Steve Buist, "Hamilton lawyer suspended from federal security panel," *Hamilton Spectator*, April 30, 2015.

37. Noor Javed, "Youth event tackles Islamophobia," *Toronto Star*, June 6, 2015.

38. Standing Senate Committee on National Security and Defence, *Countering the Terrorist Threat in Canada: An Interim Report*, Government of Canada, 2015.

39. "Register your imam, senators say," *The Globe and Mail*, July 9, 2015.

40. Steven Chase, "Senate committee on terrorism suggests certifying imams," *The Globe and Mail*, July 8, 2015.

41. Siddiqui, "Islamophobia: Paranoia infects North America," *Toronto Star*, September 16, 2011.

42. "Canadian Security Bill puts your rights at risk," Amnesty International Canada. http://e-activist.com/ea-action/action?ea.client.id=1770&ea.campaign.id=36151.

43. Dan Taekema, "Journalist group and civil liberties association start constitutional challenge to anti-terrorism Bill C-51," *Toronto Star*, July 21, 2015.

44. *An Act to amend the Citizenship Act and to make consequential amendments to other Acts*, Statutes of Canada 2014 c. 22, 2014.

45. "Challenging Misinformation: Canadian Citizenship Law Explained," Canadian Association of Refugee Lawyers, May 5, 2015.

46. Citizenship and Immigration Canada, "Protecting Canadians: Government of Canada now able to revoke citizenship of dual citizens convicted of terrorism," Government of Canada, May 29, 2015.

47. "It's official—second-class citizenship goes into effect," British Columbia Civil Liberties Association, June 3, 2015. https://bccla.org/2015/06/its-official-second-class-citizenship-goes-into-effect/.

48. Audrey Macklin, "The Return of Banishment: Do the New Denationalisation Policies Weaken Citizenship?," European Union Democracy Observatory on Citizenship. http://eudo-citizenship.eu/commentaries/citizenship-forum/citizenship-forum-cat/1268-the-return-of-banishment-do-the-new-denationalisation-policies-weaken-citizenship.

49. Thomas Wolkom, "Conservative 'barbaric practices' bill panders to fear of immigrants," *Toronto Star*, November 7, 2014.

50. Neil Macdonald, "The barbaric cultural practice of election pronouncements," CBC News, website, October 6, 2015.

51. "Concluding observations of the Committee against Torture: Canada," United Nations Committee Against Torture, June 25, 2012. http://www2.ohchr.org/english/bodies/cat/docs/CAT.C.CAN.CO.6.doc.

52. "What Omar Khadr's lawyer said: 'Mr Harper is a bigot'," *Toronto Star*, May 7, 2015.

53. "Omar Khadr should have served youth sentence, Supreme Court rules," *The Canadian Press*, May 14, 2015.

54. "PM Speaks at Eid on the Hill," The Prime Minister's Office, November 23, 2011.

55. Catherine Solyom, "Indian leader's credibility questioned," *Montreal Gazette*, November 15, 2012.

56. Robert Frank, "West Islander elected to head India Canada Organization," *The Suburban*, February 20, 2013.

57. Amanada Connolly, "Canadian Muslim leaders wary of Stephen Harper's Ramadan meal motives," *iPolitics*, June 24, 2015.

58. Susana Mas, "Justin Trudeau's 2011 mosque visit draws fire from Steven Blaney," CBC News, website, August 6, 2014.

59. "Speaking points for the Hon Jason Kenney, PC, MP, Minister of Citizenship, Immigration and Multiculturalism on the occasion of a breakfast meeting hosted by the Islamic Society of North America," Citizenship and Immigration Canada (via The Internet Achive). http://web.archive.org/web/20111228020713/http://www.cic.gc.ca/english/department/media/speeches/2008/2008-11-29.asp.

60. Michael Petrou, "Jason Kenney's speech to Islam Society of North America removed from government (and personal) websites," *Maclean's*, July 18, 2013.

61. Video of the meeting can be seen at: https://youtu.be/NwxIfg1ZDlY.

62. "Egyptian reformers deserve better than Stephen Harper's cold shrug," *Toronto Star*, January 23, 2014.

63. "Canada's Foreign Minister visits Head of Ahmadiyya Muslim Jamaat in London," Ahmadiyya Muslim Jamat International, January 25, 2012. https://www.alislam.org/egazette/press-release/canadas-foreign-minister-visits-head-of-ahmadiyya-muslim-jamaat-in-london/.

64. "Harper says Canadian Muslims condemning attacks on soldiers very important," *The Canadian Press*, December 4, 2014.

65. Siddiqui, "Resist the American way of tackling terrorism," *Toronto Star*, October 25, 2014.

66. Siddiqui, "Not much Islamic about Islamic Pakistan," *Toronto Star*, March 6, 2011.

67. "Canada should aid Syrian refugees in a fair and balanced way," *Toronto Star*, December 14, 2014.

68. "PMO sought political gain in prioritizing certain Syrian refugees: sources," CTV News, website, October 8, 2015.

69. Mark Steyn, "The future belongs to Islam," *Maclean's*, October 20, 2006.

70. "Commission statement concerning issues raised by complaints against *Maclean's* Magazine," Ontario Human Rights Commission, April 9, 2008.

71. Siddiqui, "Hate laws a reasonable limit on free speech," *Toronto Star*, June 22, 2008.

72. *Saskatchewan (Human Rights Commission) v. Whatcott* [2013], Supreme Court of Canada, 2013 SCC 11 (via Lexum).

73. Neil Macdonald, "Ottawa cites hate crime laws when asked about its 'zero tolerance' for Israel boycotters," CBC News, website, May 11, 2015.

74. Lucas Powers, New anti-terror bill could put chill on freedom of speech," CBC News, website, January 29, 2015.

75. Siddiqui, "How Harperies play their divisive anti-Muslim games," *Toronto Star*, March 10, 2015.

76. "IJV Canada Condemns Jason Kenney's Attack On Free Speech," *Independent Jewish Voices Canada*, March 9, 2012. http://ijvcanada.org/2012/ijv-canada-condemns-jason-kenneys-attack-on-free-speech/.

77. Siddiqui, "Canadian Jews wade in on Arab-Israeli conflict," *Toronto Star*, August 1, 2013.

78. Gerald Caplan, "Why won't Ottawa help Gaza's children?" *The Globe and Mail*, January 9, 2015.

79. Siddiqui, "How Harper is courting South Asians," *Toronto Star*, April 24, 2011.

80. *Ishaq v. Canada (Citizenship and Immigration)* [2015], Federal Court of Canada, 2015 FC 156 (via The Canadian Legal Information Institute).

81. Justin Ling, "We spoke to Canada's Immigration Minister About Refugees, Niqabs, and Terrorists," *VICE News*, June 10, 2015

82. Mary Allen, *Police-reported hate crime in Canada, 2013*, Statistics Canada, June 9, 2015. http://www.statcan.gc.ca/pub/85-002-x/2015001/article/14191-eng.pdf.

83. House of Commons Debates, 41st Parliament (Second Session), Government of Canada, June 11, 2015.

84. *Canada (Citizenship and Immigration) v. Ishaq* [2015], Federal Court of Appeal, 2015 FCA 194.

85. Sean Fine, "Federal court rejects Ottawa's bid to suspend niqab ruling," *The Globe and Mail*, October 5, 2015.

86. "Zunera Ishaq, who challenged ban on niqab, takes citizenship oath wearing it," CBC News, website, October 5, 2015.

87. Andrew Chung, "Quebec niqab bill would make Muslim women unveil," *Toronto Star*, March 25, 2010.

88. Bob Hepburn, "How Stephen Harper came to love the politics of fear," *Toronto Star*, March 21, 2015.

89. Sheema Khan, "Hate it if you want, but don't ban the niqab," *The Globe and Mail*, December 14, 2011.

90. Jennifer Ditchburn, "Canada stands with peaceful Muslims, Kenney says," *The Globe and Mail*, March 7, 2015.

91. Siddiqui, "Harper learning to separate Islam from terrorism," *Toronto Star*, October 11, 2014.

92. Jennifer Ditchburn, "Defence minister reaches out to Muslims," *The Canadian Press*, March 7, 2015.

93. "2011 National Household Survey," Statistics Canada, Government of Canada, 2011. http://www12.statcan.gc.ca/nhs-enm/index-eng.cfm.

94. Shanifa Nasser, "Ontario imams urging Muslims to vote in federal election," CBC News, website, April 3, 2015.

95. Stephanie Levitz, "PM's Ramadan dinner shows the importance of the Muslim voting bloc," *The Canadian Press*, June 28, 2015.

96. Murtaza Hussain, "Leading GOP Candidates to Appear at Event Hosted by Anti-Muslim Conspiracist," *The Intercept*, July 23, 2015.

97. Allan Rappeport, "GOP Field Wrestles With Questions on Islam and the Presidency," *The New York Times*, September 20, 2015.

98. Laura Stone, "Majority of Canadians support Canada's ISIS mission," *Global News*, February 13, 2015.

99. "Rania El-Alloul declines $50K crowdfunded donation," CBC News, website, March 13, 2015.

100. Lauren O'Neil, "Harper's niqab comments inspire snarky Twitter hashtag: #DressCodePM," CBC News, website, March 11, 2015.

101. *Muslim Americans: No Signs of Growth in Alienation or Support for Extremism*, Pew Research Center, August 2011, http://www.people-press. org/2011/08/30/muslim-americans-no-signs-of-growth-in-alienation-or-support-for-extremism/, and John L Esposito and Dalia Mogahed, *Who Speaks for Islam?: What a Billion Muslims Really Think* (NY: Gallup Press, 2007).

102. Aaron Wherry, "For the record: Justin Trudeau on liberty and the niqab," *Maclean's*, March 10, 2015.

103. David Schazner, Charles Kurzman and Ebrahim Moosa, *Anti-Terror Lessons of Muslim-Americans*, January 6, 2010.

104. Siddiqui, "Wars on Muslims are what's stoking terrorism," *Toronto Star*, January 28, 2015.

105. *Syndicat Northcrest v. Amselem* [2004], Supreme Court of Canada, 2004 SCR 47 (via Lexum).

106. Siddiqui, "Harper should follow our secular law on niqab," *Toronto Star*, March 14, 2015.

107. Allen, "Police-reported hate crime in Canada, 2013."

108. "Laïcité and the Skirt," *The New York Times*, May 1, 2015.

109. Sadakat Kadri, *Heaven and Earth: A Journey Through Sharia Law from the Desserts of Ancient Arabia to the Streets of the Modern Muslim World* (New York: Farrar, Straus and Giroux, 2012), 47.

110. Douglas Quan, "Zunera Ishaq on why she fought to wear a niqab during citizenship ceremony: 'A personal attack on me and Muslim women,'" *National Post*, February 16, 2015.

111. "Mulcair: 'Harper mosque comment form of Islamophobia,'" CBC News, website, February 2, 2015.

112. "Trudeau accuses Harper of stroking prejudice against Muslims," *The Canadian Press*, March 10, 2015.

Speaking to Post-secular Society: The Aga Khan's Public Discourse

1. Jürgen Habermas, "Notes on a post-secular society," signandsight.com. 2008. Retrieved November 11, 2013, from http://www.signandsight.com/features/1714.html.

2. Aga Khan, *Where Hope Takes Root* (Vancouver: Douglas & McIntyre, 2008), 120-21.

3. Adrienne Clarkson, "Introduction" in Aga Khan, *Where Hope Takes Root*, 6.

4. Karim H Karim, "At the Interstices of Tradition, Modernity and Postmodernity: Ismaili Engagements with Contemporary Canadian Society," in Farhad Daftary (ed.), *A Modern History of the Ismailis*. (London: IB Tauris, 2011), 265-94.

5. *Where Hope Takes Root*, 96.

6. Richard Neuhaus, *The Naked Public Square: Religion and Democracy in*

America. 2nd ed. (Grand Rapids, MI: Eerdmans Publishing, 1988).

7. Hayat Salam (ed.). *Expressions of Islam in Buildings* (Geneva: Aga Khan Trust for Culture, 1991), 24.

8. Government of Canada, *Canadian Charter of Rights and Freedoms* (Ottawa: Government of Canada, 1982).

9. Karim H Karim and Faiza Hirji, "Religion and State in a Pluralist Nation: Policy Challenges in Contemporary Canadian Society," *Diversity* 6:1 (Winter 2008), 109-112; Gérard Bouchard and Charles Taylor. Building the Future: *A Time for Reconciliation* (Quebec City, PQ: Government of Quebec, 2008).

10. Daniel Lerner, *The Passing of Traditional Society: Modernizing the Middle East* (Glencoe, Illinois: Free Press, 1958), 45.

11. Donald Eugene Smith, *Religion and Political Development* (Boston: Little, Brown and Company, 1970), 14.

12. Hisham Sharabi, "Islam and Modernization in the Arab World" in JH Thompson and RD Reischauer (eds.), *Modernization of the Arab World* (Princeton: D Van Nostrand, 1966), 26.

13. Habermas.

14. Northrop Frye, *The Great Code: The Bible and Literature* (Toronto: University of Toronto Press, 2006).

15. *Where Hope Takes Root*, 127.

16. Ibid, 125-26.

17. Daryoush Mohammad Poor, *Authority without Territory: The Aga Khan Development Network and the Ismaili Imamate* (New York: Palgrave Macmillan, 2014); Jonah Steinberg, *Ismaili Modern: Globalization and Identity in a Muslim Community* (Chapel Hill, NC: University of North Carolina Press, 2010); and Karim H Karim, "The Aga Khan Development Network: Shia Ismaili Islam," in Stephen M Cherry and Helen Rose Ebaugh (eds.), *Global Religious Movements Across Borders* (London: Ashgate Publishers, 2014), 143-60.

18. Aga Khan, "Address of His Highness the Aga Khan to both Houses of the Parliament of Canada in the House of Commons Chamber," Ottawa, February 27, 2014. Aga Khan Development Network website. Retrieved April 21, 2014 from http://www.akdn.org/Content/1253/Address-of-His-Highness-the-Aga-Khan-to-both-Houses-of-the-Parliament-of-Canada-in-the-House-of-Commons-Chamber-Ottawa.

19. Marc Van Grondelle, *The Ismailis in the Colonial Era: Modernity, Empire and Islam* (London: Hurst Publishers, 2009).

20. *Where Hope Takes Root*, 95.

21. Government of Quebec Bill n°60: Charter affirming the values of State secularism and religious neutrality and of equality between women and men, and providing a framework for accommodation requests (2014).

22. Aga Khan, "Speech by His Highness the Aga Khan at the Graduation Ceremony of the University of Alberta," Edmonton, Alberta, June 9, 2009. Aga Khan Development Network website. Retrieved September 19, 2012 from http://

www.akdn.org/Content/767.

23. Aga Khan, "Interview by António Marujo and Faranaz Keshavjee," Paroquias de Portugal NanoWisdoms: Archiving Knowledge from the Imamat website. Retrieved July 23, 2008 from http://www.nanowisdoms.org/nwblog/8861/.

24. *Where Hope Takes Root*, 61.

25. "Address of His Highness the Aga Khan to both Houses of the Parliament."

26. *Where Hope Takes Root*, 95.

The Framing of Canadian Muslims

1. Conservative Party of Canada. "Not the Way We Do Things Here." Edmonton West Conservative Association, April 2, 2015.

2. Lynda Clarke, *Women in Niqab Speak: A Study of the Niqab in Canada*, CCMW, January 7, 2014. See also website.

3. Quebec Bill n°94: An Act to establish guidelines governing accommodation requests within the Administration and certain institutions. Website,. Assemble Nationale Quebec.

4. "No Bill 94 Coalition Statement". Ontario Women's Justice Network. Date unknown, but see http://owjn.org/owjn_2009/-about-us/303-opposition-to-bill-94-in-quebec.

5. Quebec Bill n°60: Charter affirming the values of State secularism and religious neutrality and of equality between women and men, and providing a framework for accommodation requests. Website. Assemble Nationale Quebec.

6. Philip Authier. "Quebec releases controversial 'values charter', proposes that anyone giving, receiving public services would need face uncovered." National Post. September 10, 2013. Also see website.

7. "Secular Values, the Liberal Way: Quebec Tables New Legislation." CTV. Montreal, June 10, 2015. http://montreal.ctvnews.ca/secular-values-the-liberal-way-quebec-tables-new-legislation-1.2415703.

8. Quebec Bill N°59: An Act to Enact the Act to Prevent and Combat Hate Speech and Speech Inciting Violence and to Amend Various Legislative Provisions to Better Protect Individuals—National Assembly of Québec." Website. Assemble National Quebec.

9. Ian L Macdonald, "Harper riding terror to new popularity in Quebec". *Toronto Star*. February 21, 2015. http://www.thestar.com/opinion/commentary/2015/02/21/harper-riding-terror-to-new-popularity-in-quebec.html.

10. R. v. N.S. Supreme Court. December 20, 2012. https://scc-csc.lexum.com. Web. August 7, 2015. https://scc-csc.lexum.com/scc-csc/scc-csc/en/item/12779/index.do.

11. Multani v. Commission Scolaire Marguerite-Bourgeoys. Supreme Court. February 3, 2002. https://scc-csc.lexum.com. Web. August 7, 2015. https://scc-csc.lexum.com/scc-csc/scc-csc/en/item/15/index.do.

12. Amira El-Ghawaby, "Dr Barbara Perry on Islamophobia," *rabble.ca*. http://rabble.ca/podcasts/shows/needs-no-introduction/2012/10/dr-barbara-perry-islamophobia.

13. See http://www.nccm.ca/programs/defending-rights.

14. "Montreal Woman Launches Legal Action Seeking Clarity on Religious Freedom in Quebec Courts." http://www.nccm.ca/montreal-woman-launches-legal-action-seeking-clarity-on-religious-freedom-in-quebec-courts-une-montrealaise-lance-un-recours-juridique-pour-obtenir-clarification-sur-la-liberte-de-religion-dans-les/.

15. John Geddes, "On Chris Alexander's 'hijab' reference" *Maclean's*, February 18, 2015. http://www.macleans.ca/politics/ottawa/on-chris-alexanders-hijab-reference/.

16. Justin Ling, "We Spoke to Canada's Immigration Minister About Refugees, Niqabs, and Terrorists" *VICE*, June 15, 2015. http://www.vice.com/en_ca/read/we-spoke-to-canadas-immigration-minister-about-refugees-niqabs-and-terrorists.

17. Edward W Said, *Orientalism* (New York: Vintage, 1979).

18. Karim H Karim, *Islamic Peril: Media and Global Violence* (Montreal: Black Rose, 2000), 62.

19. David Fox, "Disney Will Alter Song in 'Aladdin'" *Los Angeles Times*. July 10, 1993. http://articles.latimes.com/1993-07-10/entertainment/ca-11747_1_altered-lyric.

20. "Zero Tolerance for Barbaric Cultural Practices Act Receives Royal Assent." Government of Canada, June 18, 2015. http://news.gc.ca/web/article-en.do?nid=989099.

21. "Perpetuating Myths, Denying Justice: "Zero Tolerance for Barbaric Cultural Practices Act'" http://www.salc.on.ca. South Asian Legal Clinic.

22. Alia Hogben, "FEMICIDE, Not Honour Killing by Alia Hogben." *Kingston-Whig Standard*, February 4, 2012. http://ccmw.com/femicide-not-honour-killing-by-alia-hogben/.

23. Amin A Muhammad, "Preliminary Examination of So-called 'Honour Killings' in Canada." Family, Children and Youth Section, Department of Justice Canada, 2010. http://www.justice.gc.ca/eng/rp-pr/cj-jp/fv-vf/hk-ch/index.html.

24. George Lakoff, *Don't Think of an Elephant!: Know Your Values and Frame the Debate: The Essential Guide for Progressives,* (White River Junction, VT: Chelsea Green Pub., 2004). xi.

25. Marie-Danielle Smith, "Weak Link Found between Religion, Terrorism for Canada." *Embassy*. http://www.embassynews.ca/news/2015/05/20/Weak-link-between-religion-terrorism-Canada/47109.

26. Alex Boutilier, "CSIS Highlights White Supremacist Threat Ahead of Radical Islam," *Toronto Star*, March 15, 2015.

27. John Baglow, "Bill C-51: Tories Cynically Surf Panic Wave for Political Ends" *Toronto Star*, February 8, 2015. Web. http://www.thestar.com/opinion/

commentary/2015/02/08/bill-c-51-tories-cynically-surf-panic-wave-for-political-ends.html.

28. Jim Bronskill, "4 Former PMs Call For Stronger Security Oversight." *The Huffington Post*. http://www.huffingtonpost.ca/2015/02/19/former-pms-call-for-bette_n_6713018.html.

29. "Support for Bill C51 Waning." *The Forum Poll*. August 7, 2015. http://poll.forumresearch.com/post/256/most-see-bill-having-negative-effect-on-their-lives/.

30. Dan Taekema, "Journalist Group and Civil Liberties Association Start Constitutional Challenge to Anti-terrorism Bill C-51" *Toronto Star*, July 21, 2015.

31. Carmen Cheung, "Either You're with Us, or You Are with the Terrorists," BC Civil Liberties Association, March 13, 2015. https://bccla.org/2015/03/either-youre-with-us-or-you-are-with-the-terrorists/.

32. Joseph Brean, "'Murderous Misfits,' or Something Else? Halifax Mass-killing Plot Relights Thorny Task of Defining Terrorism." *National Post*, February 17, 2015. http://news.nationalpost.com/news/canada/murderous-misfits-or-something-else-halifax-mass-killing-plot-relights-thorny-task-of-defining-terrorism.

33. Errol Mendes, "Politicians' Frothy Rhetoric Gives Undue Credibility to Extremists and Thugs." *iPolitics*. January 18, 2015. http://ipolitics.ca/2015/01/18/politicians-frothy-rhetoric-gives-undue-credibility-to-extremists-and-thugs/.

34. "Words Make Worlds," National Security Criminal Investigations. August 7, 2015. http://publications.gc.ca/collections/collection_2012/grc-rcmp/PS64-98-2007-eng.pdf.

35. Alex Boutilier, "CSIS highlights white supremacist threat ahead of radical Islam," *Toronto Star*. March 15, 2015. http://www.thestar.com/news/canada/2015/03/15/csis-highlights-white-supremacist-threat-ahead-of-radical-islam.html.

36. Zijad Delic, *Canadian Islam: Belonging and Loyalty*, (Ottawa: Kirtas Publishing, 2014). 56.

37. Katherine Bullock, "Toward a Framework for Investigating Muslim Women and Political Engagement in Canada," in *Islam in the Hinterlands: Exploring Muslim Cultural Politics in Canada*. ed. Jasmin Zine, (Vancouver: UBC, 2012). 107.

38. Lakeoff, xiii.

39. Ibid.

40. Ibid.

41. Daniel Kahneman, *Thinking, Fast and Slow* (New York: Farrar, Straus and Giroux, 2011). 418.

42. Peter Morey, and Amina Yaqin. *Framing Muslims: Stereotyping and Representation after 9/11*, (Cambridge, MA: Harvard UP, 2011). 216.

The Future of Islam in North America

1. This essay is dedicated to Dana Pierce, Alan Bernier, Susette McCann, John Fleener and to the memory of the following: Gerry Kramer, Neil Leader, Edna Graf, Dave Graf, Paul Henderson, Steve Cox, David Wolsk and Steve Toomey. The final form of this essay has benefited substantially from Shamas Nanji's critique of an earlier draft.

2. Remark number 309, *Philosophical Investigations* (2001), edited and translated by G. E. M. Anscombe.

3. The discussion presented here is necessarily concise due to limitations of space. I hope to present a fuller discussion of this subject in a future publication.

4. For the purposes of this essay the term "North America" refers to Canada and the United States taken together, given their common liberal democratic political, social and cultural premises and the continent-wide organizational reach of the major religious denominations. However, where appropriate, the differences between the Canadian and American polities are noted and discussed.

5. The term "denomination" is the closest American rendering of the term *madhhab* that represents, in the Islamic religious context, the institutional complex comprising religious/spiritual leadership (and its training), intellectual institutions, masjids, religious education of the young, the rules governing family, social and economic life, and other communal practices centred on a distinctive understanding of Islamic faith (*īmān*).

6. The term "Shariah" [*sharīʿah*] is an all-embracing term comparable to "American law" and "Canadian law." The specific rules of conduct and other procedures for regulating social life ("codes" and "statutes" in the American and Canadian legal systems, as in "the US Code") collectively form the *fiqh*. Jurisprudence (*usūl al-fiqh*) is the science of the foundational principles and methods of interpreting the Quran and Hadith and of deriving new rules. Legal specialists (*muftīs*) offer non-binding opinions (*fatwās*) to judges (*qāḍīs*) or to parties in a legal dispute. [Instead of giving the Arabic plural of some technical terms used in this essay, the convention adopted here is to treat the singular word as though it is an English word and attach the English suffix "s" to obtain its plural. Thus (Arabic) *khutbah* + (English) s = *khutbahs* (instead of the Arabic plural *khutab*); *fatwā* + s = *fatwās* (instead of *fatāwā*); *qāḍīs* (instead of *quḍāt*); and so on.]

7. *Time Magazine* (December 11, 2000 issue) counted Ramadan among the top 100 innovative thinkers of the 21st century.

8. This is the title of one of Ramadan's books: *To Be A European Muslim: A Study of Islamic Sources in the European Context* (1999).

9. The proposals are presented in his *Radical Reform: Islamic Ethics and Liberation* (2009).

10. I have more to say about these traditions later in this essay.

11. Williams set up his colony in 1636 on a tract of land gifted to him by the Narragansett sachems (chiefs) Canonicus and Miantonomi. In 1638 Williams, joined by other exiles from Massachusetts that included Anne Hutchinson and William Coddington, established a settlement on Aquidneck Island (Rhode Island).

12. Williams's pioneering contribution to the principle of liberty of conscience as a political principle in the American Constitution has recently been resurrected by the prominent American philosopher Martha Nussbaum from the marginalization it has suffered in the historiography of the American Constitution that accords undue influence to the English Enlightenment philosopher John Locke. Martha Nussbaum, *Liberty of Conscience: In Defense of America's Tradition of Religious Equality* (2008).

13. The settlers, led by Williams, agreed to a constitution that recognized and protected the principle of liberty of conscience. Fearing for their independence, they applied for a royal charter from England, which was granted in 1644. A second charter became necessary after the restoration of royal rule in England in 1660. Charles II of England granted the Royal Charter of 1663 to the Colony of Rhode Island and Providence Plantations. The principle of liberty of conscience was enshrined in this charter which remained in force beyond American Independence (1776) until 1843, when the state [Rhode Island] adopted the new constitution.

14. This essay is concerned with Judaism as a religious and spiritual tradition that stretches back nearly four millennia to Abraham who, according to the Quran, inaugurated monotheism and preached it to his people. The contemporary international politics of the Israel-Palestine conflict lie outside the scope that I have defined for the subject of the present discussion.

15. The other two are the Reconstructionist and Conservative movements.

16. Sally Jane Priesand became the first female rabbi in America on June 3, 1972, after graduating from the Hebrew Union College-Jewish Institute of America, which trains Reform rabbis.

17. Reform activity in the Muslim world covers a wide area and is often equated with modernization based on Western models—for example, modernizing the school system in Muslim-majority states, or state-initiated modernizations of the commercial and legal sectors as is now firmly entrenched in post-colonial Muslim states like Pakistan, Egypt and other Arab countries. Such "reforms" do not involve any fundamental rethinking of the Quran or Shariah but rather an expedient appeal to scripture to justify a decision already taken. Indeed, in most cases the typically authoritarian Muslim-majority state uses its power to impose modernization by fiat, bypassing the religious establishment altogether.

18. The Arabic word *al-qur'ān* means "the reciting." That the Quran is not a written text—"writing on parchment" (*kitāban fī qirtās*)—is declared by the Quran itself at *Al-An'ām* 6:7 (The Cattle). The best concise account of the place the Quran occupies in the daily religious life of the ordinary believer is by William A. Graham and Navid Kermani, "Recitation and Aesthetic Reception," in *The Cambridge Companion to the Qur'ān* (2006), edited by Jane Dammen McAuliffe, pp.115-141.

19. For example, when the believer recites the words of the Quran (*Al-Fātihah*, 1:6): *ihdinā al-sirāt al-mustaqīm* ("guide us along the straight path"), he or she is addressing God with words supplied by God.

20. Rabbi Harold Kushner is rabbi in the Conservative movement and one of the most prominent rabbis in America. In his book, *Living the Life That Matters: Resolving the Conflict Between Conscience and Success* (2001), Rabbi Kushner explains the concept of conscience by discussing the story of Jacob in the Book of Genesis. His insightful analysis comes not just from bookish erudition and hermeneutical dexterity—he holds a doctorate in the humanities—but also from years of experience counselling ordinary men and women and helping them find solutions to their ethical problems.

21. This is the point made by Graham and Kermani in their article, "Recitation" (note 18), pp. 119-120.

22. Ramadan has chosen to define Shariah ahistorically and abstractly as the "Way" that finds expression in history as *usūl al-fiqh* (jurisprudence), *fiqh* (rules or "statutes") and *fatwā* (legal opinion). This is a very unfortunate choice. The word "Shariah" is universally taken, by ordinary Muslims and by Muslim and non-Muslim scholars and states, to refer to the religious legal system that governs the lives of the world's billion-plus Muslims today (as it did in the past). It is the Muslim counterpart of the Jewish religious law, *halakhah*. The term "Shariah" embraces much more than just the Quran, Hadith and the textual corpus of the legal tradition. It also includes the institutional universe comprising *madrasahs* (Al-Azhar in Egypt, for example) for the training of the legal scholars many of whom later serve as judges (*qādī*) in the Shariah courts of modern Muslim states. Personal status and family law today is overwhelmingly governed by the rules of the Shariah. The intellectual traditions that are integral to the historical Shariah, such as *ijtihād* (setting aside one's personal biases and conscientiously doing the utmost intellectually to discern God's will regarding the issue at hand) and the *ijāzah* (permission granted by the expert scholar in a specific topic to his student to teach that topic), are also distinctive to it. Muslims understand the Shariah to be the expression of God's Will (which *ijtihād* seeks to discern). A much more suitable term, used by the Quran itself, to convey the abstract idea of "The Way" is *al-sirāt al-mustaqīm* (The Straight Path). The historical Shariah can then be meaningfully regarded (by Muslims subscribing to a legalist conception

of Islam) as the worldly manifestation of *al-sirāt al-mustaqīm*.

23. Ramadan describes a range of issues for which Muslims, especially the youth, seek legal rulings from religious scholars. See especially: *To Be a European Muslim* (1999); *Western Muslims and the Future of Islam* (2005); and *Islam, the West and the Challenges of Modernity* (2001).

24. Ramadan summarizes his thesis in *Radical Reform: Islamic Ethics and Liberation* (2009), pp. 1-38.

25. "It has indeed become impossible to be both a specialist in scriptural sources and perfectly acquainted with all the scientific, economic, and social knowledge of one's own time." *Radical Reform*, p. 86.

26. *Radical Reform*, p. 124.

27. *Radical Reform*, p. 83. According to Ramadan, alongside the textual Revelation (the Quran), there is a second Revelation, the Universe. The text scholars study the Quran and Hadith, while the context scholars study the Universe via the human and natural sciences (pp. 85-100).

28. Ramadan elaborates on these two categories of scholars in *Radical Reform*, pp. 130-133.

29. *Radical Reform*, p. 73.

30. *Radical Reform*, p. 130.

31. Belgium may be said to have two proprietor nations, the Flemish and Walloon, contending with each other for control of the state so as to turn it into an instrument safeguarding and advancing their respective interests.

32. I have patterned the term "proprietor state" after the term "settler state."

33. Britain is comprised of four "nations" (English, Scot, Welsh and Northern Irish) but only the English wield de facto proprietor nation control over the British state, to the growing resentment of the Scots. The rise of Scottish nationalism and its near-clean sweep in the elections of May 2015 reflect Scottish desire to become proprietors in their own right and acquire Scotland as their proprietor state. Intensifying nationalism among the four United Kingdom "nations," at present strongest among the Scots and the English, is threatening to destroy the union.

34. The "Muslim Question" echoes the European debate over the "Jewish Question" that sought to resolve the legal, civil and social status of Jews as a minority within the nation-state model. Hitler had described his scheme to destroy the Jews as "the final solution to the Jewish question." While the "Muslim Question" is very germane in Europe, to insist on seeing close parallels between the present-day situation of Muslims in North America and that of the Jews in nineteenth-century Europe, and to insinuate that Canadian and American Muslims are being subjected to European-style anti-Semitism, is to seriously misunderstand the fundamentally different set of principles governing the Canadian and American political systems. Abdulmohamed Kazempur's *The*

Muslim Question in Canada: A Story of Segmented Integration (2014), is the latest addition to this type of thinking.

35. There is a vast body of literature on nationalism and the nation-state that is impossible to summarize, let alone survey comprehensively, in the limited space available for this essay. A recent concise survey of the major theories is by Azar Gat, *Nations: The Long History and Deep Roots of Political Ethnicity and Nationalism* (2013). Benedict Anderson's very influential book, *Imagined Communities: Reflections on the Origin and Spread of Nationalism* (1986), does not distinguish between "national community" and "political community," a distinction that is central to my Proprietor State model. In fact, he equates the nation with the political community when he writes: "the nation: it is an imagined political community" (p. 15). Defined this way, the nation-state cannot treat the non-national citizen as equal to the national citizen.

36. The Peace of Westphalia of 1648 strengthened the link between religion and the nation: the parties to the treaty agreed to recognize the principle that the ruler's religion would become the established religion of his kingdom. Subjects who did not share the ruler's religion became "aliens" who were not accorded equal treatment by the state and came under pressure to leave the territory.

37. For example, by seizing and nationalizing church property during the French Revolution and requiring churches or congregations to form associations as administrative units within townships.

38. The Canadian state is not as neutral as the US. Taxpayer support for religious groups exists not just in Quebec, where it is particularly strong, but in anglophone Canada too.

39. The European Union's Preamble of the Charter of Fundamental Rights refers to "the peoples of Europe," their "common values," and their "spiritual and moral heritage," and reassures the nation-states that it respects the "national identities of the Member States." The words "national" and "States" in the same sentence betray the nation-state model governing the Charter. Predictably, the Charter locates the identity and sovereignty of the nation-state in national/cultural, not political, identity. By guaranteeing the "national identity" of proprietor nation-states, the Union has handcuffed itself and made it extremely difficult, if not impossible, to persuade or compel these entrenched "nationalities" to give up their control over the state. (The text of the Charter is available at the European Commission's web site: http://eur-lex.europa.eu/LexUriServ/LexUriServ.do?uri=OJ:C:2010:083:0389:0403:en:PDF.)

40. "Cultural identity" in this context refers to the culture of the proprietor nation as a marker of identity separating it from the culture of non-national citizen-aliens. The French (in France and in Quebec) root their collective identity in French language and culture rather than in ethnicity.

41. But in the case of mixed marriages one does say, for example, "My mother

was Danish and my father French." This usage is meaningful because the child has acquired a biologically derived dual ethnic/national identity.

42. It also explains why it is meaningful to speak of "Americanization" as a process that is distinct from "Westernization" and for which there is no European counterpart at the nation-state level or European Union level (what would "Europeanization" mean?). Americanization is not about acquiring Western culture but about acquiring political values (centred on citizenship as political identity) through which the citizen becomes a competent participant in the American political system (for example, respecting the First Amendment, joining political parties, serving on juries, engaging in informed debates about current affairs, and so on). Unfortunately, this distinction between Americanization and Westernization is lost in the book edited by Yvonne Yazbeck Haddad and John L. Esposito, *Muslims on the Americanization Path?* (2000). It is a little puzzling to find chapters in the book dealing with African American Muslims. Are the editors suggesting that African American Muslims (who have been in America much longer than either of the two editors) are not quite American enough—presumably because their Islamization has rendered their American identity suspect?—and need to be fed through the Americanization process alongside immigrant Muslims to make them complete Americans again? If not, why include them in a book that deals with *Americanization*?

43. They were de facto, not de jure, proprietors until the Civil Rights era. Euro-Americans behaved as proprietors in their dealings with Native Americans (the true and original proprietors) and African Americans (whom they owned as slaves). The historic Civil Rights legislation of 1964 clarified the constitutional distinction between political identity and ethnic/cultural identity by freeing political identity from the grip of Euro-American ethnic/cultural identity.

44. "As the Government of the United States of America is not, in any sense, founded on the Christian religion; as it has in itself no character of enmity against the laws, religion, or tranquility, of Mussulmen [Muslims]; and as the said States never entered into any war or act of hostility against any Mahometan [Mohammedan] nation, it is declared by the parties that no pretext arising from religious opinions shall ever produce an interruption of the harmony existing between the two countries." Article 11 of *Treaty of Peace and Friendship between the United States of America and the Bey and Subjects of Tripoli of Barbary*, November 4, 1796. The full text of the treaty is accessible at http://en.wikisource. org/wiki/Treaty_of_Tripoli.

45. I use the forms "proprietor ethnic group," "proprietor nation" and "proprietor group" as synonyms.

46. I have drawn from the following works for my discussion of French *laïcité*: *A History of Modern France*, by Alfred Cobban, 3 vols. (1962-65); *Religious History of Modern France*, by Adrien Dansette, 2 vols. (1961); *Revolution-*

ary France, 1770-1880 (1988), by François Furet; *France, 1814-1940* (1985), by J. P. T. Bury; "Napoleon, the Concordat of 1801 and Its Consequences," by William Roberts, in *Controversial Concordats: The Vatican's Relations with Napoleon, Mussolini, and Hitler* (1999), edited by Frank J. Coppa, pp. 34-80; and *The Birth of Judicial Politics in France: The Constitutional Council in Comparative Perspective* (1992), by Alec Stone Sweet. For information on the Constitutional Council, visit http://en.wikipedia.org/wiki/Constitutional_Council_of_France.

47. The 1905 French law on the separation of the churches and state was enacted on December 9, 1905 by the Third Republic. Prior to that, church-state relations were governed by two sets of laws. The first was the Civil Constitution of the Clergy (1790), which brought the Catholic Church under state control by making it a department of the state and effectively removing it from the authority of the Pope. Catholic clergy were transformed into de facto civil servants receiving state salary. The new republican state seized the French landholdings of the Catholic Church and dismantled the monastic and ecclesiastical orders and other institutions such as abbeys and priories. The second major event on church-state relations was Napoleon's Concordat of 1801, the agreement he reached with Pope Pius VII. The Concordat established Catholicism as the state religion and recognized the state's authority to nominate bishops and pay clerical salaries. In return, the clergy would have to swear oath of allegiance to the state, not to the Pope. The Catholic Church agreed to abandon claims to church lands that the state had seized after 1790. Napoleon supplemented the Concordat with the Organic Articles (1802)—which he promulgated in defiance of the Pope—aimed at regulating public worship in the republic. The Articles effectively gave the state the right to intervene in Catholic affairs. They included rules for public worship, clerical dress code, religious instruction in elementary schools, even how much salary the bishops would receive. The Concordat of Napoleon remained in force until it was replaced by the *laïcité* law of 1905.

48. France is not alone here: nearly every European state's highest court is in the shadows relative to the dominant role of its executive and legislative branches.

49. The French Revolution's *Declaration of the Rights of Man and the Citizen* (1789) explicitly mentions the General Will (Article 6: "Law is the expression of the general will."). Sovereignty and supreme authority rest with the nation (Article 3). Rights and liberties can be limited by the law (nation) (Article 4).

50. Here is Rousseau in his own words: "There is thus a profession of faith which is purely civil and of which it is the sovereign's function to determine the articles, not strictly as religious dogmas, but as the expression of social conscience, without which it is impossible to be a good citizen or a loyal subject. Without being able to oblige anyone to believe these articles, the sovereign can banish from the state anyone who does not believe them; banish him not for

impiety but as an anti-social being, as one unable sincerely to love law and justice, or to sacrifice, if need be, his life to his duty. If anyone, after having publicly acknowledged these same dogmas, behaves as if he did not believe in them, *then let him be put to death* [italics added for emphasis], for he has committed the greatest crime, that of lying before the law." In the next paragraph Rousseau, in spite of his own reluctance to define the dogmas of the civil religion, proceeds to list them: "The dogmas of civil religion must be simple and few in number, expressed precisely and without explanations or commentaries. The existence of an omnipotent, intelligent, benevolent divinity that foresees and provides; the life to come; the happiness of the just; the punishment of sinners; the sanctity of the social contract and the law." *The Social Contract* [translation by Maurice Cranston, 2004], Book IV, Chapter 8, "Civil Religion," p. 166.

51. The great German philosopher George Wilhelm Friedrich Hegel (d. 1831) is another major European Enlightenment philosopher whose concept of the state displays proprietarist thinking. Hegel held that the state is the most advanced manifestation of the Divine Mind in world history. Since the state embodies the Universal Will, freedom consists in surrendering one's will to the state's will. Neither the family nor civil society can fully develop the ethical capacities of the individual; only the state can accomplish this task. He admired the ancient Greek *polis* for its collectivism and cultural homogeneity. Thus the state as the expression of the collective has primacy over the individual. It is impossible here to do justice to the complexity of Hegel's political philosophy and how it treats the relation between political and ethnic/cultural identity. I shall discuss Hegel in detail in a future publication.

52. France's policy towards its Muslim citizens may be set alongside Thomas Jefferson's warnings against state intervention in the religious life of citizens. In the *Virginia Statute for Religious Freedom*, which he authored, he wrote that "our civil rights have no dependence on our religious opinions any more than our opinions in physics or geometry." Further, "to suffer the civil magistrate to intrude his powers into the field of opinion and to restrain the profession or propagation of principles on supposition of their ill tendency is a dangerous fallacy which at once destroys all religious liberty because he being of course judge of that tendency will make his opinions the rule of judgment and approve or condemn the sentiments of others only as they shall square with or differ from his own." Jefferson drafted the statute in 1776 but introduced it into the Virginia General Assembly in 1779. The Assembly adopted it as the state's law in 1786.

53. The *Charlie Hebdo* incident in January 2015 shows that these state-sponsored attempts to produce a pliant "moderate" Islam can be upended by the international context of jihadi Islam that penetrates into France.

54. Martha Nussbaum, *Liberty of Conscience* (2008); Joan Wallach Scott,

The Politics of the Veil (2007); Naomi Davidson, *Only Muslim: Embodying Islam in Twentieth-Century France* (2012); and Mayanthi L. Fernando, *The Republic Unsettled: Muslim French and the Contradictions of Secularism* (2014). All of them, in their distinctive ways, note the French state's agenda of defining and shaping the evolution of Islam in France according to its vision of an *Islam français* (French Islam).

55. The revolutionaries created a revolutionary religion by setting up Reason as the new deity, converting churches into Temples to Reason and establishing liturgies, festivals and congregations of the new religion. Adrien Dansette provides more details in *Religious History of Modern France* (1961), volume 1, pp. 91-114.

56. Mark Mazower also expresses this pessimism about the long-term prospects for Muslims in Europe in his iconoclastic book, *Dark Continent: Europe's Twentieth Century* (1998), pp. 349-350. Mazower's book is far and away the best book on the twentieth-century history of Europe, as is Josep Fontana's *The Distorted Past: A Re-Interpretation of Europe* (1995), for the pre-twentieth-century history of Europe.

57. Martha Nussbaum has also recommended the American political experience to the Europeans as worthy of their serious consideration. "The American constitutional tradition offers insights . . . to European nations newly grappling with religious difference" (pp. 13-14), and further, that this "[constitutional] tradition also suggests that the French law [banning the Muslim headscarf and Jewish yarmulke in French public schools] is an unjustified incursion into an area of religious self-expression that the law ought to protect for all citizens" (p. 14). See her *Liberty of Conscience* (2008), pp. 13-14 and pp. 348-353.

58. That the Quranic laws regulate, but do not ban, polygamy, slavery, and armed violence does not mean, as many Muslims today are at pains to point out, that the Quran promotes these social practices as ideals for a Muslim. These Quranic laws were subsequently incorporated into the body of *fiqh* texts ("statute books") of the Shariah and came to be regarded by later generations of Muslims, especially Muslim men, as license to practice polygamy, own slaves, wage *jihād*, etc.

59. Khaled Abou El Fadl discusses the *fatwās* on high-heeled shoes and "brassieres" in his *Speaking in God's Name: Islamic Law, Authority and Women* (2001), pp. 177-181.

60. The Charter of Rights and Freedoms has not been universally popular among Canada's political elites and constitutional experts. They decry what they see as the new anti-democratic "judicial activism" of the Supreme Court. They mean by "judicial activism" the authority of the Supreme Court to strike down as unconstitutional parliament's decisions and overrule the popular will. It is disheartening to discover that Andrew Petter, currently serving as president of

multiracial and multicultural Simon Fraser University in British Columbia, is one of the strongest critics of the Supreme Court's "judicial activism" and its presumed threat to social democracy. His alarmist critique, *The Politics of the Charter: The Illusive Promise of Constitutional Rights* (2010), displays no interest at all in the subject of individual rights and conscience.

61. The weakness of Canada's Supreme Court (in comparison to the American Supreme Court) is reflected in the use of the term "tolerance" to address cultural differences. The term is not part of the lexicon of American constitutional philosophy, which recognizes and protects the citizen's right to be different from other citizens. But the European proprietor state, representing the will and normative culture of the majority proprietor nation, chooses, for pragmatic reasons (for example, for domestic peace and stability), to "tolerate" cultural values and practices that deviate from its culture, which it establishes as the norm. Tolerance here means that the dominant proprietor nation chooses to refrain from imposing its will on the minority culture and force it to assimilate.

62. The proprietor nation-states of Europe make their case for a national territory—Serbia for the Serbs, Norway for the Norwegians, and so on—on the basis of their centuries-old occupation of this territory. In Canada, on the other hand, the two proprietor nations (English and French) were invaders into First Nations territories which they acquired through conquest. The original proprietors, the First Nations, were dispossessed and confined to tracts of land over which they were allowed to exercise limited autonomy at the sufferance and toleration of the two proprietor nations who control local, provincial, and federal governments. That this sufferance can be withdrawn at the whim of the proprietor nations was rudely made clear by the ugly Oka Crisis that erupted in summer 1990 over attempts by the mayor of Oka (Quebec) to unilaterally grab parts of Mohawk lands and hand them over to a private golf club. Not just the political and business classes, but also the Canadian armed forces were drafted to work in concert as they attempted, unsuccessfully in the end, to dispossess the Mohawks. European invader-settlers in America had deployed the language of the civilization-versus-barbarism paradigm to construct an image of the Indian as a savage, barbarian and wild animal they had to kill and dispossess in order to spread European civilization on the continent. The French Quebeckers expediently activated this cant of conquest—they hurled invectives such as "savages" at the Mohawks—to provide self-anointed moral justifications sanctifying the actions of the mayor of Oka and his French proprietor-nation accomplices. A serviceable entry into this subject is available at en.wikipedia.org/wiki/Oka_ Crisis. One of the best studies of the "cant of conquest" in the dispossession of Native American lands in the US is Francis Jennings' *The Invasion of America: Indians, Colonialism, and the Cant of Conquest*, 1975.

63. The sigh of relief that many Canadians breathed over the defeat of the

Charter of Values (and of the Parti Quebecois in the elections) is only partially justified, for the more troubling underlying issue revealed by the proposal for the Charter of Values is that the federal Charter of Rights and Freedoms contains a loophole that enabled Quebec's Charter of Values to be proposed in the first place. Much scholarly debate has centred on Section 1 of the Charter that allows fundamental rights to be limited under some "reasonable" conditions. But the Quebec proposal spotlights another serious weakness in the federal Charter: Section 33 (1) allows provincial legislatures to overrule sections 2 and sections 7 through 15 for five years, renewable repeatedly for another five years. Section 33 (1) states clearly that the provincial legislation "shall operate notwithstanding a provision included in Section 2 or Sections 7 to 15 of this Charter." Section 2 of the federal Charter lists the fundamental rights, among them "freedom of conscience and religion" and freedom of "thought, belief, opinion, expression." Had the Parti Quebecois won the election in 2014, they would have stood a decent chance of sustaining their argument before the Supreme Court that their proposed provincial Charter was complying with the language and meaning of Section 33 (1) of the federal Charter.

64. The fundamental idea in *ijtihād* as a Shariah principle is that of doing the utmost, conscientiously, in an impartial and self-disciplined manner, to find the correct solution to the problem at hand (typically presented by a believer). Thus, as a technical term in the Shariah, it is intended to underscore the scholar's obligation to do his utmost, conscientiously, to discern God's will regarding the problem for which the sources (Quran, Hadith and legal texts of other scholars) are silent or ambiguous. The scholar is expected—by believers, by fellow scholars and by his teacher (who grants him the permission (*ijāzah*) to engage in *ijtihād*)—to be a person of integrity who can be trusted to set aside his personal convictions and prejudices regarding the problem and instead to heed his conscience in seeking to discover what God would want done to solve it. *Ijtihād* is therefore a far cry from being a license to indulge in "free thinking." Thus the fundamental requirement in *ijtihād* is an ethical one.

65. Singular *hīlah*—tricks, contrivances and stratagems used as deceptive legal fictions intended to bypass clear Quranic and Shariah prohibitions by not seeming to violate them (*A History of Islamic Law* (1964), pp. 139-141; see also his *Conflicts and Tensions in Islamic Jurisprudence* (1969), pp. 87-91).

66. This category is expanding rapidly. The Muslim Progressive Values (MPV: mpvusa.org) is a prominent movement that supports the LGBTQ community and whose advisory board includes the well-known Reza Aslan and Karima Bennoune. A second noteworthy group in this category is AltMuslimah (altmuslimah.com), an all-women online community providing space for women to promote a female-centric practice of Islamic faith. A third group, the Women's Mosque of America (womenmosque.com), received much media

coverage in early 2015 when it was formed. It is self-consciously a women-only movement seeking to provide a safe space to "women to feel welcome, respected, and actively engaged within the Muslim Ummah." The movement seeks to offer women and girls more direct access to the Islamic legal tradition and its scholarship; it thus adheres to the legalist conception of Islamic faith and its practice.

67. Chapter 4, Verse 34. This verse has acquired the character of an "anomaly" that a paradigm is unable to resolve.

68. *Qur'an and Woman: Rereading the Sacred Text from a Woman's Perspective* (1999), pp. 69-78. Kecia Ali discusses this "difficult" verse in her *Sexual Ethics and Islam: Feminist Reflections on Qur'an, Hadith and Jurisprudence* (2006), pp. 117-126.

69. *Inside the Gender Jihad: Women's Reform in Islam* (2006), p. 200. Wadud does not mince her words: "This verse, and the literal implementation of *hudud* [*hudūd*, penal code], both imply an ethical standard of human actions that are archaic and barbarian at this time in history. They are unjust in the ways that human beings have come to experience and understand justice, and hence unacceptable to universal notions of human dignity" (p. 200).

70. Ramadan provides an extensive treatment of these two types of reform in his *Radical Reform*, especially pp. 26-38

71. The Islamic State in Iraq and Syria (ISIS) justifies its frightful savagery and depredations with legal rulings (*fatwā*) from sympathetic legal scholars who not only consult the Quran and the Shariah but also events in Islamic history. Michael Weiss and Hassan Hassan's book, *ISIS: Inside the Army of Terror* (2015), is the best book on the religious commitments of ISIS and the scriptural justifications for its savagery. (See the article in the Manchester Guardian, http://www.theguardian.com/world/2015/feb/08/isis-islamic-state-ideology-sharia-syria-iraq-jordan-pilot.) An English translation of an ISIS *fatwā* citing the Quran (for example, verses 23:5-6) to justify slavery and sex with non-Muslim minors is available at http://www.nybooks.com/articles/archives/2015/sep/24/slavery-isis-rules/.

72. The media have reported incidents in which settlers or rabbis invoke the Bible in support of their views or actions. I will cite two examples: Raffi Berg, "Israel's religious settlers," *BBC News*, August 18, 2003 (http://news.bbc.co.uk/2/hi/middle_east/3144791.stm); and Robert Stone, "Israel at 50: Drowning in History; Jerusalem Has No Past," *New York Times*, May 3, 1998 (http://www.nytimes.com/1998/05/03/magazine/israel-at-50-drowning-in-history-jerusalem-has-no-past.html). The town of Kiryat Arba, near Hebron, is one example of settlers invoking the authority of the Bible to justify their claim to the town.

73. Among those contributing was Albert Einstein, who confesses that his thought is imagistic: he initially sees images to which, in a secondary stage, he tries to give logical formulation: "The words or the language, as they are written

or spoken, do not seem to play any role in my mechanism of thought . . . [The] elements in thought are certain signs and more or less clear images . . . before there is any connection with logical construction in words or other kinds of signs which can be communicated to others." ("Letter to Jacques Hadamard," in *The Creative Process: Reflections on Invention in the Arts and Sciences* (1952), edited by Brewster Ghiselin, pp. 32-33.) Compare this to Avicenna's explanation of what he terms "prophetic inspiration": The inspirations coming from the cosmic active intelligence, which contains the forms of all things, "overflow into the imagination which symbolizes them in sense-imagery and words." *Avicenna's Psychology* (1952), Fazlur Rahman's translation of *Kitāb al-Najāt*, Book II, Chapter VI, pp. 36-37.

74. "The Name and Nature of Poetry," in *The Creative Process*, pp. 90-91.

75. "The Birth of a Poem," in *The Creative Process*, pp. 129-130.

76. The notion that the linguistic form of the Quran expresses Muhammad's *interpretation* of the formless inspiration was introduced into modern scholarship by Fazlur Rahman. In contrasting Ibn Khaldūn's theory of prophecy with the corresponding theories of the Muslim philosophers, Rahman characterizes the philosophers' theory that the prophet generates "symbolic representations" of the divine inspiration as an "interpretation by the prophet himself" of this inspiration. See Fazlur Rahman, *Prophecy in Islam: Philosophy and Orthodoxy* (1958), p. 107.

77. The metaphor comes from optics. Light passes through a prism from one side and is refracted and emerges on the other side as a spectrum of colors. On this analogy, the pre-verbal and pre-conceptual inspiration passes through the "prism" of Muhammad's cognitive system which "refracts" it into the "spectrum" of culture-carrying words (*lisān*) that constitute the Quran.

78. In a remarkable "confessionalist" moment, Muhammad utters self-censuring verses reprimanding him for his ethical lapses. These verses narrate an incident in which a poor blind man interrupts Muhammad while he is talking to some leading member of the Quraysh. Muhammad frowns (*'abasa*) at the man and turns away from him. Right away the verses came upon him, reprimanding him for showing disrespect to the poor man while being respectful to the rich and powerful: "For him who is rich and powerful, to him dost thou [Muhammad] attend with care and respect . . . But as for him who comes to thee in earnest and in fear, to him thou payest no attention." (*'Abasa*, He Frowned, 80:1-10). These verses can be understood as the voice of Muhammad's conscience—which Muhammad took to be God's words—censuring him for his conduct towards the poor blind man. In another verse the Quran urges believers to act with impartiality "even though it be against yourselves, or your parents, or your kinsmen, whether rich or poor." (*Al-Nisā'*, Women, 4:135)

79. Imam Warith Deen Mohammed (d. 2008) was the most prominent

leader in the African American Muslim community. Clearly reflecting an individual-centric conception of Islam and a rejection of the premises of "political Islam," Imam Mohammed taught that "the Qur'an does not show an effort or a plan to build a political community. The effort and plan in the Qur'an is to build people individually (*Al-Islam: Unity and Leadership* (1988), p. 55).

Of the Constitution, he writes: "The Declaration of Independence recognizes a sameness for all people and for all individuals . . . The Constitution of the United States does not base itself upon the identity of a race. It does not base itself upon the identity of a nationality. It bases itself upon the common and universal type, the person that all of us are" (p. 57).

80. This is the title of the book by Asma Afsaruddin, *The First Muslims: History and Memory* (2008). I would aver, however, that already during the Prophet's lifetime we are witnessing two qualitatively different categories of Muslims, those in Mecca whose conception of faith was non-legal and centred on the concept of *īmān* (faith), and those in Medina who subscribed to a legal conception of Islam and who lived under a developing regime of divine commandments embodying the concept of *dīn* (religion). Indeed, the Quran does not refer to the Meccan believer as *muslim* but as *mu'min*. I would therefore reserve the title "First Muslims" to the believers of the Meccan period.

81. The *zakāt* did not become obligatory until after the Prophet migrated to Medina and began to organize Muslims into a community. Prior to that, in Mecca, individual believers helped one another financially on the basis of personal ethical judgment. The masjid as a separate designated building did not exist in Mecca; the Prophet used to pray secretly in the alleys and at the home of his supporters. Later, with 'Umar ibn al-Khattāb's influence, Muhammad and his small band of believers were allowed to pray in the open beside the Ka'ba. Abu Bakr had designated a spot (*masjid*, "the place where one prostrates") for prayers in the courtyard of his home in Mecca. The other core components of the system of worship ('*ibādah*) were also introduced in Medina, where Islam became an institutional religion (*dīn*). See the helpful entries on these subjects in the *Encyclopaedia of Islam* (Second Edition) under "Adhān," "Khutba," "Masdjid," "Salāt," "Wudū'" and "Zakāt."

82. The term "physical reality" embraces more than three-dimensional material objects. It includes radiation, space-time, force fields, dark matter, and of course the laws of nature that do not themselves possess physical attributes yet are proper subjects of inquiry by the physical sciences (although the ontological status of these laws remains an unaddressed question in the philosophy of science).

Muslim scientists in the past, especially astronomers, did not adopt a literalist approach to the Quran's "physical reality" verses. The science-religion relation in Islam is closer in spirit to that in the ancient Mesopotamian, Hindu, Buddhist, ancient Iranian and Chinese religious traditions, none of which experienced the traumatic upheavals suffered by Catholic and Protestant Christianity. The fundamental reason for Christianity's catastrophic encounter with science is that both these major divisions within Western Christianity were heavily vested in the literalism of the Bible's statements about physical reality (for example, that God created the world in six days).

83. This internal "migration" (or "flight") may be construed as a metaphoric and spiritual *hijra*. The Prophet took physical flight (*hijra*) to Medina away from the oppression of the Meccans so that he and his followers might practice their faith freely in Medina. Muslims in North America would be "taking flight" (*hijra*) from the restrictive scripturalist (legalist) Shariah Islam towards a new conscience-based denomination so that they might practice their faith more freely. The several online movements that offer space to women and girls to explore and advance a female-centric approach to Islam (see note 66) may be construed to have taken "flight" from the constricting space of traditional Shariah Islam.

84. In a previous remark (note 42), I took issue with Haddad and Esposito's use of the term "Americanization." Here I would add that, viewed from the perspective of the citizen, Americanization is the process whereby political identity is created and established alongside (but ultimately sovereign over) national/religious/ethnic/cultural identity in the cognitive system of the citizen—a sign outside the US Supreme Court building the day [June 26, 2015] the Court announced its decision on same-sex marriage read: "Our Constitution is our shield against Bible based discrimination towards our gay friends & neighbors." The two identities conceptualize and give voice to conscience in different ways and constitute separate components in the cognitive system. The cognitive political identity is the "internal" counterpart of the "external" political identity defined by the American Constitution and institutionalized in the American system of government—the Constitution "constitutes" the political identity within the American citizen's cognitive system. This Constitution-created political identity defines the ideals of American citizenship, whereas the cultural/religious/ethnic identity is the repository of beliefs, values and practices that are the realities that typically fall short of these ideals or collide with them.

In the Canadian case, because the Charter of Rights and Freedoms was adopted only recently, a distinct political identity that is "sovereign" over cultural identity within the cognitive system of the Canadian citizen remains a work in progress. The Canadian Constitution is not constitutive of political identity in the way the American Constitution is constitutive of American political identity. This difference between these two political identities is reflected in the ubiquity of the American Constitution and Supreme Court in American political, economic and cultural life, in contrast to the relatively weakly registered presence of Canada's Charter of Rights and Supreme Court in Canadian politics and culture.

Bibliography

Mosques and the Making of Muslim Identity

Avcioglu, Nebahat. "Identity-as-Form: The Mosque in the West." *Cultural Analysis* 6 (2007): 91-112.

Gale, R T, and S Naylor. "Religion, Planning and the City: the Spatial Politics of Ethnic Minority Expression in British Cities and Towns." *Ethnicities* 2(3) (2002): 387-409.

Hoernig, Heidi. "Worship in the Suburbs: the Development Experiences of Recent Immigrant Religious Communities." Diss., University of Waterloo, 2006.

Isin, E, and M Siemiatycki. "Making Space for Mosques: Struggles for Urban Citizenship in Diasporic Toronto." *Race, Space and the Law: Unmapping a White Settler Society*. Edited by S Razack. Toronto: Between the Lines, 2002.

Lapidus, Ira. *Muslim Cities in the Later Middle Ages*. Cambridge: Cambridge University Press, 1984.

Leonie, Sandercock, ed. *Making the Invisible Visible: A Multicultural Planning History*. Berkeley: University of California Press, 1998.

Metcalf, Barbara Daly, ed. *Making Muslim Space in North America and Europe*. Berkeley: University of California Press, 1996.

Ramadan, Tariq. *To be a European Muslim*. Leicester: The Islamic Foundation, 1999.

Rodrigues, Pradeep. "A Not So Little Mississauga Mosque Divides a Community." *CanIndia*. December 6, 2013. http://www.canindia.com/2013/12/a-not-so-little-mississauga-mosque-divides-a-community.

Said, Edward. *Orientalism*. New York: Pantheon, 1978.

Sunier, Thiji. *Islam in Beweging*. Amsterdam: Het Spinhuis, 1996.

Walks, R Alan. "The Urban in Fragile, Uncertain, Neoliberal Times: Towards New Geographies of Social Justice?" *Canadian Geographer.* 53 (3) (2009): 345-356.

Reexamining Relations Between Men and Women

Abu-Lughod, Lila. *Do Muslim Women Need Saving?* Cambridge, MA: Harvard University Press, 2013.

Ahmed, Leila. *Women and Gender in Islam: Historical Roots of a Modern Debate.* New Haven: Yale University Press, 1992.

Ahmed, Leila. *A Quiet Revolution: the Veil's Resurgence, from the Middle East to America.* New Haven: Yale University Press, 2011.

Ayub, Muhammad. *Understanding Islamic Finance.* Hoboken, NJ: John Wiley & Sons, 2007.

Courbage, Youssef, and Emmanuel Todd. *A Convergence of Civilizations: the Transformation of Muslim Societies Around the World.* New York: Columbia University Press, 2011.

Haddad, Yvonne Yazbeck, and John L Esposito. *Daughters of Abraham: Feminist Thought in Judaism, Christianity, and Islam.* Gainesville, FL: University Press of Florida, 2001.

Haddad, Yvonne Yazbeck, and John L Esposito. *Islam, Gender, and Social Change.* New York: Oxford University Press, 1998.

Katir, Ismail ibn Umar. *Histoires des prophètes.* Traduit par Messaoud Boudjenoun. Paris: Universel, 2009.

Mir-Hosseini, Ziba. *Gender and Equality in Muslim Family Law: Justice and Ethics in the Islamic Legal Tradition.* London: IB Tauris, 2013.

Rasheed, Madawi. *A Most Masculine State: Gender, Politics and Religion in Saudi Arabia.* Cambridge: Cambridge University Press, 2013.

The Sublime Quran. Translated by Laleh Bakhtiar. www.sublimequran.org.

Who I Really Am: Communicating Islam Across Generations

Ali, Tariq. *The Clash of Civilizations: Crusades, Jihads and Modernity.* London: Verso. 2002.

Roy, Olivier. *Secularism Confronts Islam.* New York: Columbia University Press, 2000.

The Performing Identities of Muslims

Ahmed, Leila. *Women and Gender in Islam: Historical Roots of a Modern Debate.* New Haven: Yale University Press, 1992.

Balibar, Etienne. *Politics and the Other Scene.* London: Verso, 2002.

Brown, Wendy. *Regulating Aversion: Tolerance in the Age of Identity and Empire.* Princeton: Princeton University Press, 2006.

Bullock, Katherine. *Rethinking Muslim Women and the Veil: Challenging Historical & Modern Stereotypes.* Herndon: International Institute of Islamic Thought, 2002.

Burgat, François. *Face to Face with Political Islam.* London: IB Tauris, 2002.

Butler, Judith. *Gender Trouble: Feminism and the Subversion of Identity.* New York: Routledge, 1999.

"The Future of the Global Muslim Population—Projections for 2010-2030." *Pew Research Centre.* January 27, 2011 http://www.pewforum.org/The-Future-of-the-Global-Muslim-Population.aspx.

"GTA woman has niqab pulled off in assault." *CBC News.* November 22, 2011. http://www.cbc.ca/news/canada/toronto/story/2011/11/22/toronto-niqab-mall-assault-video.html.

Jiwani, Yasmin. "Doubling Discourses and the Veiled Other: Mediations of Race and Gender in Canadian Meida." *States of Race: Critical Race Feminism for the 21st Century.* Edited by Sherene Razack, MS Smith, and S Thobani. Toronto: Between the Lines, 2010. 59-86.

Jones, M R. "Spatial Selectivity of the State? The Regulationist Enigma and Local Struggles Over Economic Governance." *Environment and Planning* A 29 (1997): 831-864.

Karim, Karim H. *The Islamic Peril: Media and Global Violence.* Montreal: Black Rose Books, 2000.

Mackey, Eva. *The House of Difference: Cultural Politics and National Identity in Canada.* Toronto: University of Toronto Press, 2002.

Mamdani, Mahmood. *Good Muslim, Bad Muslim: America, the Cold War, and the Roots of Terror.* New York: Pantheon Books, 2004.

Massumi, Brian, ed. *The Politics of Everyday Fear.* Minneapolis: University of Minnesota Press, 1993.

Said, Edward W. *Orientalism.* New York: Pantheon Books, 1978.

Scott, Joan Wallach. *The Politics of the Veil.* Princeton, NJ: Princeton University Press, 2007.

Sharma, Nandita. "White Nationalism, Illegality and Imperialism: Border Controls as Ideology." in *(En)Gendering the War on Terror: War Stories and Camouflaged Politics.* Edited by Krista Hunt and Kim Rygiel. Aldershot, UK: Ashgate Publishers, 2006. 121-44.

Thobani, Sunera. *Exalted Subjects: Studies in the Making of Race and Nation in Canada.* Toronto: University of Toronto Press, 2007

Contributors

Mohamed Abualy Alibhai is an independent scholar and former editor of the quarterly journal *Islam in America*. He obtained a joint honours degree in physics and mathematics from the University of Dar es Salaam (Tanzania), and a master's degree in geophysics from the Imperial College of Science and Technology (University of London, England). He then switched to the graduate program in Islamic Studies at McGill University and proceeded to Harvard University, where he obtained a doctorate in Islamic philosophy. He returned to McGill University in the mid-1980s as faculty member, lecturing on and conducting graduate seminars in Neoplatonic and Islamic philosophy. He eventually settled on a career as computer programmer and systems analyst. He divides his time between Vancouver and Seattle.

Mayank Bhatt immigrated to Toronto from Bombay (Mumbai) in July 2008 with his wife Mahrukh and son Che. In Bombay he worked for many years as a journalist. The communal violence of 1993, which he witnessed firsthand, had a deep impact on him. His short stories have been published in *TOK 5: Writing the New Toronto*, *Canadian Voices II*, and *Indian Voices I* and he has recently completed a novel, to be published in 2016. He blogs at www.generallyaboutbooks.com.

Amira El-Ghawaby obtained an honours degree in Journalism and Law from Carleton University in 2001. Since then, she has worked as both a full-time and freelance journalist, writing and producing stories for a variety of media including the *Globe and Mail*, the *Toronto Star*, the *Ottawa Citizen*, CBC Radio and New Canadian Media. In 2012, she was hired as the Human Rights Coordinator of the National Council of Canadian Muslims to advocate for the human rights and civil liberties of diverse communities.

Safia Fazlul was born in Dhaka, Bangladesh and raised in Oslo, Norway. When she was ten she moved to Toronto with her family and had difficulty adhering to traditional Muslim and Bangladeshi values while trying simultaneously to become a "Canadian." She studied history and sociology at the University of Toronto, during which period she began writing *The Harem*, a novel inspired by her own struggle in maintaining a cultural identity and belonging. Safia currently works in the financial industry and is also writing her second novel.

Ihsaan Gardee A graduate of the University of Windsor and the University of Western Ontario, Ihsaan Gardee was involved with the National Council of Canadian Muslims as an occasional volunteer from its early years and is now its Executive Director. He appears regularly on local and national news media and programs on issues related to Canadian Muslims and Islam, and his writings have appeared in major Canadian and international publications. He has appeared as a witness before several Parliamentary and Senate committees on proposed legislation on national security.

Karim H Karim is the Director of the Carleton Centre for the Study of Islam and a Professor at Carleton University's School of Journalism and Communication. He has also served as Director of the School, and of the Institute of Ismaili Studies in London, England, and has been a Visiting Scholar at Harvard University. Earlier in his career, he worked as a journalist and as a senior policy analyst in the Canadian Government. Karim has been a distinguished lecturer at venues in North America, Europe, and Asia. He won the inaugural Robinson Prize for his book *Islamic Peril: Media and Global Violence*. His most recent publications are *Re-Imagining the Other: Culture, Media and Western-Muslim Intersections* and *Engaging the Other: Public Policy and Western-Muslim Intersections*.

Monia Mazigh is an academic, author, and human rights advocate. She was born and raised in Tunisia and immigrated to Canada in 1991. Mazigh was catapulted onto the public stage in 2002 when her husband, Maher Arar, was deported to Syria where he was tortured and held without charge for over a year. She campaigned tirelessly for his release. Mazigh holds a PhD in finance from McGill University. In 2008, she published a memoir, *Hope and Despair*, about her pursuit of justice. In 2014, she published her first novel *Mirrors and Mirages*. Her second novel, *Du pain et du jasmine*, came out in September 2015. You can follow her on Twitter @MoniaMazigh or on her blog www.moniamazigh.com

Ameen Merchant was born in Bombay and raised in Madras, India. In 1989, he came to Canada for graduate work in English Literature and Cultural Studies at the University of British Columbia. Within two years of his arrival at the university, he began hosting a weekly Indian/ Bollywood music hour on CiTR Radio called *Geetanjali*, the first such student radio show in Western Canada. What began as a small, musical experiment in multiculturalism lasted a decade. By the time Merchant gave up his hosting duties in 2002 to concentrate on his writing, the show had expanded to two hours and been renamed *Rhythm's India*.

His work has appeared in Canadian and international journals, including *Books in Canada*, *Apples Under The Bed—Recollections and Recipes from B.C. Writers and Artists*, ed. Joan Coldwell (2008), "Body of Evidence" and "Dressing Up for Jesus" in *Vislumbres* 1 & 2 (2009, 2010), *The Indian Express*, and *Femina*. Merchant's debut novel *The Silent Raga* was shortlisted for the Commonwealth Writers' Prize, 2008.

Ameen Merchant lives in Vancouver BC, where he is working on his next novel.

Narendra Pachkhédé, is a Commonwealth Scholar, with a broad-based scholarship in anthropology, foreign affairs, cinema, contemporary art, architecture, and public policy. He has pursued his doctoral studies in Canada and is a multidisciplinary artist, curator, and critic. His films have been shown internationally, including at the Rotterdam Film Festival, and he sits on various juries of international film and arts festivals in Canada and Europe. He has published across disciplines and practices, including the retrospective *Transpose*, an international Conference on Cultural Production in Contemporary Canada, Regina (2007); *International Geographic*, a retrospective of video art, edited with Catherine Russell, Trinh T Minh-ha and Coco Fusco (2006); the anthology, *Fringe Benefits: Cosmopolitan Dynamics of a Multicultural City*, edited by Ian Chodikoff (2008); and *Euphoria & Dystopia: The Banff New Media Institute Dialogues 1995–2005*, edited by Sara Diamond & Sarah Cook (2011).

Asma Sayed received her PhD in Comparative Literature from the University of Alberta, Canada. She has taught comparative literature, women's studies, cultural studies, and communication studies at a number of Canadian universities. Her interdisciplinary research focuses on South Asian Canadian diasporas in the context of global multiculturalism. Her books include *MG Vassanji: Essays on His Work* (2014), *Writing Diaspora: Transnational Memories, Identities and Cultures* (2014), *World on a Maple Leaf: A Treasure of Canadian Multicultural Folktales* (2011). *Screening Mothers: Motherhood in World Cinema* is her forthcoming book.

Haroon Siddiqui is Editorial Page Editor Emeritus of the *Toronto Star*, Canada's largest newspaper, where he was columnist, national editor, news editor, and foreign affairs writer. Earlier, he was managing editor of the *Brandon Sun*, in Manitoba. He has covered or supervised coverages of Canada for more than 45 years, and reported from nearly 50 countries, including the Soviet invasion of Afghanistan, the Iranian revolution, and conflicts in the Middle East.

Siddiqui is the author of the best-selling *Being Muslim*, a post-9/11 assessment based on his travels across North America, Europe, the Middle East, South Asia, and the Far East. He has contributed to *Canada and Sept. 11*; *Writing in a World without Peace*; *Belonging and Banishment*; *Great Questions of Canada*; *Multiculturalism and Rights in Canada*; and *Drawing Fire, The State of Political Cartooning*. He is the editor of *An Anthology of Modern Urdu Poetry*.

A former president of PEN Canada, he has also served on the board of PEN International. He is a member of the Order of Canada and the Order of Ontario, and holds an honorary doctorate from York University.

Zainub Verjee is a writer, critic, curator, contemporary artist and public intellectual. At the forefront of the two decades of cultural politics of the 1980s and 1990s in Canada, Zainub was the co-founder and Festival director of the critically acclaimed In Visible Colours: An International Film/ Video Festival & Symposium for Third World Women and Women of Colour (1988–90). Verjee was co-guest editor of the *Capilano Review* and has published in numerous academic, cultural, and critical fora including, *Leonardo Journal* (MIT), *Kinesis, Parallelogram, Fuse, Horizon*, and the *Journal of Art and the Public Sphere*. She is invited to speak nationally and internationally, on cultural policy, contemporary art and cultural diplomacy.

As a contemporary artist, she locates her practice in the politics of identity, culture, and technology. Her pursuits cover Canadian contemporary art, contemporary Asian art, Islamic art, and contemporary Arab art. Her work has been shown nationally and internationally, including at the prestigious Venice Biennale on its 100th anniversary and the Museum of Modern Art (MoMA), New York, and resides in private and public collections such as the Vancouver Art Gallery, Canada. Currently, she is engaged in a research project at York University on the making of Muslim identity in Canada post 9/11 and is the Executive Director at the Ontario Association of Art Galleries.

Nurjehan Aziz is the publisher and a director at Mawenzi House Publishers, and was formerly publisher at TSAR Publications. She has edited the anthologies *Her Mother's Ashes: Stories by South Asian Women in Canada and the United States*, Vols. 1, 2, and 3; and co-edited, with Sanjay Talreja, the collection of essays, *Strangers in the Mirror: In and Out of the Mainstream of Culture in Canada.*